Climbing Your Family Tree

Climbing Your Family Tree

Online and Offline Genealogy for Kids

LIBERTY ELLIS ISLAND

TM © 1982, 1987 S O L E I F, INC.

The Official Ellis Island Handbook

Completely revised and updated version of
Do People Grow on Family Trees?

by Ira Wolfman

Foreword by Cyndi Howells   Introduction by Alex Haley

Illustrations by Tim Robinson

Workman Publishing • New York

OCT 3 1 2002

Dedication

This book is dedicated to my most direct ancestors, Bea and Artie Wolfman. Both children of immigrants, they have given me life, love, and an enduring appreciation of those who came before me. And to my children, Evan and Perry, the precious newest branches of my very own family tree.

Copyright © 1991, 2002 by Ira Wolfman and the Statue of Liberty–Ellis Island Foundation, Inc.
Text by Ira Wolfman
Illustrations © 2002 by Tim Robinson

Library of Congress Cataloging-in-Publication Data
Wolfman, Ira.
Climbing your family tree : online and off-line genealogy for kids / by Ira Wolfman ;
foreword by Alex Haley ; illustrations by Michael Klein.
p. cm.
Rev. ed. of: Do people grow on family trees? c1991.
Includes bibliographical references and index.
ISBN 0-7611-2539-6 (alk. paper)
1. Genealogy—Juvenile literature. I. Klein, Michael, 1960 Nov. 6- II. Wolfman, Ira.
Do people grow on family trees: III. Title.

CS15.5 .W64 2002

929'.1—dc21   2002016797

Book design by Ty Cumbie, Adriana Cordero, and Michael Fusco
Cover illustration by Reynold Ruffins

Workman Publishing Company, Inc.
708 Broadway
New York, New York 10003-9555
www.workman.com

Manufactured in the United States of America

First printing September 2002
10 9 8 7 6 5 4 3 2 1

A Treeful of Thank You's

Anyone who sets out to learn about his or her ancestors quickly discovers that genealogists depend on the kindness of strangers. In fact, those strangers often turn into friends, and even, sometimes, relatives. This revised edition of *Climbing Your Family Tree* would not have been possible without the help and advice of many people. They have made it a much better book. So heartfelt thanks to the following:

Cyndi Howells, for her foreword and for sharing her incredible knowledge of genealogical Internet information; Gary Mokotoff, whose generosity has done wonders for Jewish genealogists everywhere; Eileen Polakoff, a talented genealogist and a good friend; the incredible crew at jewishgen.org, who enriched me with their passionate discussions, diligent data-gathering, and ongoing love of genealogy; Peg Zitko at the Ellis Island Foundation; the late Alex Haley, whose great spirit lives on in the many stories about his kindness, and in his introduction to this book; my many colleagues and friends at the Jewish Genealogy Society, whose conventions and corrections taught me so much; the late Rabbi Malcolm Stern, whose guiding influence continues to nurture a new generation of genealogists; the New York City LDS Family History Library, where I made discoveries I will cherish for the rest of my life; David Gordon, my Chicago landsman.

Ted Kesler, a remarkable third-grade teacher who helped me reimagine important pieces of this edition; Ted's third-grade class, who taught him and me an enormous amount about the diversity of this country; the many people who shared their family-history stories, including Jessica Pearlman, Eric Adler, Anny and Lily Holgate, and John, Laurie, and Orion Taylor. A special thanks to Natasha and Magda Bogin, for opening my eyes to the unique challenges and beauty of adoptive families.

Linc and Joan Diamant, who encouraged me in so many ways for so many years; Louise Gikow and Ellen Weiss, the matchmakers who brought me to Workman Publishing; Sally Kovalchick, dear departed, my editor on the original edition of this book; Sue Kassirer, who smartly read and reread this manuscript; Margot Herrera, for keeping this book on course down a long and winding road.

Finally, a huge thank you to my family: Bea and Artie Wolfman, my wonderful parents, for their constant encouragement and love; my dear sister Sharon Zarom, her husband Ilan, and daughters Lauren and Kerry; my supportive in-laws, Abe and Molly Small; Hyman Small, my late grandfather-in-law, who so clearly filled his 105 years with integrity and kindness; and my incredible sons, Evan and Perry, who fill every day of my life with surprise and struggle and delight.

Most of all, thank you, Ronda, for gracing my life with that beautiful smile.

CONTENTS

Foreword

By Cyndi Howells

The idea of a genealogy book written just for kids and young people thrills me because my own love for genealogy took root when I was in high school. Actually, it began the year that I was born, with the gift from my Grandma Nash of a family-tree book (although, of course, I didn't know it at the time).

During my last year in high school, sadly just a few months after my last grandparent had passed away, I was given a new project for a social studies class. We were to create a chart on poster board, depicting our family tree. I was very excited about this new assignment. I remembered looking at Grandma Nash's book many times through the years.

I went home and dug the book out of the trunk, packed with photographs and family memories, and

Cyndi Howells is the creator of the genealogy website *cyndislist.com*, where more than 100,000 genealogy web pages can be accessed.

spent time reacquainting myself with the red, vinyl-covered book, lettered in gold. My mom told me that the year I was born her mother had purchased five of these books, all blank, and that she gave one to each of her four children and kept a copy for herself.

Grandma's book was filled with her handwriting and stuffed full of newspaper clippings, letters, and cards. The copy that was given to my mom was also filled with hand-written information, but I was drawn to the book that had once been used by my grandma. She was the same grandma who once made me toast with her special jam. The same grandma who gave me a necklace that her own grandmother had given her years earlier. The same grandma whom I miss more and more as time passes. This book was a connection to her, and now I know it was my first connection to all of my ancestors.

I began to draw a chart based on the information in Grandma's book. At first, I copied what she had written in her book. Then I found letters, as old as I was, stuck in the back of the book, which were from Grandma's cousins. One letter described how our Swedish ancestors, my great-great-grandparents, came to America, and gave details for the number of children they had, where they lived, and when and where they died. Another letter told of my great-great-great-grandfather, who fought in the Civil War. I still remember the feeling that washed over me at that time. I felt like I was uncovering a long-lost mystery and discovering family secrets about these ancestors. And I immediately wanted to learn more.

But I had no idea how to go about learning more. What I wouldn't have given to have this book to get me started on the right research path! I completed the chart for my school project and received an "A" for my efforts—or rather, for Grandma Nash's efforts.

The genealogy bug had bitten me. I realized that there must be more information about my ancestors, and I wanted to find it all. But I needed help and advice on how to find new information—where to look and what to do with it all once I had it. *Climbing Your Family Tree* does all of this for today's budding genealogists. Kids working on their family trees today have things quite a bit easier than I did more than 20 years ago. Computers and technology make record keeping and correspondence easier than ever before. The Internet has managed to shrink the world, as cousins can find each other online and reunite branches of the family tree that have been out of touch for years. As I write this, two more descendants of my Civil War ancestor have just contacted me through e-mail: two more cousins for me to get to know and with whom I can share our heritage through pictures and documents. I can't help but wonder what Grandma would think of all this. Letters that were written by her and to her, with pen and ink, have inspired electronic replies to her granddaughter several decades later. I am sure that Grandma Nash would be very happy to see where her efforts have led me through the years.

Now it is time for me to inspire my son, my niece, my nephew, and my cousins, just as Grandma inspired me all those years ago. I had the help of that one, red-vinyl book to introduce me to my ancestors. Fortunately, they will have an advantage over me, because they will not only have that one personal family book, but this wonderful guide as well.

—Cyndi Howells
February 2002

Introduction to the First Edition
By Alex Haley
(1921–1992)

How I wish I could have read this book when I was a child. If I had, I would have been so much more aware that my grandparents were a source of riches beyond belief. I would have known that the stories they told—stories about themselves, their parents, and their grandparents—were gifts more precious than the greatest of treasures.

If I'd been aware of these things as a child, I would have known to listen much more closely to my family and to keep a notebook of what they said. I would have known what further questions to ask—questions seeking anything and everything they knew about our history.

And I know they would have loved telling me.

Because both of my parents were teachers, they saw to it that most of my presents were books. It tingles me today to think that if I had been given this book, I would have plied my elders about every aspect of their lives. Where did they live? What work did they do? What clothing did they wear? What games did they play as children? Tell me, I could have asked, what was it like when your family went to church?

Alex Haley on a visit to Sengal, Africa. Haley wrote *Roots,* a book that inspired millions to get started in genealogy.

I could have kept notebooks from early on. I could have sketched and written descriptions of what my elders told me about how they dressed, or their games, or the horses and mules and wagons and buggies that were their transportation. And of the cotton and tobacco farms where they worked.

It strikes me as significant that two of the most popular books of modern times were written by authors who had once been grandchildren in southern families, sitting and listening as their elders frequently, proudly, told family stories.

One of these grandchildren was a little girl from Atlanta, Georgia, whose name was Margaret Mitchell. For years, Margaret heard the family stories and was taken as a child to visit Civil War sites on the outskirts of Atlanta. She would grow up to write a book that, along with its later motion picture, would fascinate the whole world. The book and the film were, of course, *Gone With the Wind.*

The second book was my own *Roots,* which was born on the front porch of a gray-frame home in the very small town of Henning, Tennessee. After the death of my grandfather the year that I was five, my deeply grieving grandma Cynthia Palmer wrote asking her five sisters to come and visit the next summer. And they all did.

A pattern quickly developed: After supper in the evenings, they would gather on the front porch in their rocking chairs. Dipping snuff, which they skeeted out over the honeysuckle vines and the blinking fireflies, they talked night after night about their own childhoods as the children of former slave parents Tom and Irene Murray. Their daddy was a strong, stern blacksmith. And they talked most of all about his daddy, their grandfather, my great-grandfather, a most colorful slave gamecock fighter whose name was George Lea and whom everybody called by his nickname of "Chicken George."

They recalled his mother, who lived in Spotsylvania County, Virginia, and was called Miss Kizzy. And then her parents—the Big House cook Miss Bell and the master's buggy driver, an African, who said that his African name was Kinte.

I sat listening night after night, until the ancestral family stories became fixed in my memory. It would be 40 years later that I would remember and decide to try to research the skeletal story I'd heard. The eventual result was the book and its television miniseries, *Roots.*

And now I'm astonished to think how much more I could have learned from those dear old ladies on the front porch if only I'd known to ask them questions, as I would have—if only I had read this book.

—Alex Haley
1991

CHAPTER ONE

Ancestor Detectors at Work

Tales of Kids and Adults Who Tracked Down Their Families

In this chapter, you will learn:

- How I became an ancestor detector
- The kinds of discoveries you can make through genealogy
- How kids and adults made their discoveries
- Some of the many places to look for clues about your family

It was a hot summer day in Washington, D.C., but I hardly noticed the temperature. While other people were working or touring or going to the beach, I was on a manhunt.

I was looking for my grandfather.

I was in a library in the National Archives of the United States of America, a majestic building where historic American documents and records are kept. In front of me was a list of people who had come to America by ship in the early 1900s. These lists, called "passenger lists" or "ship's manifests," were part of the curious mystery I was examining.

I'd recently learned that three men—all of them with exactly the same name as my father's father—had entered the United States between 1900 and 1910. They were born in different years, so I was sure that only one could be *my* grandfather. But which one?

I was determined to find out.

The men had arrived on three different ships. I found the passenger list of the first ship, the S.S. *Belgravia*. It had left Hamburg, Germany, for New York City on December 12, 1902, with more than 1,350 people on board. The list was

Morris and Ida Wolfman and their son Ben, around 1916. On line 30 of the boat manifest, note Morris's name (Moische Wolfmann) and his age (21).

gigantic: 45 pages long, with 30 names on each page. And every name was written in the same cramped, hard-to-read handwriting.

I took a deep breath, then started on page 1. Around me, other people appeared to be working hard on their own mysteries.

After about an hour, I came to page 30, line 30. And then, even though I was in a library, I yelled.

There he was! I was sure this was *my* grandfather because the manifest named the tiny town—Lapiz, Russia—from which I knew he had come.

I can't explain what made seeing my grandfather's name so special. But finding him in that long list thrilled me. I read every bit of information the manifest had about him. He was 21 years old, single, and could read and write. His trade was listed as "tailor," his

Your Many Families

When we talk about tracing your family history, it sounds as if you have only *one* family. But that's not true. You actually have many families.

You start, of course, with your immediate family—your parents and yourself. But very soon you'll be thinking about your four grandparents, each of whom came from a different family. Your research, therefore, will include your mom's mother's family and your mom's father's family and your dad's father's family and your dad's mother's family.

How can you research so many families? The answer is, you can't. As you dig deeper into the past, you will find that one branch of your family is easier to trace than the others. That's the one you will work on most. (But, of course, if at any time you come across clues about another branch, you should follow that trail as far as you can.)

One of the nice things about genealogy is that it is a lifetime hobby, so over the years, your research can move from one part of your family to another.

nationality as "Hebrew." He was to stay with an uncle in Brooklyn. And he had three dollars with him.

I'd known my grandfather as a kind old man who moved slowly and spoke English softly, with an accent. But until this moment, I'd never thought of him as a courageous young man who—by himself—had taken a giant ship and traveled thousands of miles in the middle of winter to move forever to a new country where people spoke a language he didn't understand.

I wanted to hold on to this bit of family history. I made copies of the page and took them with me. When I shared them with my parents, they were as excited as I was.

EXCITING DEVELOPMENTS

Finding my grandfather's name was one of my first experiences as an *ancestor detector*—my name for anyone who's interested in tracking down the story of the people who make up his or her family. As the years went on, I discovered a lot of exciting family information. I found out exactly when all four of my grandparents arrived in America. I learned a lot about the little towns in Europe that my grandparents had once called home. I uncovered all kinds of documents about my relatives' past. I also discovered the names of relatives who had long been forgotten—including those of my great-great-great-great-grandparents, who were born in the 1750s!

At Morris and Ida's home, around 1954.

I learned that my family was made up of many families. All four of my grandparents came to the United States in the early 20th century. They all left behind their parents and many relatives in the small hometowns that today are in the countries of Poland and Belarus.

I began tracing my grandparents' stories by talking with my parents. I searched for and examined any special items that my grandparents had owned that were now in my parents' possession: photographs, books, clothing, religious objects. I spoke with cousins and uncles and other relatives, and I asked to see their artifacts. I wrote to records centers and asked for copies of important documents. I even visited some of those centers.

When I found my grandparents' names on ships' manifests, I was thrilled. When I discovered marriage licenses, naturalization papers, and census records, I was amazed.

I finally took everything I had learned about genealogy and put it into a book—this book. *Climbing Your Family Tree* was originally published in 1991. It was filled with my excitement over the kinds of discoveries anyone can make in genealogical research.

After the book came out, I heard from genealogy fans all over the country. They wanted to share their family stories and to learn more about how to find their missing ancestors.

Then I discovered computers and the Internet. I'd done so much work on my family tree without using computers that I didn't realize what an amazing genealogical tool was now at my fingertips. But in the years since, I've used genealogy software to improve my record keeping. Even more important, I've made dozens of discoveries online about the people, times, and places in my family's long history.

I was extremely impressed by the immense power of the Internet to connect families all over the world—simply with the click of a mouse. I realized that this book

A Website Just For You

We've built a website just for the readers of this book: *www.workman.com/familytree*. It will help you make your own family charts, get copies of family documents, and visit genealogy websites without lots of typing. Here's what you'll find:

Links—Want a one-click link to nearly every website mentioned in this book? Come here and you won't have to type in all those long URLS. You also won't have to worry about one typing mistake messing you up.

Downloadables—This is the place for blank pedigree charts, family group sheets, research logs, alternative family trees, and more. You'll also find checklists like "family treasures" and "questions to ask at family-history interviews."

Other fun stuff—Try out our genealogy tips, lists, updates, quizzes, and other nifty family-history activities.

It's all free—so come to *www.workman.com/familytree* and check it out!

needed to be revised to include information about how to use this new and invaluable genealogical tool. At the same time, I would be able to add ten more years of genealogical discoveries and stories. Finally, I realized that I could make an important addition to the multitude of genealogical websites by creating an electronic tie-in to this book—*www.workman.com/familytree* (see box at left).

You hold the results in your hands—a book that has been revised, revamped, re-edited, reconceived, and brought fully into the electronic age, all of which I hope makes it even more valuable to 21st-century ancestor detectors.

DETECTOR STORIES

Over the years since I first wrote this book, I've met many ancestor detectors who have made exciting discoveries about their families. In this chapter, you will meet a few of them—famous and not famous, kids and grown-ups. Listen to their tales of genealogical journeys. Then read the rest of the book, and you will be able to join them in your own family history treasure hunt.

A Very Big Bedtime Story: Charlotte Finds a Family Legend

As a young girl, Charlotte Littlejohn noticed something odd when she visited her grandmother, Almeda Elizabeth Ware Fenley, in Texas. "My grandmother was

The Great Bed of Ware.

a short woman, but all her brothers were very tall," Charlotte recalls today. "I was intrigued by the tallest ones, Uncle Oscar and Uncle Ira. They were six feet nine and seven feet tall!

"When I asked my grandmother about them, she told me that somewhere in England there was a giant bed built especially for one of her ancestors."

Grandma Almeda had been told about the bed by *her* father, J. C. Ware. He said it was built around 1600 and that it was gigantic—about nine feet long. Her father claimed the bed had to be put together in the room where it was to be used because no one wanted to think about moving it.

"My grandma had no dates for what happened

afterward," Charlotte notes, "but she said she'd heard that the man who had the bed made moved to Ireland and couldn't take it with him."

Grandma wasn't sure whether the bed still existed.

This story stayed in Charlotte's mind. Years later she met with Eileen Mundy, a cousin who had just returned from studying the family history in England. Eileen told Charlotte, "That bed exists. I found a notation about it in a book—it's known as the Great Bed of Ware—and I've been told it's still in England somewhere. I just don't know where."

Then Charlotte and her husband, Jack Waggoner, took a trip to England. One day they were looking at a map and noticed a little town outside London named Ware. "Let's go see," Charlotte said. They drove to Ware and walked around town, asking if anyone knew about a huge bed. It wasn't until they met an elderly man in a pub that they got their answer. "Oh yes, that was here for a long while. They kept it in an inn, but it's gone now. It's at the Victoria and Albert Museum in London."

The couple rushed back to London, and Charlotte made a beeline for the museum. She asked a guard for directions, and he took her to a corner of the museum. There it was: the Great Bed of Ware, a nine-foot-long by nine-foot-wide bed with a huge wooden canopy, made before 1600.

Charlotte stared and stared. "I had this wonderful feeling that there was a basis to my family stories."

She had only one regret: "I just wish my grandma had been there to see it too."

The *Roots* of Popular Genealogy: Alex Haley's Story

"I'd always heard my grandma tell stories about our ancestors," Alex Haley told me. "Then one Saturday afternoon, I was in Washington, D.C., poking along on the sidewalk of the Mall. I looked up and saw a big building with the words *Archives of the United States* written across its front.

"I wandered in without any specific reason. Someone startled me by asking, 'Can I help you?' I heard myself say, 'I wonder if I could see the 1870 census records for Alamance County, North Carolina.'

"I went to the microfilm room, put the census on the reader, and turned and turned the handle. I was fascinated. Here were all these names of people long gone and descriptions of their families. I felt as if I were standing on the side of the road, watching them.

"And then I found something that astonished me: the name of my grandma's daddy, Thomas Murray. How many times had I heard Grandma talk about him? And there he was, her daddy, a blacksmith. His wife. Their children.

"That was my first bite of the genealogical bug, for which there is no cure."

When Haley began this trip into his genealogy in the 1960s, he didn't quite know what he was looking for or

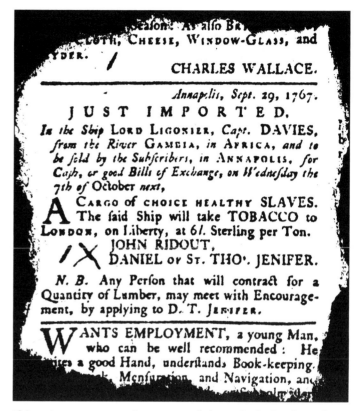

This 1767 newspaper ad announced the arrival of a slave ship. Alex Haley's ancestor was aboard.

where it would lead. Haley had spent many nights listening to his grandma tell stories about his ancestors. He knew that his family had been in America for nearly 200 years, and he had heard ancestors' names and the names of a few places, like 'Naplis and Alamance County.

"When I walked into the archives, the idea of writing a book was as far away from me as the man in the moon,"

On a visit to Africa, Alex Haley met his sixth cousins. All the people in this photo were thought to be descended from the same great-great-great-great-great-grandparent.

At left, Levar Burton as Kunta Kinte in the enormously popular television series, *Roots*. At right, Alex and his brother, George Haley, talk family history with "cousin" Georgia Henderson.

Haley recalled. But when he found his great-grandfather's name on official records in Washington, D.C., it changed him. Soon he began to work on a book about his family.

Nine years later—after thousands of hours of research and trips across the United States, to England, and to Africa— *Roots,* Haley's book about his family, was published.

Alex Haley, author of the best-selling book *Roots.*

Roots tells, in dramatic fashion, the story of Kunta, a young African boy who was kidnapped and brought to the English colonies in America in September of 1767. The book traces the painful and courageous lives of Kunta's descendants through slavery, the Civil War, emancipation, and the world wars. It follows the descendants right up to the 1970s. One of those descendants was, of course, Alex Haley.

Haley's story startled America. A descendant of slaves could find his own ancestors? How was that possible? Wasn't genealogy only for rich people, for aristocrats?

Haley convinced many Americans that even a descendant of poor people could find and tell his own distinguished and important story. *Roots* became a bestseller and one of the most popular TV shows ever broadcast.

"All human beings belong to some family that has ancestry and a native land," Haley recalled. "The need for knowing who you are is universal.

"I've traveled around the world since *Roots* came out. Everywhere I speak—Egypt, Mexico, Peking, Paris—people come up to me with their family charts. Everyone can gain something—something that is immense—from knowing where they came from."

Jessica Pearlman: Using the Internet to Find My Ancestors

"In fifth grade, my teacher had us all do a family history project," recalls 17-year-old Jessica Pearlman, a high school student in California. "I had a pretty good head start: On my mother's side, one of my cousins a generation back had done extensive research. I learned that my ancestors participated in the Civil War for the North and that one had even played the drum during battles!

"When I was in sixth grade, we got connected to the Internet. Almost immediately I began logging on to *ancestry.com* and Mormon family-history websites. I had fun plugging in my family surnames and seeing what would come up."

On many genealogy websites, Jessica points out, you can leave information about your ancestors—their names and where they came from. Other visitors to the site can see the information. If they think they may be related to you, they can send you an e-mail.

"A couple of years ago, I got an e-mail from someone who said he knew who I was—his fifth cousin!" Jessica remembers. "I connected him with my grandmother and they began talking regularly. Apparently, my grandmother and he may have seen each other when they were very little. He even had pictures of my grandmother and her parents that we had never seen before.

"On my mother's side, I was able to trace back to 1503 and my ancestors Richard and Allison Bowlby in Helmsley, York, England. The Internet helped me extend my family tree, correct wrong or missing information, see pictures of my ancestors and the places they lived, and learn about how and why they came to America. I even found a portrait from the early 1700s of my eighth great-grandmother!"

Jessica knew where her father's family had come from. "I wanted to know more," she says, "more about their lives, not just where they had come from. I

Jessica Pearlman (holding oboe, in photo with her family) and her genealogy discoveries: Her great-grandfather Yankel during World War I, and the gravestone of her great-great-grandmother Hanna.

started checking books out from the library and searching the Internet for that kind of information. I now know a lot about the history of Old England, Lithuania, Australia, and Poland."

Learning about her heritage has changed her, says Jessica. "It's given me the understanding that my self is rooted deeper than my personality, values, and ideas—it is the life of every mother and every father in my family tree. It is the languages my ancestors spoke and the jobs they had, what they stood up for and, as in the cases of those who were Jewish, what they died for, too.

"My research has helped me learn some of what they might have told me about their lives," she says proudly. "I can visit the places they walked, the graves they are buried in. That's what makes genealogy so special for me: It's my family's history—nobody else's. Of course, that means no one has a magical textbook with all the answers, but the plus side is that I have

Hundreds of Thousands of Ancestors!

How many ancestors do you think you have? If you start with your parents, then count their parents, and their parents' parents, how many people are there? And what if you go a few steps beyond that?

Each level of your family is called a "generation." Go back one generation and you find your parents. Look back two, and there are your grandparents. When you look back three generations, you reach your grandparents' parents—your great-grandparents.

A chart showing only your parents, grandparents, and great-grandparents would include fourteen people (two parents, four grandparents, and eight great-grandparents).

But each of your eight great-grandparents had two parents, and each of those sixteen great-great-grandparents had two parents. By the time of your great-great-great-

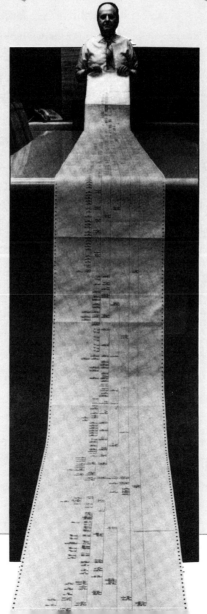

great-grandparents (what genealogists call your "fourth great-grandparents"), there would be 126 people on the chart. And if you went back three more generations, your chart would have more than 1,000 people on it!

If you were able to go back 20 generations, you'd arrive somewhere before the year 1400. In that time, you might find yourself with over 2 million direct ancestors!

Actually, however, genealogists estimate that the number of *different* people in your family tree would more likely be only about 1 million because many distant cousins marry each other without being aware that they are related.

That's still a lot of family!

Gary Mokotoff unrolls a 30-foot-long computer printout of his family tree, which includes thousands of ancestors!

been able to create and research everything and learn how it relates to my family and me specifically."

Coming to America and a New Family: Natasha's Story

"I knew I was adopted as a baby from St. Petersburg, Russia," Natasha Bogin recalls. "But when I was assigned to do a family history project for my third-grade class, I had a problem: The family tree we were given to fill in didn't make sense for me."

The blank family tree (actually called a pedigree chart), with its branches off to either side for "Father's family" and "Mother's family," was fine for some families—but not for Natasha's. It wasn't just that she was adopted: "All my friends had a mother and a father, but I don't. I was adopted by a single mother."

Bringing baby home: Natasha and Magda in Russia.

Natasha wanted to do the assignment in a way that would show her pride in her family. So she and her mom spread a huge piece of paper on the floor and thought about what sort of "family tree" design could do that. A house? A circle?

As they talked, they hit on a pleasing solution: "We decided to use the shape of a flower, which also symbolizes life," Natasha remembers. "And we put lots of petals to show the people closest to me."

Natasha drew the flower on a long stem, then placed a photograph of herself in the center. Next, she drew lots of petals around the flower. On the petals nearest to the center, she wrote in the names of the people she considered most important in her life: her mother Magda, her mother's parents, her aunt, her babysitter. In the next ring, she wrote the names of "ancestors"— her mother's grandparents and great-grandparents, who had immigrated to America. She also added people whom she rarely saw but who mattered to her, such as a cousin in France.

There was one more name to add. Because Magda had shared the details of the adoption with Natasha, the third grader could write in someone else in a very special place: "I put the name of my birth mother, Lyubov, on a leaf."

Natasha says she learned a lot from looking at the materials her mother had saved for her from the time of the adoption. "I found a copy of my own Russian passport. I also found the papers that made me a citizen when I was a baby."

As she researched her family history, Natasha was excited to discover that she had a special link to her mother's grandparents—and to the larger story of history: "When I did this project, I realized that I am an immigrant, just like all those people I was studying in school. It sort of amazed me! And it's special to me that I have ancestors who were also immigrants to America, from Russia!"

Not every child who has been adopted will be able to, or want to, share all this information, Natasha's mom points out. "Putting together a family tree can be very touchy for some adoptive families," Magda says. "But for our family, it opened up a wonderful conversation." (For more information about adoptive children and family research, see Chapter Ten, "My Story's a Little Different.")

Natasha and Magda Bogin's "Family Flower," showing Natasha's birth mom's name (Lyubov) along with her adoptive family.

Family Flower diagram labels: God / Mother / Adriana Ortiz-Ortega; God / Mother / Claudia Hinojosa; God / Mother / Josefina Tavares; God / Mother / Electa Arenal; Julius Weissglass Grandfather; Rose Fleischer Great Grandmother; Magda Bogin My Mother; Leon Fleischer Great Grandfather; Julia Frankel Great Great Grandmother; Rita Alperovich Babysitter; Rebecca Bogin Great Great Grandmother; George Bogin Grandfather; Eva Sugan Great Great Grandmother; Maurice Bogin Great Grandfather; Alain Buttard uncle; Ruth Bogin Grandmother; Philip Katz Great Great Grandfather; Jennie Rosenberg Great Great Grandmother; Masha Varkshavskaya Blood Sister; Nina Bogin Aunt; Georgyi Gnovier Dear Friend; Georgyi Bogin Great Great Grandfather; Cecilia Buttard and Valentine Buttard Cousins; Sophie Bogin Great Grandmother; Rudolph Fleischer Great Great Grandfather; Gershon Bogin Great Great Grandfather; Lyubov Birthmother.

Books About Kings, Queens, and . . . Me?: Dafna's Discoveries

"When I was very young, I was fascinated with family trees of the royal houses of Europe," recalls Dafna O'Neill. "I would spend hours looking at those complicated trees, figuring out who was related to whom. I thought it was especially interesting that so many members of the ruling families of England and Greece and Germany and Russia had married one another.

"I come from a big family, but I never thought of tracing my own family tree," she remembers. But when Dafna was about 13 years old, a distant cousin visited her family. "I was sitting with a book in my lap, looking at some royal family tree. She noticed my interest and asked, 'Did you know that someone has put together a book of *our* family's genealogy?'

"I got very excited. Together with my grandmother, I found a cousin who had a copy. The book was written in Berlin, Germany, in 1928. It goes back to the 1770s!

The man who had put together this book made about 50 copies and sent them to family members. "The copy I found is one of two I know of that survived World War II. It was written in German, of course. I spent the next three years translating it and adding an index," Dafna says.

"Over the years, I made contact with members of the oldest generation mentioned in the book. Now I am adding to the book—writing about our family's new children and spouses, talking about the ways life has changed over the years. And I find that I have a treasure box full of photos and documents for the newest generation of our family."

Dafna says she gained a lot from doing this when she was a teenager. "I felt a stronger sense of who I was—I was part of a family that had so much history! The most important experience was meeting many people who share common roots with me but are also very different. (Sometimes that common root was very noticeable in the way they looked!)

"Doing my genealogy, I also came to see that life offers many choices and that what you make of your life is up to you. I learned much from the experience of my older family members—lessons that have helped to guide my own choices and attitudes."

Orion Taylor, about five years old, with his dad, John, and his grandfather Telford.

Finding Out About a Famous Ancestor: Orion's Story

Orion Taylor had what seemed like a simple assignment from Ted Kesler, his third-grade teacher: Fill in as much as you can of a family pedigree chart, then do a research project about one of your family members. Orion had heard that his grandfather Telford had done some important things. But he didn't know *what* he had done. "I was in kindergarten when he died. I didn't know much more than that he was in World War II," says Orion, who lives in New York City.

So Orion went to his father, John, and asked for details. "My dad had lots of stuff about my grandfather, and he showed it to me. There were books about him and books written by him. My dad also had a box of Telford's stuff."

Orion looked over books and articles about his grandfather. He conducted interviews about Telford with his dad, his grandfather's second wife (his step-grandmother), and Telford's friend Junius Scales (who was also Orion's godfather).

Doing his research, Orion discovered that his grandfather had been the chief prosecuting lawyer at the historic trials of Germany's Nazi leaders in the years after World War II. "I didn't even know that he was a lawyer!" Orion says. "And I didn't know anything about the Nuremberg trials."

By the project's end, Orion had filled in his family pedigree chart. He wrote an essay about his grandfather. He even put together a small exhibit about Telford's life. The exhibit included articles about Telford and a few artifacts, including a cigarette case Telford brought back from Germany.

"It was exciting exploring all these important events," Orion remembers. "I learned a lot about the Second World War—not just about my grandfather. Now I am very interested in finding out about the rest of my family; my mom showed me some computer CDs that let you make a really big family tree, and I want to do that."

Doing this research also made Orion think about a lot of things. "I wondered what it was like for my dad, being Telford's son, and how my mom felt about Telford."

Orion's parents, John and Laurie, were thrilled with his project. "I'm so pleased at all that Orion has learned about a grandparent he won't ever see alive again," says John. "I hoped he might come away from this with a sense of history as a living thing, and I think he has."

To read about Orion's famous grandfather, go to *www.cardozo.net/life/fall1998/taylor/*.

A Boy Scout Learns to Ask the Right Questions: Eric's Story

"I started doing genealogy when I was eleven years old," remembers Eric Adler of Kileen, Texas. "I was a member of the Boy Scouts of America, and I was working on getting a genealogy merit badge. As I went about earning the badge, I learned two important skills. The first was how to talk to relatives about family. It is easy to teach a child what questions to ask and why to ask them.

"The second skill was basic research," he says. "As part of the merit badge, we actually went to a Family History Center [genealogical libraries run by the Church of Jesus Christ of Latter-day Saints, or Mormons; see Chapter

The genealogy merit badge of the Boy Scouts of America

(continued on page 18)

A Word for Beginners About Websites

Genealogists today can find a lot of information on the Internet . . . if they know where to look. You can't simply go online and find your family's records, all neatly located at a few addresses. They just aren't there. But you *can* uncover useful and interesting information if you do your research carefully and use the Internet smartly.

All of Chapter Eight is devoted to helping you get the most out of the Internet's genealogical riches. Here we offer a few tips for getting started online.

One resource that is particularly helpful in genealogical research—or, in fact, in any online research—is a search engine. Search engines are websites that help you locate information across the Internet. At most search engines, you enter a word or a few words into a "search" box. The site then looks for those words across the Internet. Within seconds, it shows you a list of web pages where your chosen words appear. Many good search engines can be found on the Internet, including general ones like *yahoo.com*, *google.com*, and *altavista.com*. There are also genealogical search engines such as *www.genealogytoolbox.com* and *gensource.com*.

To help you look for the family data that's most important to you, we've included addresses for different genealogical websites throughout this book. Before you head online, however, take a careful look at those addresses. If you were visiting a house, you'd make sure you had the right address. It's exactly the same with websites. If Internet addresses—called URLs, or uniform resource locators—aren't correct, they're worthless.

A URL is a string of letters, sometimes mixed with numbers. It can be as simple as *myancestors.com*, or as complex as *www.myancestors.com/index2~books*.

In a URL, every letter, space, and bit of punctuation is important. Here are some rules about typing in web addresses:

• **Type the URL** exactly as you see it on the page. Include every period, comma, or slash (/). Sometimes you need to type *www.* at the beginning of a URL, sometimes not.

• **Don't add spaces** between letters if they aren't in the listing.

• **Double-check** what you've typed before you submit it. Watch out for periods, commas, or other punctuation that may accidentally get typed in. A comma that doesn't belong will make the address useless.

• **IMPORTANT!** *Please note that web addresses sometimes change—or even disappear—with time.* If a URL given in this book does not take you to the desired site, it's probably because the site has moved

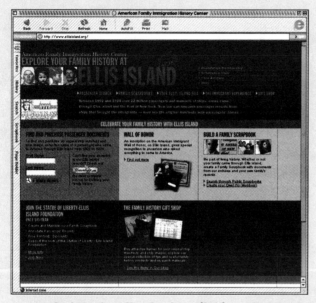

Are you looking for *ellisisland.org* (left) or *ellisisland.com*? When you type a web address, every letter is important.

or been discontinued. The next step is to try searching for a new site using a search engine.

Long URLs usually include extra information that will send you to a specific place on a website. If you get an error message on a long URL, try deleting any information that comes after the .com (.org, or similar three-letter extension following a period) and submit again. (For example, in the URL on the previous page, you would delete *"index2~books."*)

If you want to return to a website, "bookmark" it. Using the software that helps you surf the Internet, find the place on the menu bar where you can keep a permanent record of that URL. That way, you won't have to try to remember it. And you won't have to type it in again, which eliminates making a small typing mistake that makes the whole address useless.

For more information about genealogy online, turn to Chapter Eight.

Lily Holgate (top left) and her sister Chloe. On the I.D. card of their great-grandfather Rosario, Lily found an X—"his mark"—instead of his signature.

Nine]. I used copies of the pedigree charts they gave us until I bought software in 1998. "I've made a lot of progress in genealogy over the last fifteen years, and I look forward to researching for 50 or 60 more years."

To see the requirements for the genealogy merit badge, visit the official website of the Boy Scouts, *www.usscouts.org/mb/mb056.html.*

Surprises in a Box of Documents: What Lily Learned

"The only thing I knew about my great-grandfather before I started doing my family history was his name: Rosario DeGange," says nine-year-old Lily Holgate. But Lily knew that her mother had a box filled with some of Rosario's papers, so she began researching his life. Lily

learned that Rosario had emigrated from Sicily, in southern Italy, in the early 1900s. Looking through his papers, she found his passport. She also uncovered a more unusual document, his "alien identity card." Because Italy was fighting against the United States during World War II, Italian immigrants who were not citizens had to register with the U.S. government between 1941 and 1945.

That surprised Lily. She was even more surprised that Rosario signed the card with an X because he didn't know how to sign his name. "I thought that was pretty weird, that he did not know how to read or write, because he was an adult and was working. How did he live?" she wondered. In fact, U.S. government statistics show that many immigrants were illiterate when they arrived, and some stayed so their whole lives.

With all its surprises, tracking down her family history was fun for Lily. "I loved that I could learn more about my family at the same time that I was doing work for school," she said.

WHERE WILL YOUR SEARCH TAKE YOU?

Your family history research may not lead you to find a legendary family artifact, write a book, discover a famous ancestor, or go back to the 13th century. But it *will* put you in touch with the people you came from. And it will make their past come alive.

"The relatives I never knew were just names to me," recalls genealogist Miriam Weiner. "But then I researched them. What I learned made me admire them so much. It reconnected me to who I am."

Great personal discoveries also await you. As you trace your family's path, you will see how it fits into history's larger picture. You will read about the great tale of immigration to this part of the world. You will come to understand the struggles and courage of both your ancestors and the many other people who risked a great deal to become Americans.

Finding all this information takes time. If you are going to find your family's stories and facts, you need to have a plan. How do you make that plan? You'll find out in Chapter Two.

Detector's To-Do List

Every chapter in this book offers tips about tracing your family history. At the end of each chapter, you'll find these lists to remind you of the steps you can take to move your research along.

❑ Ask your parents and others about family stories. Are there any famous (or notorious) relatives in your family? (See Chapter Three for lots of ideas about the best way to record these stories.)

❑ Ask about family artifacts. Are there any old documents, such as Lily's great-grandfather's identity card, or precious hand-me-downs, like Dafna's family book? (See Chapter Two for more about how to use these.)

❑ Has anyone in your family already started researching the family history? Ask around. *Their* history will become a part of *your* history!

CHAPTER TWO

Getting Started

The First Steps in Your Family Search

In this chapter, you will learn to:
- Draft a first version of your own story
- Make your first Pedigree Chart
- Use family charts and other documents
- Create personalized family trees
- Find your family's treasured items

Y ou've heard about others' discoveries. Now it's time to begin to learn how to make your own.

You are going to become an ancestor detector. You will work backward into the past from what you already know to what you want to know—just as a detective does. You will be collecting data, looking for clues, and following up on tips and snips of information. Eventually the clues will lead you to exciting discoveries.

"You won't be able to find much," someone in your family may say. "Our ancestors came from a country where very few records were kept."

"I doubt you'll get far," someone else might warn. "No one really remembers that much about where our family came from."

Another family member may tell you, "The records that did exist are gone; they were destroyed during World War II."

All those comments are reasonable. But one of the great joys of genealogy is showing family members that what they think is impossible—finding pieces of your past—really *is* possible. Someone in your family may remember more than anyone knows. And a surprising number of old records do exist—in the United States and in other countries, too.

You've started on a jigsaw puzzle for a lifetime, because genealogy is a hobby that never ends. You can work on it for a while, then leave it for weeks or even months. But looking into your family's past is thrilling, and there's always more to learn. You'll come back to it time and again.

Finding out about your ancestors won't always be easy, however. You might pursue a certain piece of your puzzle for a very long time, following all the leads, doing everything exactly right, and come up with nothing. There will be times when you won't have a clue about what to do next.

But there will also be rewarding times. One day you might uncover a piece of information—something you've been trying to verify over months or even years— and suddenly a whole section of the puzzle will fall into place. You might make connections that add new people, places, or events to your family's story.

Most important, there will be unforgettable moments. Imagine digging up a wonderful story about your grandfather's childhood, or learning how your family played a part in a famous event. Just think of what it would be like to read a note one of your ancestors wrote a hundred years ago, or to find the name of a long-forgotten family member.

GETTING STARTED: WRITING YOUR OWN STORY

Your own long and fascinating history is waiting to be discovered. But exactly how do you begin to unearth your family's secrets? Well, the basics of genealogical research are as simple as 1-2-3:

1. Gather all the facts you know or can find out about your family. By talking to relatives, you will locate lots of information about your family's past. You might also discover that they have documents that can lead you to more information.

2. Organize what you discover. Put all your information in one place, arranged so that you can find it easily and refer to it. Make sure everything is accurate.

3. Using what you've learned, look for new information. Based on the information you have found, look for new sources of facts and stories about your family. Interview newly discovered relatives. Use what you've learned to search the Internet. (See Chapter Eight, "Catching Your Ancestors with a Net.") Write away for

Color-Coding Your Families

Doing genealogical research means handling many pieces of paper—even if you use computers for much of your family hunt. You need to keep track of many different family surnames (last names). And you need to keep the information together in a way that allows you to find what you need when you need it.

The best solution? Set up a color-coded genealogical filing system.

Choose one color for each of your four grandparents' last names. (Remember, your grandmothers' last names were likely different before they married your grandfathers.) If you are using a loose-leaf notebook for your family information sheets and the typed-up transcripts of interviews, use color-coded dividers to separate each grandparent's last name.

For any material—birth certificates, boat manifests, death certificates, citizenship papers, and so on—that doesn't fit into a notebook (or if your records are mostly computerized), use four color-coded file folders. Mark each of these files with your grandparents' last names. If your files get too full, you may want to make subfiles as you search back in time and branch out with more and more surnames. Just be sure to use the four-color code, which will help you keep track of how each family fits into the overall family picture.

government documents, school documents, and other records. Explore sources of information about the places and people most important to your family. Make sure this information is accurate, then add it to your records. And start the process over again.

Of course, you'll need some kind of record-keeping system. You want a place where you can safely record information as you learn it. When you discover new facts, you need to be able to add that information—easily—to what you've already learned.

You can simply use a loose-leaf notebook, a package of loose-leaf paper, some section dividers, and a pencil. If you are using a computer, you might set up a series of folders on your computer. But whether you are writing or typing, you will eventually need to set up a filing system with file folders. (For help with this, see the "Color-Coding Your Families" box above.)

FAMILY RECORD

Family records can be as simple as a list of names—or fancier, like this family tree of hearts and fruits.

Now you are ready to take your first step—putting together your first genealogical document.

An important rule in genealogy says, "Go from the known to the unknown. Let what you know lead you to what you don't know." Things that you know about your own life will lead you to information about your parents' lives. Facts about your parents' lives will give you clues to your grandparents' lives. In this way, you will delve deeper and deeper into the past.

You will craft your first document alone. You don't need to log on to the Internet, conduct an interview, visit a records center, or go to the library. You just need to gather information from the person you know best: yourself.

Find some quiet time and start writing the facts of your life. See "The Story of Me" on page 40 or go to *www.workman.com/familytree* and click on Downloadables, then "The Story of Me." You should start at the very beginning ("My name is _____ and I was born on _____"). You can fill in a copy of "The Story of Me," or you can just record the answers on your loose-leaf paper or on your computer.

Fill in as much of this information as you know. Then check with your parents or other relatives on the sheet and ask them to check your answers and to fill in any blanks that they can.

When you finish, examine this, your first genealogical record, carefully. What information are you not 100 percent sure of? Mark those bits of information with a question mark. What information is missing?

Once you've answered those questions, you're ready for the next step: transferring this information onto your first genealogical chart.

FAMILY TREES AND PEDIGREES

There are lots of ways to show what you know about your family's history. Some of the most common are family trees, pedigrees, lineage charts, and family diagrams. Although people sometimes use them interchangeably, the terms do mean different things.

Pedigree Charts show only the direct ancestors of an individual (parents, grandparents, great-grandparents, etc.). They don't include brothers and sisters (siblings), cousins, or uncles and aunts.

The Pedigree Chart is the most basic genealogical document. You'll find a blank Pedigree Chart on page 28. The instructions on how to fill it in follow here. You can also download and print out a copy at *www.workman.com/familytree.*

Family trees, also called family charts, are much less formal than pedigree charts. They are basically picturelike lists of family members. A family tree can include a dozen names or a thousand. It can tell a lot about every family member—or just his or her name.

Family trees can show brothers and sisters, cousins, and aunts and uncles. They may sometimes include the names of very close family friends, very distant relatives, and even (I've seen it done!) pets. Family trees come in all kinds of designs. Many are drawn to look like (naturally!) trees. But families have also created their "trees" in the shapes of fancy fans or flowers, organ pipes or peacocks, bridge cables or candelabra. And whatever shape your family is—two parents, single parent, step-parent, adopted, and so on—your family tree can proudly reflect that fact.

One rule of family charts is that they have to be readable. Everyone listed should be able to find his or her name fairly easily. Some trees even include photographs of family members.

You can easily put together a family tree of your own. In fact, you already began when you put together your "Story of Me."

Putting Your Pedigree Together

To do research about your ancestors, you will find it useful to fill in a Pedigree Chart like the one on page 28. These charts are usually used to identify your biological ancestors—people to whom you are related genetically. If any of your direct ancestors had not existed, you would not exist.

Computer programs make putting together a Pedigree Chart faster, neater, and easier. There are many software programs that do the job nicely; you can check out some suggestions in Chapter Eight, "Catching Your Ancestors with a Net," to find one that is best for you.

If you already have a software program, follow the instructions for inputting the names of all your family members. Be sure to double-check your typing.

If you go to *www.workman.com/familytree* you will be

Branching Out: Unusual Family Trees

Family trees can be displayed in many creative ways. People don't just write them down. They sew them, paint, crochet, appliqué, embroider, and computerize them. There are photo family trees using pictures of each generation. There are calligraphy trees made out of the names of all the family members.

In a booklet called *The Living Family Tree,* Marie Schreiner offered suggestions for unusual family trees. Among her ideas:

- **Artifact tree.** Make a tree using items that relate to each person: a lock of hair, a fingerprint, a baby tooth.
- **Meaningful-shape tree.** A family tree doesn't have to look like a tree. Why not use a shape that reflects your family? The Schreiners used organ pipes to list their names. Marie suggests books on a shelf for a family of avid readers or an airplane outline for the family of a pilot.

Picture this: a family tree filled with photos.

- **"Palm" tree.** Maryloo Stephens created a tree out of 81 handprints. Relatives sent tracings of their hands to her, and Maryloo cut out the shapes using a different shade of blue fabric for each generation. She embroidered the name of the hand's owner on each print and added a number indicating the order of birth. The handprints were then attached to a tree trunk, which Maryloo appliquéd and placed on a quilt. This quilt was presented to Maryloo's mother and father as a gift for their sixtieth wedding anniversary.

Other projects include a Popsicle-stick tree, a cross-stitch tree, and several family tree quilts.

For today's families, many shapes can be appropriate. You'll find fan- and pyramid-shaped charts in this chapter. Or look at Natasha's family flower in Chapter One. Try coming up with your own inventive shapes. And see what your computer software offers.

What Shape Is Your Family?

This book aims to help you paint a picture of your family, past and present. As you trace your genealogy, you will come across charts and other forms that assume some things about your family. Those assumptions may not always fit.

For example, Pedigree Charts show who your direct ancestors are. They may seem to say that this is your "real" family. But, of course, families come in all shapes and sizes. That's certainly true today, when many people don't live in a family with the two parents to whom they were born and four living grandparents who gave birth to those parents.

Every family is "real." Here are some types of families you might find in the United States today:

Two parents living with the children they gave birth to.

Blended families made up of parents living with children from their present marriage and children from previous marriages. In blended families there may be stepbrothers and stepsisters, half-brothers and half-sisters.

Families created through adoption. Sometimes an adoption is an "open" one in which everyone knows who the birth parents are. Other times the adoptive family knows very little about the birth family, perhaps because they went to another country to find their child. Children in the United States today have been adopted from many places, including China, Korea, Russia, India, and Latin America.

Single parents with their birth children. In most cases, the single parent is a mom, but there are single-dad families, too.

able to download and print out multiple copies of the blank Pedigree Chart and an alternate chart for nontraditional families.

If you fill out your Pedigree Chart by hand, be sure to use pencil so you can erase if need be. As you continue your research and information gathering, you'll discover new facts that will make it necessary to revise your charts. You don't want to have to revise an entire page because some information turns out to be incorrect.

Before you start filling in the chart, mind this simple genealogical rule when writing down dates: Always put the day first, the full name of the month second, and the full year third. For example, 25 June 1847 and 30 January 1988. This is not the way we Americans are used to writing dates, but it works best for genealogy.

Single parents with adopted children. Again, in most cases the single parent is a mom, but there are also single dads who adopt children.

Families in which the grandparents are raising the children. There may be no other parent in the household.

Families of divorce, in which one or both parents may have remarried and the children live with each parent at different times.

All of these families are obviously real families, even if they don't all fit easily on a Pedigree Chart. The Pedigree Chart is valuable for showing your direct ancestors, but it isn't the only important chart. In making a family tree, you are free to create any shape or form you want. You might want to try a Family Fan or a Family Pyramid, shown here. (There's a bigger fill-in version of the Family Fan at the end of the chapter.)

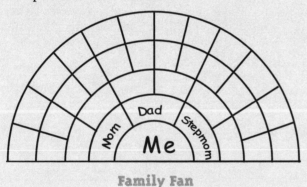

Family Fan

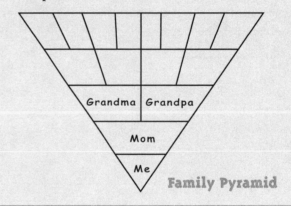

Family Pyramid

Writing out the month can help prevent confusion. Shorter methods can lead to mistakes: Does 6/11/86 mean June 11, 1986, or November 6, 1886?

Begin filling in your chart. At the far left-hand corner, write your name next to Number 1. Always write the last names in CAPITAL letters and first names in upper and lower case (Evan LEVINE). At "Born," write your date of birth. Next to "Place," write where you were born, including the town and state or country: Albany, New York; London, England; Helena, Montana; or Lomza, Poland, for instance.

If you know the county or province of a birthplace, write that down, too. This will make it easier to locate a small town. For example, Bedford, Taylor County, Iowa, is easier to find than simply Bedford, Iowa. This is especially true with common names—there are at least three

PEDIGREE CHART

This is chart number _____.

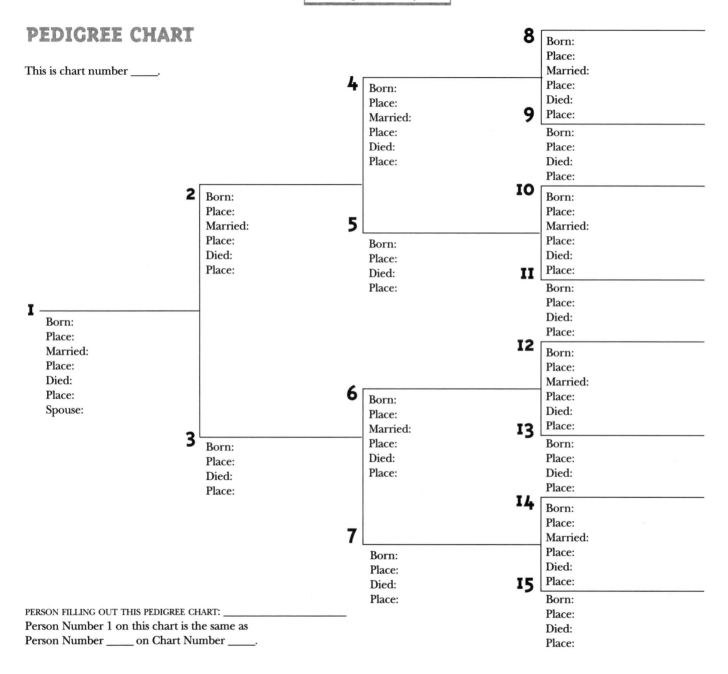

8
Born:
Place:
Married:
Place:
Died:
Place:

4
Born:
Place:
Married:
Place:
Died:
Place:

9
Born:
Place:
Died:
Place:

2
Born:
Place:
Married:
Place:
Died:
Place:

5
Born:
Place:
Died:
Place:

10
Born:
Place:
Married:
Place:
Died:
Place:

11
Born:
Place:
Died:
Place:

1
Born:
Place:
Married:
Place:
Died:
Place:
Spouse:

12
Born:
Place:
Married:
Place:
Died:
Place:

6
Born:
Place:
Married:
Place:
Died:
Place:

13
Born:
Place:
Died:
Place:

3
Born:
Place:
Died:
Place:

14
Born:
Place:
Married:
Place:
Died:
Place:

7
Born:
Place:
Died:
Place:

15
Born:
Place:
Died:
Place:

PERSON FILLING OUT THIS PEDIGREE CHART: _____
Person Number 1 on this chart is the same as
Person Number _____ on Chart Number _____.

This is chart number _____.

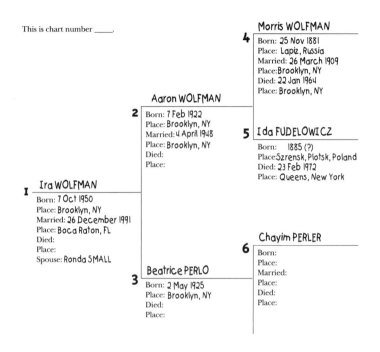

Morris WOLFMAN
4
Born: 25 Nov 1881
Place: Lapiz, Russia
Married: 26 March 1909
Place: Brooklyn, NY
Died: 22 Jan 1964
Place: Brooklyn, NY

Aaron WOLFMAN
2
Born: 7 Feb 1922
Place: Brooklyn, NY
Married: 4 April 1948
Place: Brooklyn, NY
Died:
Place:

Ida FUDELOWICZ
5
Born: 1885 (?)
Place: Szrensk, Plotsk, Poland
Died: 23 Feb 1972
Place: Queens, New York

Ira WOLFMAN
1
Born: 7 Oct 1950
Place: Brooklyn, NY
Married: 26 December 1991
Place: Boca Raton, FL
Died:
Place:
Spouse: Ronda SMALL

Chayim PERLER
6
Born:
Place:
Married:
Place:
Died:
Place:

Beatrice PERLO
3
Born: 2 May 1925
Place: Brooklyn, NY
Died:
Place:

Pedigree charts are used to show your biological anestors.

villages in Ohio called Oakwood. So whenever you can, indicate the county.

After you've filled in your personal information, do the same for your parents. Write your father's name next to Number 2, and next to Number 3 write your mother's first and maiden name (her last name *before* she was married). This number pattern—even numbers (2, 4, 6, 8) for men and odd numbers (3, 5, 7, 9) for women—is the way to keep all your genealogical records. (The only exception to the odd/even rule is for Number

1. Put yourself there whether you're male or female.) List every woman under her maiden (unmarried) name.

Under your parents' names, write their dates and places of birth. The date and place of your parents' marriage is listed under your father's information.

By the time you come to your grandparents (numbers 4 to 7), even your parents may not have all the answers. And when you reach your great-grandparents (8 to 15), there will almost certainly be gaps of information. You probably won't know some of the names for these slots—especially the maiden names of your great-grandmothers.

In your genealogical hunt, you will be adding to this Pedigree Chart all the time. Unless you are storing your charts electronically, make photocopies of it and keep them in your loose-leaf notebook.

Where Do You Put Extra Ancestors?

If you manage to trace your family very far back, you won't be able to fit all the generations on one chart.

But on any Pedigree Chart, you can add a note that says, "Person Number 1 on this chart is the same as Person Number _____ on Chart Number _____." This is called a "cross-reference," and it's the key to keeping your records in order.

So if you find an ancestor who goes back further than the spaces in your chart, just expand to another page.

First Cousins, Second Cousins, and Removed Cousins!

Did you ever wonder what a second cousin was? Or a first cousin once removed? How do you get a cousin removed, anyway? And can you get a second cousin once removed, moved a second time? These terms are a shorthand way of explaining how you are connected to other relatives.

The chart on the next page can help you figure out how you are related to your many cousins. But before you learn how to use the chart, you need to understand what "second" and "third" and "removed" mean.

Cousin is a term for someone who is descended from a common ancestor with you. Almost all of your relatives are cousins of one sort or another (except your sisters, brothers, parents, grandparents, children, or spouse). The children of your parents' brothers and sisters are your cousins. So are the children of your parents' cousins. But one is a first cousin, and one is a second cousin.

A *first cousin* is someone who has two of the same grandparents as you. A *second cousin* is someone who has the same *great*-grandparents. As you go further back, the relationship becomes more distant. So your *third cousin* is someone whose *great-great*-grandparents are the same as yours. You probably even have eighth and ninth cousins somewhere.

Removed means that you and your relative are from different generations. Someone *once removed* would be a child of your grandparents' siblings. For example, my father's first cousin is my first cousin once removed; my grandfather's first cousin is my first cousin twice removed.

Say you discover information about Number 16 (your great-great-grandfather) that leads you to *his* father. You could then put Great-great-grandpa at spot Number 1 on another chart, which you'd label Chart Number 2. Your new discovery (Great-great-great-grandpa) would be written in at the Number 2 spot.

And at the bottom of the new chart, you'd write, "Person Number 1 on this chart is the same as Person Number 16 on Chart Number 1."

A Family Group Sheet

Another useful chart for genealogists is the Family Group Sheet, which is used to organize information about all the members of your family, including the many who do not get entered on your Pedigree Chart. Sisters, brothers, cousins, uncles, aunts, great-uncles, and great-aunts are not direct ancestors, so their records should be entered on these sheets.

Make several copies of the blank Family Group

Here's how the chart works:

1. Figure out what relative ("X") you have in common with another relative.

2. Find your relationship to "X" in the far left-hand column.

3. Have your relative find his or her relationship to "X" in the very top row.

4. Now figure out where your row and column meet. That's the formal term of *your* relationship.

Example: Sharon and Evie are both related to Ida. Sharon is Ida's granddaughter (far left column, number 2). Evie is Ida's great-granddaughter (top column, number 3). Sharon and Evie are first cousins once removed.

		1	2	3	4	5	6
	COMMON ANCESTOR	CHILD	GRAND-CHILD	GREAT-GRAND-CHILD	G-G-GRAND-CHILD	G-G-G-GRAND-CHILD	4G-GRAND-CHILD
1	CHILD	BROTHER/SISTER	NEPHEW/NIECE	GRAND-NEPHEW/INIECE	GREAT-GRAND-NEPHEW/NIECE	G-G-GRAND NEPHEW/NIECE	G-G-G-GRAND-NEPHEW/NIECE
2	GRAND-CHILD	NEPHEW/NIECE	1ST COUSIN	1ST COUSIN ONCE REMOVED	1ST COUSIN TWICE REMOVED	1ST COUSIN 3X REMOVED	1ST COUSIN 4X REMOVED
3	GREAT GRAND-CHILD	GRAND-NEPHEW/NIECE	1ST COUSIN ONCE REMOVED	2ND COUSIN	2ND COUSIN ONCE REMOVED	2ND COUSIN TWICE REMOVED	2ND COUSIN 3X REMOVED
4	G-G-GRAND-CHILD	GREAT-GRAND-NEPHEW/NIECE	1ST COUSIN TWICE REMOVED	2ND COUSIN ONCE REMOVED	3RD COUSIN	3RD COUSIN ONCE REMOVED	3RD COUSIN TWICE REMOVED
5	G-G-G-GRAND-CHILD	G-G-GRAND-NEPHEW/NIECE	1ST COUSIN 3X REMOVED	2ND COUSIN TWICE REMOVED	3RD COUSIN ONCE REMOVED	4TH COUSIN	4TH COUSIN ONCE REMOVED
6	4G-GRAND-CHILD	G-G-G-GRAND-NEPHEW/NIECE	1ST COUSIN 4X REMOVED	2ND COUSIN 3X REMOVED	3RD COUSIN TWICE REMOVED	4TH COUSIN ONCE REMOVED	5TH COUSIN

Sheet on page 43, or download and print it out from *www.workman.com/familytree*. Make up one Family Group Sheet for every "nuclear family"—that is, each group of parents and children. The family name should be written in large letters at the top of the page, followed by the husband's name, with all of his information on the lines directly below. Place the wife's name and her information on the designated lines. Below, place the name of each child of that marriage, in order of birth.

Fill in the Family Group Sheet for your father, mother, any brothers or sisters, and yourself. When you come to the "Children" section, start with the firstborn in your family. Then list the other children in order of birth, down to the youngest. Names—including your own—should be written last name, first name, middle name, and then any other given names or nicknames.

Every member of your family should end up on at least one group sheet. Some will be on two—one as a child, then another as a parent when they have their own families.

You don't have to use this particular Family Group Sheet. Maybe you want to include baptism, communion, bar or bat mitzvah, or other religious ceremony dates. You might even want to include a physical description or a photograph. Design your own Family Group Sheet, or use the back of the sample sheet for those kinds of things. Just be sure to use the same style throughout.

Keep all your Family Group Sheets together in your loose-leaf book. Group them according to last name, and keep them in chronological order—either oldest or youngest family on top, followed by the rest in order. That will make it easier to find them. And you *will* need them. These sheets are where you are going to keep much of the information you find. Later you can use the information to make other Pedigree Charts and family trees.

Keeping Track of Your Family's Addresses

Another chart you will want to create is a family address log. This is a list of addresses where family members lived and the dates they lived there.

Set up a record so that there is plenty of room to write in new addresses for every few years. Addresses that have been forgotten can be found on many documents—birth certificates, marriage licenses, wills,

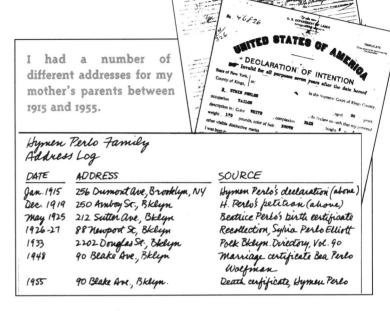

I had a number of different addresses for my mother's parents between 1915 and 1955.

Hymen Perlo Family
Address Log

DATE	ADDRESS	SOURCE
Jan. 1915	256 Dumont Ave, Brooklyn, NY	Hymen Perlo's declaration (above)
Dec. 1919	250 Amboy St., B'klyn	H. Perlo's petition (above)
May 1925	212 Sutter Ave, B'klyn	Beatrice Perlo's birth certificate
1926-27	88 Newport St, B'klyn	Recollection, Sylvia Perlo Elliott
1933	2202 Douglas St, B'klyn	Polk B'klyn. Directory, Vol. 90
1948	90 Blake Ave., B'klyn	Marriage certificate Bea Perlo Wolfman
1955	90 Blake Ave., B'klyn.	Death certificate, Hymen Perlo

and such. Perhaps you will find letters that your parents or grandparents saved or old phone books and city directories, which many local libraries carry.

Next to the date and the address, write where you got the information. This "Source" column is very important. You must keep track of where every bit of information comes from because you may get conflicting information later. Knowing where you got the data will help you decide which is more trustworthy. A good place to keep this log is on the back of the Family Group Sheet.

FAMILY ARTIFACTS: SPECIAL PIECES OF YOUR HISTORY

Where should you go to find new information about your family, information you can add to all of your

Genealogical Jewels

Here's a list of locations where family papers and treasures may be found. Ask your relatives if they have any of these items and, if so, whether you could see them.

- Announcements and invitations
- Books (baby books, diaries, family histories, family recipe books, other old books, school yearbooks, autograph books)
- Certificates (birth, christening, bar or bat mitzvah, confirmation, school, military, marriage, divorce, and death)
- Deeds and wills
- Family Bibles

- Family trees or charts
- Heirlooms (quilts, jewelry, old books, candlesticks, furniture)
- Identification cards
- Letters
- Newspaper clippings
- Photo albums
- Scrapbooks
- Trophies, plaques, or other awards

family charts? The obvious answers might include government offices, records centers, and databases on the Internet.

Some of the most interesting, exciting, and often surprising family information, however, is located in your own home and in the homes of your relatives. Precious pieces of your family story are waiting in photo albums, scrapbooks, baby books, and family Bibles. You'll also discover family history in the clothing, toys, and religious items that have been in your family for decades.

In fact, *anything* that mattered to one of your relatives is worth seeking out and studying for clues about an ancestor. So ask your parents and other relatives if they have any of these kinds of things (see "Genealogical Jewels," above), and if you can look through them.

Many of these "treasures" may be old and in very fragile condition. Handle them with great care. Don't touch photographs except on the edges. Handle old books very gently; their pages may crack or the spines may break if you are too rough with them. Look at the inside front cover and the last pages. There may be an inscription or notes made by the previous owners. If the owner of a family artifact is nervous about you handling it, suggest that they turn the pages or hold the item while

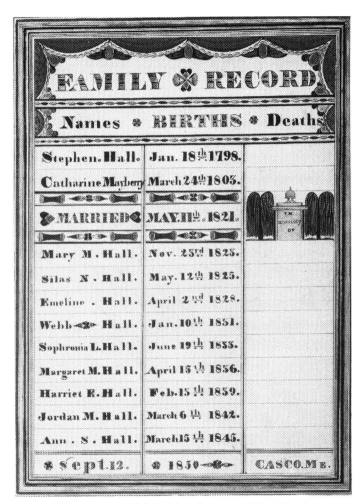

Discovering a wonderful old family record like this document from Maine would make a genealogist jump for joy.

Documents such as citizenship papers, passports, old driver's licenses, and school records often include a person's date and place of birth. They may also list the names of both parents (including the hard-to-find grandmother's maiden name).

Photo Opportunities

Family photo albums can be wonderful resources. You may hear stories about the circumstances under which a photo was taken or about the people in the picture. Just seeing photos of ancestors sometimes jogs people's memories and may bring to mind a long-lost name.

Ask your relatives to talk about the people in the pictures. After they've identified who's who, you may want to ask them about the way the people were dressed. Before about 1920, taking pictures was considered a great occasion and people often wore their best outfits. What were your ancestors wearing? What do the clothes say about them? Were the clothes serious or cheerful, worn or new, dressy or casual?

Where was each photograph taken? Check to see if the name of the photographer's studio, its location, or a date is on the back.

If there is more than one person in the photograph, are the people related? Is everyone dressed the same way? Are their hairstyles the same? Are the women wearing head scarves and aprons, and are the men wearing hats? If so, are they in the style of America or the Old Country?

you just look. Write down any significant dates you find on your Family Group Sheets, noting where you found the information.

Handling Old Family Photographs

Photographs are not merely pieces of paper. They are chemical compositions, usually coated with gelatin and silver. Photos can be harmed by light, air, or dust. For that reason, they need to be protected.

Here are some points to remember:

- When you look at old photographs, handle them with great care. Be sure your hands are clean, and touch old photos only on the corners. Oil or dirt from fingers can ruin photographs.

- Keep old photos out of temperature extremes. Don't store them in an attic or basement where it's hot or damp.

- If you can identify the photos in any way, it is a good idea to label them on the back. But *never* write with a ballpoint pen. Instead, use a Stabilo art pencil, which you can pick up in any art store for about two dollars. These pencils leave less of an impression than regular pencils. When you write, be sure not to press hard, and don't write on the area where people's faces are. Another possibility is to buy gummed labels and write the information on them, again using a Stabilo. Then you can carefully transfer the label to the back of the photo.

- Do not store photos one on top of the other. This is especially important if anything has been written on the back; ink can come off and ruin your pictures. Place acid-free paper between old photographs.

- Never fix an old photograph with cellophane tape; it cracks and leaves a residue. Also, don't attach photos with paper clips, bunch them together with rubber bands, or glue them into books.

- If you can scan pictures into your computer, do so—but be sure to treat the originals with care.

Our Own Artifacts

The most precious articles in your family may not be rare or expensive but, rather, those handed down from one generation to another, from father or mother to son or daughter. These items are special mainly because of their history, and they are highly valued simply because they are beautiful or because they played a part in a family's past. Be on the lookout for them.

Old samplers (decorative pictures sewn onto cloth) or quilts that have been in the family for a long time may have names and dates of birth embroidered onto them.

Gently look underneath and behind pieces of furniture. Ask if you can look at the backs of paintings. Sometimes you may find notes or inscriptions on those, too.

Perhaps you will come across a clock that your great-grandfather made. Does anyone know when great-grandpa made it, or why? Did he make others? How did the person who owns it today receive it? Is there a story behind it?

You may find hundreds of other fascinating items in family collections: crocheted tablecloths or handmade dolls, a hat with a funny history, a portrait of a parent left behind in another country, a book brought across the sea by a young woman who loved to read.

Whenever you find any information, be sure to record it in your notebook. This could be as simple as writing a line or two on your great-uncle's Family Group Sheet about the trumpet he played in order to smuggle it past border guards. Or you could start a special Treasure Sheet, a page in your notebook filled with your impressions of artifacts you examine. Write down the name of the person who showed the treasure to you and where and when you saw it. You *must* keep track of where every bit of data comes from, because you may uncover conflicting information later. Knowing each source will help you decide what information is trustworthy.

The author of this book could not make the wedding pictured above; his parents were getting married. But a few years later, he did manage to pose for the portrait at right.

A Special Book: The Family Bible

Once, nearly every family had its own "family records center," but it wasn't computerized, fancy, or expensive. It was a copy of the family Bible, the one book almost every home was sure to have. Within the pages of a King James Bible or an Old Testament (sometimes called a *Chumash* in Jewish families), someone in the family wrote down the names and dates of important events. This was the practice in millions of families, and not just in the United States.

Some Bibles came with pages already provided for recording birth, marriage, and death dates. In other Bibles, the owners just wrote on blank pages. If your family has any Bibles that have been handed down, look them over carefully. Check the inside covers and the pages between the Old and New Testaments, which were the most common spots for registering information.

The most valuable Bibles are those that were kept as a running record of family history. Some were passed down from parent to child, from generation to generation. If you come across an old Bible, ask yourself:

- Are the dates all written in the same handwriting?
- Is the color of the ink always the same, even for different dates?

Look for handwritten information in family Bibles and books.

If both answers are yes, your Bible may be a summary rather than an ongoing record. Often family members copied dates from one source to another. If you suspect this is so, check the front of the Bible for a date of publication. If that date is more recent than any of the births, you're looking at a summary.

But if the dates seem to have been written *as they occurred,* you may have found a special and accurate record of your family's vital events. Make a note of all the information, being sure to indicate whether it came from an original record or from a summary.

Internet Links

For these and other clickable links, go to *www.workman.com/familytree*.

GENEALOGICAL CHARTS

www.pbs.org/kbyu/ancestors/charts
At this site, you can easily download various blank forms—Pedigree Charts, Family Group Sheets, a personal time line sheet, a checklist of places to look for family information, and research logs. The site is run by the people who produced *Ancestors*, a PBS-TV show on genealogy.

www.workman.com/familytree
Created for readers of this book, this site contains blank forms for pedigree charts, family group sheets, and a research log. It also includes sample family trees and links to other genealogy websites.

www.ancestry.com/save/charts/ancchart.htm
Here you will find lots of free, downloadable charts that you can print out and use, including Ancestry (Pedigree) Charts, Family Group Sheets, research calendars, all kinds of research extract forms, and a "source summary" form to note where you got your information.

www.familytreemagazine.com/forms/download.html
Log on to this site for tons of downloadable forms, including five-generation Pedigree and Family Group Sheets, research calendars, time lines, and census forms.

BEGINNER INFORMATION

AOL Genealogy Forum, Keyword: Roots
www.genealogyforum.com/gfaol/beginner/beginner.htm
This is an information-rich area about genealogy for subscribers to America Online. It includes beginners' information, online courses, and databases. Some of this information is also available on the web to non-AOL members.

www.familysearch.com/sg/
Here you will find how-to guides, a glossary of genealogical terms, and a catalog helper from one of the biggest sites on the Internet, the LDS (Mormon) church's *familysearch.com*. (See Chapter Nine for more about the LDS.)

www.usigs.org/index.htm
Check out the United States Internet Genealogical Society for lots of resources with articles, encouragement, and useful information.

Richer Than Jewels

You now have information about your family, and you know some of what you DON'T know. You've also looked for family jewels in your own home, and perhaps you've found some there or in relatives' homes.

Now comes the richest part of your genealogical treasure hunt.

This hunt isn't for golden coins or jewels but for something even more precious: memories and information that reveal things about your family, past or present. You will find them through the stories and memories your relatives share with you.

You will find these special memories and items by talking to your relatives, by visiting them in their homes, and by watching and listening very carefully.

In the next chapter, you will learn how to create a successful interview. You'll discover what to look for, how to find what you're looking for, and how these things can help you discover much more about your family.

Detector's To-Do List

❑ Put together the first draft of your life story.

❑ Work with your parents and other family members to answer questions left unanswered.

❑ Look into getting a genealogical computer software program.

❑ Start filling in blank charts by photocopying the ones in this book, downloading some from the web, or entering information into a genealogical software program.

❑ Begin entering data on your family charts.

❑ Think about the kind of family tree you might like to create.

❑ Pull together your genealogical supplies: loose-leaf notebook, pencils, multicolored file folders. Set up your folders.

❑ Ask your parents and other relatives if they have any family artifacts.

The Story of Me

PERSONAL HISTORY OF _____

Today's date (day/month/year) _____

My name is _____. I was born on (day, month, year) _____
in (city, county, state, country) _____. I was named after _____.

MY PARENTS

My parents' full names are:

Father _____   Mother_____

Date of birth _____   _____

Place of birth _____   _____

My parents were married on (date) _____ in (place) _____.

MY HOME

I now live at this address (building number, street, city, state, zip code): _____

I have also lived at the following addresses:

_____

_____

WERE YOU ADOPTED?

If so, include this information:

I was adopted by my parents or parent on (date) _____ in (place) _____.

Other facts about my adoption: _____

BROTHERS AND SISTERS (and step- and half-siblings)

Here are the names of my brothers and/or sisters (if any), and when and where they were born:

Name _____

Date of birth _____

Place of birth _____

This child was named after _____.

Name _____

Date of birth _____

Place of birth _____

This child was named after _____.

Name _____

Date of birth _____

Place of birth _____

This child was named after _____.

Name _____

Date of birth _____

Place of birth _____

This child was named after _____.

(Add more siblings, if any.)

GRANDPARENTS

My grandparents' full names are :

FATHER'S PARENTS

Grandfather _____   Grandmother _____

Date of birth _____   _____

Place of birth _____   _____

Date of marriage _____   Place of marriage _____

MOTHER'S PARENTS

Grandfather _____   Grandmother _____

Date of birth _____   _____

Place of birth _____   _____

Date of marriage _____   Place of marriage _____

FAMILY FAN

An Alternative Family Chart

If a pedigree chart isn't right for your family, try this fan chart. Place your name at the center, then write in important family members in the spaces above—divided any way you choose. The second level can include only one parent, or be divided for three or more names for stepparents, birth and adoptive parents, or other relatives. (See page 27 for an example.)

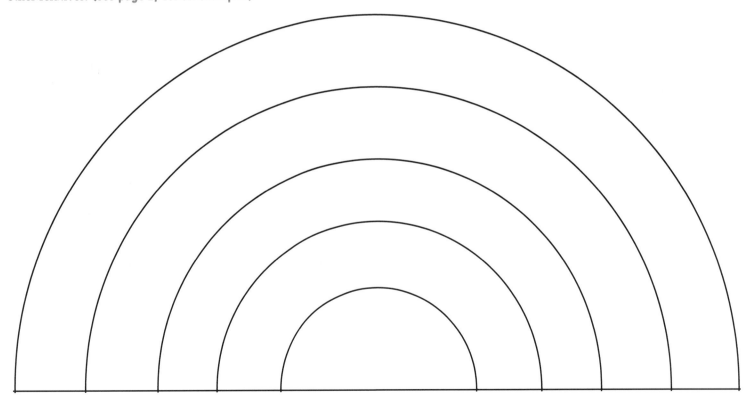

FAMILY GROUP SHEET

HUSBAND		WIFE	
Born	Place	Born	Place
Married	Place	– –	
Died	Place	Died	Place
Buried	Place	Buried	Place
Husband's Father		Wife's Father	
Husband's Mother		Wife's Mother	
Husband's Other Wives		Wife's Other Husbands	

CHILDREN Last Name, First Name, Middle Name, Nickname or Other	WHEN BORN Day/Month/Year	WHERE BORN Town/County/State	DATE OF FIRST MARRIAGE To Whom	WHEN DIED Day/Month/Year
			– – – – – – – – – –	_____
			– – – – – – – – – –	_____
			– – – – – – – – – –	_____
			– – – – – – – – – –	_____
			– – – – – – – – – –	_____
			– – – – – – – – – –	_____
			– – – – – – – – – –	_____

Sources of Information

CHAPTER THREE

Let's Talk About . . . Us!

How to Do Great Family Interviews

In this chapter, you will learn how to:
- Interview your family members
- Ask the best questions
- Bring the right materials
- Record the interview in the easiest way
- Use your family treasures

"What was it like growing up in a small town in Poland—before cars or planes or television?"

I was sitting in the living room of my "Tanta" (Great-aunt) Blima's home. More than 90 years old, she still lived by herself in an apartment in New Jersey. That afternoon I learned that my great-aunt had a sharp sense of humor. And that she remembered . . . a lot.

"I was the youngest one, the baby," she replied. "When I was still young, my father went to America, and he said he would send for my mother and me. We had to make a living while he was gone, so my mother ran a little grocery in the town. She would bake bread, and we sold beer to the people. But it was a little undercover, because I don't think that we were supposed to sell the beer. I was maybe 13, 14 years old."

"Did you ever drink the beer?" I asked.

"No," she answered, "but I washed my hair with it."

Tanta Blima was the oldest person I knew of in my family and one of the first people I called when I began researching my genealogy. When I asked if I could come talk to her about the old times, she said, "Sure, sure!"

The author's great-aunt—"Tanta" Blima—as a young woman.

I couldn't believe my eyes. I was holding an old piece of paper covered with writing in German and Russian. I don't speak either language, and I couldn't make out what the document was. But I could read the date on the bottom of the page: 25 October 1913. This document was about 75 years old! And Tanta Blima had taken it out of a drawer and given it to me as if I had asked for a glass of water or an apple—nothing special, just "Look at this."

I later found out a lot more about what my great-aunt had given me. That piece of paper had been her passport to go from Russia to Germany on her way to the United States. An obvious clue might have been a photograph on the document—but there was none. As I later learned, in 1913, most passports didn't have photos. Instead, they used words to describe the person. When I had it translated, this is what it said:

Weight:	Large	Small	Medium
Eyes:	Blue	Brown	Black
Mouth:	Large	Small	Unremarkable
Nose:	Large	Small	Unremarkable

This description was what officials in Russia and Germany went by to decide if she was really Blima Fudelowicz, the 16-year-old girl who was on her way with her mother to America.

Blima told me how her father would travel between Russia and Germany in the years before he left for New York. She remembered the boat trip to America with her mother when she was 16 years old, and how she had felt sick for some of the days at sea.

Then I asked, "By the way, do you have any papers or documents, things from the Old Country?"

"I think so," she replied. She walked off to look in the drawers of her dresser. In a moment, she returned with a faded piece of paper. "Here, look at this," she said.

One of the best ways to fill in gaps in your family history is to interview relatives. If you can, bring along a tape recorder.

When I left Tanta Blima's home a couple of hours later, I thought about all that had happened that afternoon. First of all, I had fun talking with my great-aunt, whom I had never visited before. I thought she, too, had enjoyed our conversation. But there was more: I had also opened a door to the past. I had been given a peek into a young girl's life in the early 20th century. I learned a little bit about someone I had known, but not really known, my entire life. And I had uncovered documents and facts about my family's history!

That is the magic of family interviews.

PREPARED TO FIND TREASURE

Afternoons like the one I spent with my Tanta Blima are not rare when you are tracing your family history. As you can see, your greatest source in genealogy is not the Internet, government records, or genealogical libraries. The richest storehouse of information about your family is . . . your family! And memories are the most precious of all family treasures. Nothing can capture the story of your family the way your grandparents and other relatives can. They have lived through some historic moments and if you take the time to ask them, they can recall them for you firsthand. They may remember the smallest details of significant family moments, details that aren't recorded anywhere else. And these details can bring ancestors to life.

When these spoken recollections are gathered, organized, and preserved, the information is called an "oral history." Oral histories do not grow out of rambling reminiscences—they are collected through carefully directed interviews. That's where you come in. As an ancestor detector, *you* get to ask the questions.

Whom do you think you should interview? Most genealogists would say, "Everyone in the family." After all, probably every family member knows something no one else knows. And one of those memories may help you solve a piece of your family puzzle.

The best place to start is with the people you feel

Record It!

Tape or video recorders can really help you document your family history. If you possibly can, bring a recorder to every interview.

Some people may feel a little self-conscious talking with a recorder on. Small tape recorders ease this problem; they are usually forgotten after a short period of time. Camcorders, on the other hand, are more intrusive and often require a second person to operate them.

Whichever recording device you use, it's a good idea to engage in small talk before you turn the recorder on, just to make the talker feel comfortable. Then ease gently into the interview—with the recorder on. Ask simple questions, like "How long have you lived here?" or "Can you tell me a little bit about this photograph? When was it taken? Who are the people in it?"

Before you begin, write the name, date, time, and place of the interview on the outside of the tape. Also speak those words into the recorder so that they are the first thing you hear when you play the tape back: "Interview by Billy Jones with Aunt Gertrude (Gus) James, 2:30 P.M., Saturday, December 14, 2000, at her home on Collins Avenue in Miami, Florida."

When you end the interview, say this same information before shutting off the recorder.

most comfortable with. Begin by interviewing your mom and dad, then move on to other relatives you know well. When you feel like you are an experienced interviewer, you'll want to talk with your oldest relatives. They know the most about the earliest days of your family. They are, in fact, a precious link to the past. Someone born in 1930 not only can give you memories of the 1940s but may have heard firsthand tales of the 1890s from someone who was 70 years old in 1940. You may connect 100 years in one conversation!

You won't always be able to sit down with your subjects. Some of them may live far away from you. In those cases, your interviews can take place over the telephone, by e-mail, or by letter-questionnaire.

However you do it, conducting a successful oral history interview isn't always easy. How well you do depends partly on your relatives: what they know, what they are willing to talk about, and how much they remember. But much depends on you and your ability to combine the best attributes of caring friend, hard-nosed reporter, and sensitive psychologist. You've got to get your relatives talking.

Thirteen Tips for a Successful Interview

In normal conversation, both people talk. Ideas are exchanged. Each person contributes information. The talk flows in unpredictable ways.

Interviews are different. One person has a goal: to get information from another person (let's call him or her "the talker"). You want the talker to feel comfortable, but you also need to direct the conversation to the points you are interested in.

You also have to be flexible. Sometimes an unexpected topic can turn out to be wonderful. Other times you'll need to lead your talker back to the main point—without hurting his or her feelings. This can be difficult, but you will become better at it as you go along—practice will make you skilled. Be patient with yourself and expect some mistakes. To make things easier, keep these tips in mind:

1. Before any interview, give advance warning.

Explain what you want to do, why you want to do it, and why the talker is important to you and your research. You can call or write a letter or e-mail. Here's an example of the kinds of things you should say:

Dear Aunt Gus:

I'm working on a history of our family, and it would be very helpful if I could sit down and talk with you. I'm particularly interested in your memories of my great-grandparents (your mother and father) and the family's early years in Minnesota. I'd also love to look at any old photographs or documents you have.

I won't need much more than an hour of your time and would like to hold our talk at your home. Any weekend day would be fine. Can you let me know a date that is convenient for you?

Thanks so much for your help.

By writing this letter, you've given your relative a chance to start thinking about the topics you're interested in, and you may have even jogged her memory. Of course, not all your relatives will be close by, and your arrangements may be more difficult than "any weekend day." That just makes your writing—and planning—even more important.

2. Prepare before your interview. Find out whatever you can about the talker *before* the interview. Where does she fit in the family? What documents might she have? What other genealogical jewels might she have? (It's a good idea to send her a copy of the list on page 33 before you go.)

Did she meet someone no one else knew? Where did she live? Who else was close to her? Gather as much information as you can ahead of time about her relationship to everyone in your family. Your parents can probably help you with this.

Left: The bustling marketplace in the Polish village of Lomza in the early 1900s. Right: The author's great-grandfather, who helped his son Max emigrate from Lomza, Poland.

3. Think out all your questions beforehand.

Interviewing requires structure. Write your questions on a sheet of paper, organized by subject. One easy way to organize what you want to ask is by year: Start with your relative's earliest years and then move on from there.

"So, Aunt Gus, you lived in the house in a town outside Minneapolis till you were 10—about 1922, right? Then where did you move?" Or "You say Great-grandpa worked as a tailor in St. Paul. Did you ever visit his shop? Where was it? What years did he have the business there?" As this interviewer did, it's a good idea to summarize what you already know so that your subject can verify your facts. Then move on to a request for more detail.

Sometimes the simplest questions can hit the jackpot. I asked my great-uncle Max, "How old were you when you went from Poland to America?" I didn't get an answer; I got a story:

I must have been about 15 when I went to Warsaw to get a visa to emigrate. I got the visa, but then the counselor at the examination said, "Listen, boy, you are underage. You can't go without your father." He crossed out my stamp.

(continued on page 52)

Saving Your Own Life

One of the best ways to practice putting together the story of your ancestors is by telling your own story. You may not think you have much to tell, but you do. Think of someone 100 years from now and imagine the questions he or she will have: Who were you? Where did you come from? What was your life like? What did you do with your days? What kind of home did you live in? Who else was in your family? What mattered most to you? What did you hope to accomplish?

You don't have to answer those particular questions. There may be others that give more of a sense of who you are. You choose. Then sit down and try to write about yourself—something that will tell your descendants 100 years from now what it felt like to be you at this time.

You can use more than just words in this life history. Photographs are very helpful. So are relevant documents. There are dozens of possibilities here, in fact: your birth or baptismal certificate; a report card; an award for athletic or academic achievement; a map you draw of your neighborhood; letters you wrote or letters someone wrote to you; a list of your favorite books, sports teams, movies, or music.

Describe what you look like: how tall you are; what color your hair and eyes are; what kind of clothes you like to wear. Include whether you're quiet or outgoing, optimistic or pessimistic, energetic or slow-moving. List your friends and the things you do for fun; what you do with your family; where your family has lived. You can list addresses and what you remember about each home.

Be sure to include stories about yourself. Don't just tell what *you* remember; think about things you've

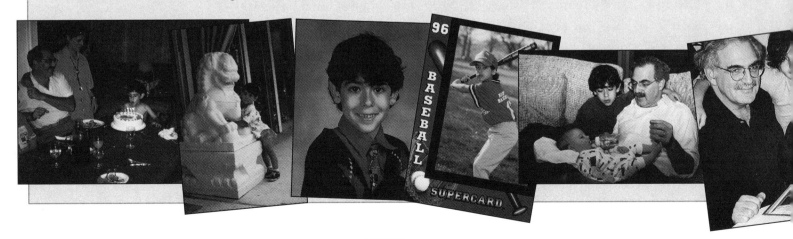

heard about yourself from members of your family. Mention things you're proud of, as well as things you've done that you're not so proud of. A little bit of the less-than-perfect side of your life will make your history much more honest and realistic.

Try to give a picture of day-to-day life. What does an apple cost? A bicycle? How much is a meal in a restaurant? What kinds of foods do you eat? How many hours a week do you go to school or work? How much free time do the people in your family have? Do your parents work outside the home? What do they do?

Write about customs and rituals in your life: how you celebrate birthdays and holidays, what you do on weekends, whether you are religious and, if so, how you practice your religion.

You will also want to give your future relatives a sense of the larger world you live in. What is life like in the early years of the 21st century in your family, in your town, in your state, and in your country? Maybe you should include the front page of a local newspaper, a copy of a news magazine, or a list of stories covered on the national TV news one night. Did any of those news stories affect you? Explain how.

Once you've finished the report, date it. Then put it away somewhere safe. This document is going to be very valuable to you for a couple of reasons.

First of all, it will be a model to use when you write about your relatives. See if you can describe their personalities, their day-to-day lives, and the flavor of their times in the same spirit with which you captured your own.

Second, this report will be a wonderful record for you of this moment in time. Years from now, you will find it fun to reread and see who you were when you wrote it. In fact, you may want to write a new one every few years.

I went back to our town and told my father. He said, "Don't worry, we'll take care of that."

My father was a religious man, but he also knew how to get things done. He called a policeman from our town and asked him to make me older.

I got new papers. Now I turned from 15 to 18 or 19. I went back to Warsaw, and I was able to leave. And on February 20, 1920, I took the boat Susquehanna *from Danzig to New York.*

Remember to also ask open-ended questions. "What do you remember most about the apartment on Division Street?" or "Tell me about your relationship with your brothers" may yield something unexpected and wonderful.

This photo could remind someone of a great family story.

4. Bring a video or tape recorder if possible. A small tape recorder usually doesn't disturb anyone, and it catches every bit of information, including the way your talkers sound and exactly how they answer questions. If you don't have a tape recorder, ask your parents if you can borrow or rent one. Even better is a videotape camera. If you plan to videotape, be sure someone comes with you to run the camera. *You* need to focus on your talker. (See "Record It!" on page 47 for some suggestions.)

5. In any case, bring a notebook and pen. Even if you have a recorder, *always* take handwritten notes. Recorders can break down.

During the interview, write down names and dates and double-check them with your subject. Facts are important, but the most important information your talkers offer are their stories. Try to capture the way they talk and their colorful expressions: "That ship was rolling on the ocean like a marble in your hand."

There's another good reason to bring pen and paper with you. You won't have to interrupt when you think of a question; just write a note to yourself so you'll remember to ask it at an appropriate time.

6. Start with easy, friendly questions. Leave the more difficult or emotional material for later in the interview, after you've had time to gain your talker's trust. If things

No Truth Without Proof

Although the family stories you hear may be fascinating, they may also not be true. Is there any proof that your ancestor fought in the Civil War and that he won a medal? If not, then it might be just a wonderful story—not a fact, but a fine family legend. (Family legends are fine, as long as you label them as such.)

If you don't have proof for a piece of information—where someone was born, what he did in the war—then you can't claim it as a fact.

You may find yourself with two different facts for the same event, like two different birth dates, far apart, for the same person. In that case, you'll have to evaluate the clues and decide which one is right. The important thing is to know where you got each piece of information. Eventually you'll probably amass enough support material to be able to tell what is valid and what isn't.

A story backed up by a document becomes a "quite-possible" story. Your job is to determine which stories are "possibles," which are "probables," and which sound terrific but are more a testimony to family imagination than to family history.

Aaron Wolfman, the author's father, during World War II.

---

aren't going well, you may want to save those questions for another time.

It's also a good idea to begin with questions about the person you're interviewing. You may be more interested in a great-grandfather if he is the missing link in your Pedigree Chart. But first get some background information about your talker—your aunt, for example. This serves two purposes. First, it lets her know she's important to you, that you care about her, and that her life is interesting, too. Second, as she talks, she may reveal some other information that you would never have known about otherwise.

Also, when asking for dates, relate them to your talker. "How old were you when Uncle Bill died?" is often a better way of discovering when the event happened than simply asking, "What year did Uncle Bill die?"

(continued on page 56)

Good Questions for Family Interviews

When you visit a relative, you should have lots of questions prepared. Many will grow out of the particular history of the relative you are interviewing or from the kind of information you hope he or she can give you. However, there are dozens of areas that you can cover in an interview. Here are a number of questions that I have found useful to ask my family members:

• **Home and community life.** "What do you remember about the house you lived in? How many bedrooms did it have? Where did most of the family activities go on? What was the neighborhood (village) like? What kind of people lived there? What did you do for fun? Who else lived in the neighborhood (village, etc.)? What kinds of activities went on there?"

• **Personalities and relationships.** "Tell me about your parents: What kind of people were they? What was most important to them? Did they have a good marriage? What do you remember best about them? What was your relationship like with your mother/father/sister/brother?"

• **Economic conditions.** "How did the family earn money? Who worked? How did your family compare to others in the neighborhood—richer or poorer or in the middle? Who handled the family finances? Were there any major economic setbacks? Were there any big successes? What kinds of things did the family spend money on?"

• **Family characteristics.** "Were there a lot of people in the family who looked like each other? What were the most outstanding family characteristics? Are there any diseases that run in the family? Any physical oddities? Was anyone in our family famous or notorious? Was there a 'black sheep' in the family? Do you remember any big family celebration or event or a crisis in the family?"

Questions that explore the links between family members can turn up wonderful anecdotes. Be sure to ask about family "characters," and try to get a sense of how they were received within the family.

• **Family facts.** You will always be trying to fill in the blanks on your Pedigree Chart and Family Group Sheets. Show your subject the charts and ask: "Who were you named after? Do you know the names of your parents' parents? Do you know anyone who would know more than you do about that branch of the family?

"Where are members of our family buried? Is there a family burial plot? What did Great-grandma die of?"

• **Life in the Old Country** (for immigrants). What do you remember most about your life before you came to America? What did you do for entertainment in the Old Country? Do you remember going to school there? What kind of work did your family members do? What kind of work did you do? Did any members of your family leave the Old Country before you did? Who? When and why did they leave? Who decided to move your family to the United States?

• **Coming to America** (for immigrants). Do you remember anything about your trip to America? How did you come? How long did it take? Where did you eat and sleep during the trip? Do you remember when you entered the United States?

Where did you come? What was your first impression? Who met you when you arrived? Where did you go on that first day?

If you are lucky enough to have relatives who remember their immigration, question them carefully. There's a lot of richness—and family history—in their memories. These relatives may also have fascinating family artifacts. Looking over these items is like touching a story because often they have family tales connected to them. (Before each interview, take a look at the information about family artifacts on pages 32 and 33.)

Great old family photos—with clues for your research—may be hidden away in a shoebox.

and want to rush in with another question when your talker stops speaking. *Don't.* Silence is an important part of interviewing, and it can sometimes lead to very interesting results. Because people find silence uncomfortable, they often try to fill it if you don't—and in doing so, they may say something you might not have heard otherwise.

Sometimes silence is also necessary for gathering thoughts. Don't forget—you are asking your subjects to think back on things they may not have considered for years. Calling up these memories may spark other thoughts, too. Allow your subject time to ponder. You may be thrilled by what he or she remembers.

9. Ask the same question in different ways. People don't know how much they know, and rephrasing a question can give you more information. This happens all the time. "I don't know," a relative will tell you, sometimes impatiently. They *do* know—they just don't know that they know. The most common version of this occurs when an interviewer asks, "What was your father's mother's name?" The relative answers, "I never knew her. I don't know." Then a few minutes later, in response to "Whom were you named after?" this answer comes: "My father's mother."

Try to find a couple of ways to ask important questions. You may feel like you're being repetitive, but you never can be sure what you will learn.

Talk to older family members; there is no better source for wonderful bits of information about your heritage.

7. Bring family photographs with you. Use the pictures during the interview. Look for photos, artwork, or documents that will help jog your subject's memory. Bring the pictures out and ask your talker to describe what's going on. "Do you remember when this was taken? Who are the people? Where was it taken? What was the occasion? Who do you think took the picture?" You may be amazed at how much detail your relative will see in a photograph and also at the memories that come spilling forth.

8. Don't be afraid of silence. You might feel uneasy

10. Ask about family treasures. Do your relatives own anything old and special? When your talkers bring out an heirloom, ask them to describe what you're looking at. What is it? How was it used? Who made it? Who gave it to them? Ask if there are any stories connected with it, or any documents.

11. Be sensitive to what you discover. Sometimes people become emotional talking about the past. They may remember long-dead relatives or once-forgotten tragedies. If your talker is upset by a memory, either remain silent or quietly ask, "Is it all right if we talk some more about this? Or would you rather not?" People frequently feel better when they talk about sad things; you should gently give your relative the *choice* of whether or not to go on.

12. Try not to interrupt. If your talker strays from the subject, let him or her finish the story and then say, "Let's get back to Uncle Moe" or "You said something earlier about . . ." By not interrupting, you make the conversation friendlier, and the story may lead you to something you didn't expect.

Of course, there is always the exception to the rule. If a story goes on forever and seems useless, the best way to handle it may be to say, "Gee, Aunt Gus, could you hold the rest of that story for later? I'd like to get the facts out of the way and then come back to that."

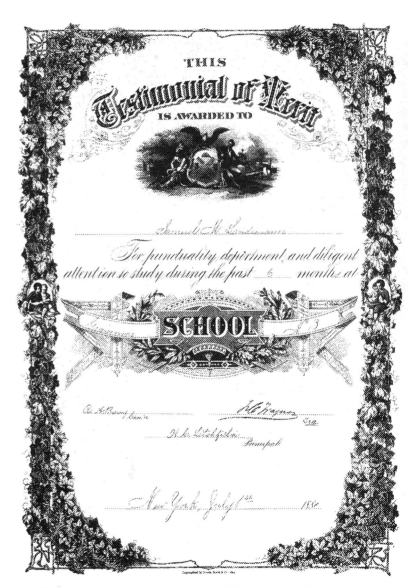

In the 1880s, this was just a boy's certificate for good behavior. Today, it's a piece of precious family history.

Internet Links

For these and other clickable links, go to *www.workman.com/familytree.*

Oral History Questions

genealogy.com/00000030.html?Welcome=983765712

Here's a good list of interviewing questions on a variety of topics. Included are growing up, religion, the family's physical characteristics, occupations, historical events, and immigration stories.

Journal Jar: Recipe Questions for a Life History

www.omnicron.com/~fluzby/sister-share/journal.htm

This site has more than 400 questions for family interviews. But it also offers a clever family-history project: a "Journal Jar." This is a different way to inspire someone to tell you his life story. You place family-life questions on strips of paper into a jar. A family member can then pull them out, one at a time, and write down (or tell you) his or her answers.

A Script for Family Interviews

rootsweb.com/~lineage/famhist.htm

This site presents dozens of questions, arranged by topic, in a kind of conversational order. It includes useful follow-up questions that you logically should ask after specific answers. Print out the list and use it to do an interview with older family members.

Guide for Interviewing Family Members

rootsweb.com/~flgso/intvwqus.htm

Genealogist Dick Eastman assembled this collection of family-history interview questions. Topics covered include grandparents, childhood, the family house, friends and games, school, the family's philosophy, and others.

---

13. Ask for songs, poems, unusual memories. You may discover something wonderful when you ask your subject if she recalls the rhymes she used to recite while jumping rope as a little girl or the hymns she sang in church. Probe a little here—ask about childhood games and memories, smells and tastes and sounds. (See box, "Good Questions for Family Interviews," page 54.)

After the Interview

Your interview should not last more than about an hour. People do best when they're not tired. If you think there's more to talk about, schedule another interview. That will give you time to review your notes and consider any other questions you might want to ask. It will also give your relative time to remember more things.

After you've done the interviewing, your hardest, most important work lies ahead. You have to go through the information and analyze it. What have you learned? Did you discover any new relatives or find out about something worth following up? How accurate is what you have learned?

If you recorded the interview, transcribe it—that is, create a written document of the important things your talker told you. You don't have to write down or type every word Aunt Gus said, but try to hold on to the *way* she said it. If you didn't record the interview but only took notes, rewrite or type them so they're neat and legible.

Review the information. Take out your Family Group Sheets and see if you can add to any of them. Maybe you'll have the name of a third son in a family you've never heard of or the address of a home that your grandparents lived in. Write everything in its appropriate place, and be sure to indicate where the information came from. This will come in handy when you want to verify the accuracy of what you've learned.

There's one last, very important step: thanking your talkers. They have been generous with their time, energy, and memory. Sending them a thank-you note and a copy of the interview (for corrections and additions) is a way to show that you value what they've shared.

One of the goals in researching your genealogy is to make your family aware of each other and of their common history. If your relatives' experiences during the interviews are good ones and if you are thoughtful in showing appreciation, they may be inclined to give you even more help.

Detector's To-Do List

☐ Interview your parents about their family history. Practice interviewing with them.

☐ Make appointments to interview other family members.

☐ Prepare your questions. Use the lists in this chapter as a guide. If you'd like the entire list, print it out at *www.workman.com/familytree*. Check off the questions that are most relevant. Write your own list.

☐ Type up your notes from interviews. Ask the relatives you interviewed to review them and correct or add to them.

☐ Write a thank-you note to every family member you interviewed.

CHAPTER FOUR

What's Your Name?

The History, Mystery, and Meaning of Family Names

In this chapter, you will learn how to:

- Research the history of all your family names
- Say the name "Smith" in 25 languages
- Find out what your last name means
- Search for your name across the Internet

"Hello," the man in the white coat said as he walked into the room. "I'm Bill Doctor."

It took a minute to sink in. Was this man really called Dr. Doctor?

Yes, he admitted with a good-natured shrug. "If someone asks, 'Is there a doctor in the house?' I guess I should answer twice."

Why is that funny? What makes us laugh if we meet a Judy Tailor who works as a tailor or a Billy Baker who specializes in cakes? What makes us do a double take when we see a sign that reads "Law Offices of Ellen Law"?

There is one simple reason: We don't expect names to *mean* anything. But they do. Names are filled with meaning, symbolism, and history. First and middle names frequently have family tradition behind them. Family names may reveal where ancestors lived, what they looked like, how they acted or spoke, how they earned a living, or who their parents were.

Start with your own name. Do you know the original family names of your grandparents? They probably hint at the country (or countries) your family comes from, but their meanings may be hidden from you because the names are in the language of your relatives' original homeland.

Even if you don't know the meanings of your ancestors' names, there are ways to go about deciphering them. In the Appendix, you'll find a dictionary of almost 400 last names adapted from the *New Dictionary of American Family Names*. You may find one or more of your own family names there. "Finding Out About Your Names" on page 70 offers more suggestions on how to proceed in your name search.

You'll also find great resources about names on the Internet. You can join mailing lists dedicated to studying specific last names. You can find lots of information about where your last name is most common. And you can check out interactive surname maps, the history of names, and sites that explain which nicknames most commonly went with which names back 100 or even 200 years ago. See the box "Internet Links" on page 71 for specific URLs.

Tracing the History of Names

Last names are a modern invention. From the earliest days of human beings until recently, people across the world had only one name. They were John or Ivan, Abdul or Shoshana, Sese or Haile, Isabella or Roberto—and that was enough. Parents gave children unique names, made up just for them. Almost everyone lived in the countryside or in villages with very small populations, so one name suited most folks just fine.

What kind of work did your ancestors do? Family names such as Farmer, Plowman, Tiller, and others may offer clues.

But as the years went on, villages grew larger and became towns. Towns turned into cities. Some people began naming their children after famous heroes or religious figures.

As a result, many towns had people with the same name. In 14th-century England, for example, two out of every three men in the country had one of five names—

First Names

Where did your first name come from? Were you named after someone special? Is your name part of a family naming tradition?

You may not be aware of it, but your first name is loaded with meaning. Your parents thought long and hard before choosing it.

In the earliest days of naming, parents often chose names that would bless their children with special qualities. Faith, Hope, and Grace are just three examples among English-language names. In American colonial times, daughters in particular ended up with names like Patience and Charity.

Boys' names also carried meanings, but many of them have been lost to us. Robert means "famous" or "bright"; Peter means "rock"; Curtis, "courteous"; Seth, "the appointed one"; Richard, "powerful ruler"; and Donald, "world ruler."

First names also have meanings *within* families. Certain names occur again and again in one family's history. For example, in some families, firstborn sons are named after the father or grandfather. In Catholic families, names may be taken from saints. And Jewish parents frequently name their children after relatives who have recently died.

These naming patterns may be genealogical clues. Be sure to ask all your family members what they know about their own first names.

Henry, William, Robert, John, and Richard. This made for some pretty interesting situations.

Imagine an English village around that time. Someone new arrives in town and asks a native, "Excuse me, but where can I find William?"

"Which William?" the native responds. "Are you looking for William who has a house at the lake? Or William whose father is that loud rascal John? Or maybe you mean William who runs the mill? Or the William who has the flaming red hair?"

Across Europe, scenes like this were common. More and more natives ended up describing their neighbors. Soon, within the town, people didn't just say "William" anymore—they automatically referred to "William whose house is at the lake," "William son of John," "William the Miller," and "William the Red."

Over time, long-winded phrases such as "whose house is at the" were dropped, and only "William Lake" remained. William, John's son, became William Johnson; William the Miller became William Miller; and William the Red became William Russell, the Old English word for "red-haired." Last names had arrived.

The growth of family names spread over the next few hundred years. Governments began insisting that people take second names because they needed those names to tax their citizens and draft young men into their armies.

But as late as 1800, many people were still without surnames. It was only over the course of the next 100 years that countries in eastern Europe and Scandinavia finally insisted their people adopt permanent family names.

Four Kinds of Names

Permanent names were decided upon in a few ways. In many cases, people chose the one they wanted, then the government recorded it. At other times, the officials picked the name.

Names often came naturally. A man was given a nickname in addition to his first name, the nickname stuck, and it was eventually adopted as a permanent name that was passed on from father to son. Daughters were expected to take their dad's surname until they married; then they were to take their husband's name. And that's the way it has been until recently (see "Hyphenated Names" on page 68).

But where did all those last names come from? Let's go back to the medieval English village and its many Williams. Their names came from one of four sources:

- **Dad's name (patronymic).** The father's name with "son" immediately after it.
- **Place name.** Words that identified where a person lived.
- **Job (occupational) name.** What a person did for a living.
- **Nickname.** Names based on a person's characteristics (personality or appearance).

There is an excellent chance your name comes from one of these four types because they account for more than 90 percent of the names in America today. Here are some examples.

John Porter of HY = JOHN PORTER (son) OF HENRY
John Ellor (Jacob Son) = JOHN ELLOR (JACOB SON)
John Wood (of John) = JOHN WOOD (son) (of John)
John Wood of James = JOHN WOOD (son) of James
John McLeod Self + Estate = JOHN McLEOD SELF AND ESTATE
Jonathan + Wm Eady = JONATHAN AND WILLIAM EADY

On this old list, you see permanent family names and patronymics, like Jacobson on line 2.

The Mighty Smith

The most common family name in the world is Chang (also spelled Zhang). More than 75 million Chinese carry that moniker. But the name that is most common in Western countries is—are you surprised?—Smith.

There are about 3.3 million Smiths in the United States; at least 500,000 in England and Wales; nearly 100,000 in Scotland; more than 75,000 in Canada; over 30,000 in Ireland; and probably another 50,000 in Australia and New Zealand. In each of those countries, about 1 out of every 100 people is named Smith.

The name Smith comes from the Old English word *smite*, which means "to strike." Smiths worked with metals, using hammers or other tools to smite the metal and make something useful, such as horseshoes, plows, tools, or swords. These implements were important to people in the village, which must have made Smith an important person in town.

That must be part of the reason why in every nation there are people whose names translate as "Smith." For example:

Patronymics (dads' names) are carried by about one in every four Americans. Numerous English names evolved like this: Bill, son of Robert, became Bill Robertson or Robinson. Other names are similar: Wilson, Johnson, Jameson, Jackson. There are a few cases in which names were given after the mother—Allison (Alice's son) is one English-language example—but they are rare.

Sometimes a father's name was adopted with just an "s" at the end: Peters, James, Rogers. There are even cases in which the father's name was adopted as is: Robert, son of George, became Robert George; Tommy, son of John, became Tommy John.

The word *patronymic* comes from the Latin word *pater*, which means "father." Patronymics occur in most European languages. In Sweden, Norway, Denmark, and German-speaking countries, they are easy to spot: Hansen is Hans's son; and Ludwig's son is Ludwigsohn.

Arabic: *Haddad*
Armenian: *Darbinian*
Bulgarian: *Kovac*
Catalan: *Feffer*
Czech: *Kovar*
Dutch: *Smid, Smidt, Smit, Smed*
Estonian: *Raudsepp, Kalevi*
Finnish: *Rautio, Seppanen*
French: *Lefevre, Lefebvre, Ferrier, Ferron, Faure*
German: *Schmidt, Schmitt, Schmid, Schmitz*
Greek: *Skmiton*
Gypsy: *Petulengro*
Hungarian: *Kovacs*
Irish Gaelic: *Gough, Goff*
Italian: *Feffaro, Ferraro*
Norwegian: *Smid*
Persian: *Ahangar*
Polish: *Kowal*
Portuguese: *Ferreiro*

Romanian: *Covaciu*
Russian: *Kuznetsov, Koval*
Spanish: *Herrera*
Swedish: *Smed*
Turkish: *Temirzi*
Welsh: *Goff, Gowan*

There are also a number of specialized Smiths: Mr. Goldsmith, Mr. Hammersmith (he made hammers), and Mr. Naismith (he made nails). And in addition to the millions of just plain Smiths in the United States, there are Smithers, Smithsons, and Smythes. Originally, all of them were workers in metal or children of those workers.

Amid all those metal-minded people, there is one Smith type whose ancestors may never have picked up a hammer. Smithfields got their name from a location; in Old English, the name means "smooth field."

In Spanish, the ending *ez* indicates "son of"—as in Rodriguez and Fernandez, the sons of Rodrigo and Fernando.

In Slavic countries (Russia, Poland, Lithuania, Yugoslavia, Czechoslovakia), "son of" is indicated by a variation of *ov, vich,* or *wicz*: Romanov, Ivanovich, and Janowicz are the sons of Roman, Ivan, and Janos.

For a list of different attachments that indicate "son of" or, occasionally, "ancestors of" in other languages, see "Daddy's Boys" on page 66.

Place names. More than 40 percent of all Americans have names that have to do with a location. There are two types of these names: local and long distance. The first had to do with a physical description of a local resident's home; the other was adopted for people who moved in from another town or country.

A "local" name came from the physical characteristics of the land where someone lived. For example,

Daddy's Boys:
Patronymics Around the World

Here is a list of the attachments (mostly endings) that indicate "son of" or "ancestor of" in other languages, plus examples of how they are used:

aitis, onis, Lithuanian; son of (Gerulaitis, son of Gero)

ak, ack, Polish; descendant of (Agustyniak, descendant of August)

akis, akos, Greek; descendant of (Theodorakis, descendant of Theodore)

Ap, Welsh; son of, comes before the name (Ap Richard turned into Pritchard, Ap Owen into Bowen, Ap Howell into Powell)

Ben, Hebrew; son of, comes before the name (Ben Gurion, Ben Yehuda)

chuk, chik, Ukrainian; descendant of (Kovalchik, Adamchuk)

enko, Ukrainian; son of (Shevchenko, son of Shevcho)

es, Portuguese; son of (Lopes, son of Lope)

escu, Romanian; of our family (Romanescu, Antonescu)

ez, Spanish; son of (Perez, son of Pedro, Juarez, son of Juan)

William who lived at the hill became William Hill. If he lived at the marsh, William Marsh. And if William lived near a great gathering of trees, he might have been dubbed William Forest or Woods.

The same thing held true in many other languages. In German, Mr. Woods would have been Mr. Wald; in French, Mr. DuBois; in Italian, Mr. Bosco.

A "long-distance" name had to do with the town or country from which someone came. If Heinrich moved from Vienna to another city, his neighbors might refer to him as Heinrich from Vienna (Wien)—or, in German, Heinrich Wiener. This is how many names came about, including the Italian Di Napoli (from Naples), the Russian Minsky (from Minsk), the German Salzburger (from Salzburg), and the English Sunderland (from the southern lands of Scotland).

Job (occupational) names are carried by about 15 percent of Americans. People commonly took these names from their work: butchers, bakers, butlers, tailors, and so on. James the Baker became James Baker; James

Fitz, English (Norman); son of, comes before the name (FitzGerald)

ian, Armenian; son of (Khatchaturian, Manoogian)

Ibn, Arabic; son of, comes before the name (Yusuf Ibn Khalid, son of Khalid)

Mac, Scottish; descendant of (MacDougal)

Mc, Irish; descendant of (McGlynn)

O', Irish (Gaelic); descendant or grandson of (O'Connor, O'Keith)

ov, Slavic (Russian, etc.); son of (Romanoff, Romanov)

poulous, Greek; son of (Andropolous, son of Andros)

s, English; son of (Edwards, Williams, Peters, Adams)

sen, Norwegian, Danish; son of (Peterssen, Carlssen)

sohn, German; son of (Mendelsohn, Sarasohn)

son, Swedish; son of (Swenson)

vich, Russian; son of (Denisovich)

vici, Romanian, Serbian; son of (Marcovici)

wicz, wiecz, Polish; son of (Karkowicz)

zoon, Dutch; son of (Anderzoon)

the Tailor became James Taylor. Mr. Tailor would be Signore Sartori in Italian, Herr Schneider in German, Monsieur Tailleur in French, and Pan Krawczyk in Polish. Baker is Becker in German, Piekarz in Polish, Fornari in Italian, and Boulanger in French.

A few occupational surnames are specifically female and were probably given to a family in which the woman was well known for her talent. Baxter was a female baker; Thaxter was a woman known for her work thatching roofs.

Nicknames. This fourth type of surname, held by about 15 percent of all Americans, is based on personal characteristics. To this day, people get nicknames for their personality traits (Wild Willie) or their physical attributes (Big Mike). You may have had—or given—one of those names yourself. When surnames were being taken, some people ended up with nicknames that have lasted hundreds of years. For example, among Old English names, Hardy, Short, and Long refer to physical characteristics; Goodman, Savage, and

Hyphenated Names

For the last few hundred years, there was a strict rule about surnames: Men had the enduring ones, and women followed.

A single woman carried her father's name, and when she married, she took her husband's last name. Bill James's daughter Sue was known as Sue James. When she married Bob Jones, she instantly turned into Sue Jones.

There were a few occasions when famous female last names were preserved. If Jack Nobody married Linda Distinguished—who came from a wealthy and well-respected family—sometimes Jack would take on Linda's last name. In Great Britain, the solution to this problem was to attach the woman's high-class name to the man's: Armstrong-Jones, Coverly-Smith, Scott-Moncrieff.

But in most of Western society, the male name was the one that survived. Until the last decades of the 20th century, that is. As more women pursued careers of their own, some began to resist losing their birth names. Should a well-known painter, lawyer, doctor, or engineer change her name overnight because she marries? If a woman works hard to build up a good name in her field, why should she give it up?

Two solutions were arrived at. One was that old British standard, the hyphenated name, a joining of both families. If Ann Sayers married Peter Slocum, she could become Ann Sayers-Slocum. The children could then be named either Slocum or Sayers-Slocum.

The other solution was simpler. "I'll keep my name; you keep yours." So Ann Sayers remained Ann Sayers, and she would say, "I'd like you to meet my husband, Peter Slocum." Generally, the kids still took the father's last name.

Nowadays, the second solution seems to be the more popular one. Many women still take their husband's names, and some women and men create hyphenated offspring. What did your parents decide to do?

Truman refer to an individual's personality.

Other European languages follow the same pattern. Hungarian Mr. Nagy (big) was a large fellow; Germans must have thought Lustig was a happy guy; the Poles regarded Mr. Halas as a noisy, bustling type; and the French thought Mr. Belcher was . . . no, not rude, but *bel cher,* or "well loved."

Hundreds of negative names were given out, but many of them disappeared over the centuries because people chose to change their names to something more pleasing. In other cases, no one remembers negative meanings. Besides, those negative meanings have nothing to do with the characteristics of people today. Think about this: Kennedy means "large or ugly head" in Irish Gaelic. Names reveal the past but don't determine the present.

Other Types of Names

In addition to these four major types, there are a number of other kinds of names in the United States today.

Mr. Smith got his name from working with metal.

Asian names generally don't follow the standard Western patterns. In China, where surnames have a very long history, they are almost always one-syllable words that may be taken after the name of an old ruling family (Song) or a verb like Tung (to correct). There are few occupational or location names. Vietnamese names like Ky, Thieiu, and Nguyen grow out of the Chinese tradition.

In Japan, names have been created more recently, usually combining two unrelated, often poetic words. Suzuki means "bell" and "tree"; Nakada means "middle" and "rice field"; Nakamura means "middle" and "village."

Jewish names sometimes are made up of acronyms, abbreviations that combine a number of words. The common Katz often comes from *kohen tzedek,* two Hebrew words that mean "righteous priest." Segal, also Chagall, stands for *segan leviah,* meaning "priest of righteousness." And Schatz comes from *shaliah tzibur,* Hebrew for "representative of the congregation."

African names have been very rare in America

American kids carry last names from many cultures and many languages.

until recently. Most slaves were forced to take names that their masters were comfortable with. As a result, many African-American surnames today are of British origin, reflecting the backgrounds of the masters.

In the last half of the 20th century, some African-Americans have returned to ancestral names. The well-known writers LeRoi Jones and Paulette Williams both changed their names; they are now Amiri Baraka and Ntozake Shange.

Other African-Americans have taken names that reflect their conversion to the religion of Islam. Boxer Cassius Clay is now world famous as Muhammad Ali, and basketball star Lew Alcindor changed his name to Kareem Abdul-Jabbar.

FINDING OUT ABOUT YOUR NAMES

There are over 1.6 million different family names in the United States, and each one has its own history. Here's how to begin to search for the history of the names in your family:

• **Is the name original?** Before you do anything else, find out if the names you are researching—your last name, for example, or those of your grandparents—are the ones your ancestors had before coming to this country. Many have been altered. Sometimes immigrants made changes in order to feel more American or to try to avoid prejudice. Often names changed because English-speaking clerks had problems understanding the sounds of foreign languages.

Whatever the reason, you want to know about any change and, if you can, find out not only how but also why it occurred. This may give you a good story or personal insight into your ancestors.

Start by asking your parents or your oldest relatives. They may even know the precise spelling of Old Country versions of your family names.

• **What language is it?** You probably know the ethnic heritage and language of your last name. If for any reason you don't, your parents should be able to tell you.

Once you know which language your name comes from, you can look it up in a dictionary of that language.

Internet Links

For these and other clickable links, go to *www.workman.com/familytree.*

Here are a few fun websites that may help you find interesting information about your family surnames and names.

18th- and 19th-century American nicknames

www.cslib.org/nickname.htm

Do you know that Peg or Peggy is often short for Margaret? Or that Jack is often used as the nickname for John? Names change to nicknames in ways that aren't always obvious. This site gives you a list of many name-to-nickname changes that were common 100 years ago in the United States.

General surname mailing lists

rootsweb.com/~jfuller/gen_mail_surnames-gen.html

A list of genealogy resources on the Internet. Here you can subscribe to any of the hundreds of mailing lists where people share information about a specific surname they are chasing.

How common is my family's name?

www.census.gov/cgi-bin/namesearch.pl

Find out where your last name ranked among all American families in the 1990 census. Visit this site, enter your name, and you'll get a ranking, from number 1 (Smith) to, say, number 556 (Small) to 44,850 (Wolfman) and so on.

Surname Links

http://www.CyndisList.com/surnames.htm

Cyndi Howells has collected links to all the individual surname newletters, websites, etc., that she's found on the Internet. Check this page to see if anyone is writing about any of your family members' last names.

http://directory.google.com/Top/Society/Genealogy/Surnames

Google, an excellent general search engine, also offers specialty pages. Here you'll find links to last-name websites. Click on any letter and go to a page dedicated to surnames starting with that letter. Or click on links to different ethnic group name pages.

American names with roots in England, Spain, and Germany—among others.

The translation may tell you right off what your name means—or at least hint at the meaning.

• **Check the list in the Appendix.** There are nearly 400 names in this list, and you may be lucky enough to find yours there (page 198). But if you need to keep looking, consult the classic book on the subject, Elsdon C. Smith's *New Dictionary of American Family Names.* It includes nearly 20,000 names!

• **Go online.** Log on to one or more of the websites listed in the box "Internet Links" in this chapter.

• **Still can't locate your name?** Since so many names are approximations of the originals, try saying yours out loud in different ways. This requires some imagination.

For example, Janos is pronounced Yan-osh in Czech; it could easily have ended up being spelled that way. W's in German are pronounced "V"; Weber could have easily been turned into Vayber.

Be on the lookout for these letters, which were often confused or changed: F/V; W/V; B/V; P/B; J/Y.

The names all around you are filled with meaning. Write down your friends' names. Can you figure out their origins, their meanings? The United States is a great country for studying names—thanks to immigrants from so many nations.

Detector's To-Do List

❑ Get all the information you can about your family surnames. Try to track down the original spellings. Ask family members what they think the names mean.

❑ Look up your family names in the listing in the back of this book and on the Internet.

❑ Explore your family naming traditions. Ask your parents what they know about why they were given their first names. Ask them why they chose *your* first name.

CHAPTER FIVE

How We Got Here

The Great American Immigration Story, Yesterday and Today

In this chapter, you will learn:
- How people came to the United States
  - When they came and why
  - Where they came from
- Where they entered and where they went
- What the trip was like for some immigrants
  - How to start tracing your family's
    immigration story

ry as she might, 13-year-old Maryashe could not fall asleep. Her mind was buzzing, thinking about how her life was about to change.

"Excitement kept me awake. . . . In the morning, I was going away from Polotzk, forever and ever. I was going on a wonderful journey . . . to America. How could I sleep? . . . A million suns shone out for every star. The winds rushed in from outer space, roaring in my ears, 'America! America!'"

What could be more thrilling than imagining a new life in the United States of America, that magical land across the sea? No wonder Maryashe, living in the little Russian village of Polotzk in the 1890s, was so excited, as she remembered years later in her book *The Promised Land*.

Millions of people—young and old—have had the same reaction to coming to America. Since the 1600s, the land we call the United States has been a magnet for the rest of the world. Over the last 200 years, more than 60 million people from 140 countries have left their homelands to move here.

This immigration has been the greatest movement of people from one place to another in world history. Immigrants have changed the United States from a small country with 4 million people in 1790 into a huge super-power that is home to nearly 300 million people. Immigration continues today, with as many as 1 million people a year still coming to the United States from all over the world.

Sometime in the great parade of newcomers, your

Millions of immigrants came to America by ship. The people above are waiting for theirs in the port city of Danzig in 1920.

Comings and Goings

Two words that are sometimes confused are "emigrant" and "immigrant." They mean different things, but they have a lot in common: Every emigrant is also an immigrant.

To *migrate* means "to move from one place to another." The prefix *em* means "away from." The prefix *im* means "going into." *Emigrants* leave their country to live somewhere else permanently. *Immigrants* arrive from another land, hoping to make their home permanently in the new country.

Calling people "emigrants" refers to where they came from. When you hear talk about immigrants, that refers to where they went.

Min Jae's family left Korea to resettle in the United States. They emigrated from Korea and immigrated to America. To the Korean government, they were emigrants. To the American government, they were immigrants.

family arrived. They might have come with the Pilgrims in 1620, on a slave ship in the 1700s, on a steamship in 1902, or on a jet airplane last month. But no matter when they got here, your family history is now forever tied up with American history.

"All of our people, except the pure-blooded Indians, are immigrants or the descendants of immigrants, including those who came over on the *Mayflower*," President Franklin D. Roosevelt noted in 1944. So just about every American's family history includes stories of immigration.

In this chapter, you will learn about the many places that Americans have come from—and are still coming from. You will discover some of the reasons that have led them to leave their familiar homelands and come to a new culture, a new land, a new way of living. You will explore the story of how the United States has been built by people from all corners of the earth. And you will learn how you might discover more about your family's part in this great story.

COMING TO AMERICA

Long before this country existed as the United States, millions of people dreamed of coming here. The voyages of Italian-born explorer Christopher Columbus in the 1490s first made Europeans aware of a "new land" across the sea. Explorers who followed Columbus returned to Europe with stories about a place filled with great forests, sparkling rivers, open land, and natives they called "Indians."

By 1600, the first wave of settlers had arrived. Many stayed temporarily. They trapped beaver and other animals for their fur and established trade between the "Old World" and America. These pioneers, mostly from Spain, France, Holland, and Belgium, planned to make their fortunes, then return to Europe to live in comfort. Only a few ended up staying for good.

Other groups came to settle permanently in the "New World." Attracted by reports of good, fertile soil, they established farms. The great majority of these immigrants were from the British Isles—

Escaping to freedom: On a November day in 1956, this Hungarian family crossed the border to Austria, escaping the Russian crackdown in their homeland.

Why They Left: Family Stories

Nearly every immigrant comes to America for one of three big reasons: economic opportunity, religious freedom, or political liberty. But all immigrants also have private reasons for leaving home, and these reasons are frequently the beginning of a family story. Here are some examples:

- "Our great-grandfather wanted to live a 'modern' life, and his parents were very traditional. He felt the only way he could fulfill his desire was to move far, far away—to America."

- "I knew that if that no-good brother of mine could succeed in America, so could I."

- "Great-grandma read letters from a relative who had emigrated. They made America sound like a wonderful place."

- "I knew my children would have more opportunity here than in Korea."

- "I didn't want to go into the Russian army."

- "Great-grandfather heard there was gold in California, and he wanted to strike it rich."

- "Great-great-grandpa always wanted a farm of his own. Then he heard that in America they were giving land away—free!—to people who agreed to work it. He packed his bag that night and left Norway the next morning."

- "My grandmother's best friend was going, and she didn't want to be left behind."

- "Great-aunt Tessie heard there was a good job for her in Boston."

- "One of my children was killed in a pogrom. I wanted to live in a country where pogroms did not exist."

There was also one type of person with a very simple reason:

- "I had no choice. I was four years old."

Scotland and Wales and England. Some sought religious freedom. Others were looking for economic opportunity. Still others came because they wanted political freedom—the right to speak out against the government without fear.

From the 1600s until the late 1700s, the land on the east coast of North America was a colony of the British Empire. Then, in 1776, the American Revolution broke out between colonists and their British rulers. Seven years later the colonists won and proclaimed a new and free nation. In the Declaration of Independence, the Founding Fathers had said they believed that "all men are created equal." It wasn't clear exactly whom they were talking about—after all, they didn't include women, Native Americans, or African slaves. But they did say their nation was based on freedom and democracy. These principles made America stand out as an inspiration in a world where most nations were ruled by kings and queens.

Word spread throughout the countries of Europe that there were opportunities across the sea. America needed people to build its cities, settle in its wilderness, and work in its factories.

The new nation began to develop over the next few decades. There were no rules restricting who could come, so thousands of immigrants started pouring into the United States. In the years between 1820 and 1880, a second wave of immigrants came.

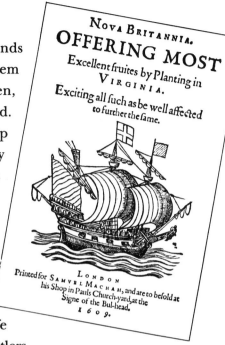

This 1609 booklet urged Englishmen to emigrate to America.

Hundreds of thousands arrived, most of them from Norway, Sweden, Germany, and Ireland. They traveled by ship —crowded, unsanitary vessels that took weeks to get to America.

These immigrants learned that life in their new country was difficult but that it also held much more opportunity. Life *felt* freer, too. The settlers wrote to their friends and families to tell them so.

"I am living in God's noble and free soil," a Swedish immigrant who settled in Iowa in 1850 wrote to his family in the Old Country. "I have now been on American soil two and a half years, and I have not been compelled to pay a penny for the privilege of living. Neither is my cap worn out from lifting it in the presence of gentlemen."

Letters like this had a powerful effect on people all over Europe. A family would receive mail from a relative in America. Villagers might gather to hear the letter read, or perhaps a local newspaper would publish it.

The First Americans

About 5,000 years before an Italian sailor named Cristoforo Colombo "discovered" North America, hundreds of thousands of people were already living on the continent. Today, we call these people Native Americans or American Indians.

Scientists believe the first Americans came from Siberia, the part of Russia that is closest to Alaska. We think (no one knows, since there are no written records) that they were Asian peoples searching for new lands.

These wanderers crossed a land bridge that existed at that time between Siberia and Alaska, and moved slowly southward. Over thousands of years, they put down homes all across North America.

By the 1400s, there were probably millions of people living in North America. They hunted and grew food—maize, pumpkins, and beans—on their own farms. They built shelters, wove, made pots, and made animal skins into clothing.

When Europeans began arriving in large ships with white sails, the native peoples were curious. Sometimes there were conflicts, but in many cases the Indians helped the settlers, teaching these "white people" how to hunt wild animals and grow plants.

But many settlers saw the natives as obstacles. The Europeans had come a long way for new land, and they didn't want to share it. Some purchased land from the natives, but many just took the land and killed any natives who stood in their way. European diseases, to which the Indians had no resistance, killed many more.

Over the next few hundred years, American Indians were pushed out of their homelands. Hundreds of thousands were killed in battles with European soldiers and settlers or were forced to move by the new government. Many promises were made to Indians by the U.S. government, but almost all of them were broken.

Today some Native Americans live on special reservations that the government set aside. Others live in cities or towns. And millions of other Americans are descended from marriages between these natives and European settlers.

Soon everyone was talking about their countryman's great success across the sea.

As interest grew, more information about the New World started appearing. Shipping companies sent representatives to villages across Europe, telling people about the waiting opportunities. Some states in need of a labor force began recruiting through brochures and posters, inviting workers to come over. Local newspapers gave immigrants advice about the easiest way to leave for America. Tickets were mailed by relatives to other members of a family so that they could follow as quickly as possible. Before long, millions of Europeans were on their way to America.

The Young Nation Expands

The country these immigrants arrived in had changed a great deal since the first European settlers reached its shores in the 1600s. Now there were busy, bustling cities like New York, Boston, New Orleans, and Philadelphia. By 1840, steamboats were whistling up and down American rivers. The northern states had factories and mills. The southern states also had vast, rich farms where, beginning in 1619, much of the work was done by slaves who had been kidnapped in Africa and brought here.

America was expanding. At first, newcomers settled along the eastern coast of the new nation. Practically the only people living in the lands to the west were Native

To European settlers, the American West looked like a giant, open wonderland. This lithograph was made in 1870; millions of settlers would come over the next few decades.

Americans, the "Indians." But settlers began exploring the land, and by the 1840s, thousands of pioneers were moving west to start a new life.

Then in 1848, a discovery was made near Sacramento, California. Word spread that gold had been found near John Sutter's sawmill, and by 1849, people from all over the world were flooding into the area. So many prospectors came with dreams of striking it rich that this period is known as the Gold Rush.

Among the people who came at that time were large numbers of Chinese workers, many from the Canton province in the south of China. They stayed to work in the San Francisco area or on the building of the transcontinental railroad.

(continued on page 82)

Famous Early Immigrants: The Pilgrims

One of the earliest and most famous groups of immigrants who came to America were known as the Pilgrims. They were Englishmen and -women who did not agree with the way the Church of England was run. They secretly set up their own separate church, but that was illegal in England, and several of their leaders were jailed.

The "separatists," as they were called, decided that the only way they could pray as they wished was to leave England. In 1608, a group of them sailed to Holland. They could pray freely there, but they felt like outsiders.

After hearing about the New World, the separatists decided to move there. They got permission from the King of England to establish a colony in Virginia and arranged to take two sailing ships from Plymouth, England, to North America. One ship, the *Speedwell*, broke down, so 102 passengers—68 adults and 34 children—and a crew of 30 jammed onto the second ship, the *Mayflower*.

These travelers spent 66 days at sea before spotting what is now known as Cape Cod on

The title of this 1867 painting by Henry Broughton is *Pilgrims Going to Church.*

November 9, 1620. A month later, they established Plymouth colony, named in honor of their town of departure.

When genealogy first became popular in late-19th-century America, many people claimed that they were descended from *Mayflower* passengers. "A Brewster was on the ship," someone might say. "That was my great-great-grandfather Brewster." It was possible, of course. But just having the same last name is *never* proof that anyone is related to you. To clarify exactly who was who, the Society of Mayflower Descendants was founded in 1894.

Listed on the next page are the names of the original *Mayflower* passengers. For more information about these families, contact the General Society of Mayflower Descendants, P.O. Box 3297, Plymouth Center, MA 02361, or check their website, *mayflower.org*. You can also go to *rootsweb.com/~mosmd/mayfpas.htm* or contact the New England Historic Genealogy Society, 101 Newbury Street, Boston, MA 02116.

Mayflower Passengers

Alden, John

Allerton, Isaac, his wife, Mary, and their three children,
    Bartholomew, Remember, and Mary

Allerton, John, a seaman

Billington, John, his wife, Eleanor,
    and two sons, John and Francis

Bradford, William, and his wife, Dorothy May

Brewster, William, and his wife, Mary,
    and their two sons, Love and Wrestling

Britteridge, Richard

Browne, Peter

Butten, William,** servant to Samuel Fuller

Carter, Robert, a servant to the Mullins family

Carver, John, and his wife, Katherine

Chilton, James, his wife, Susanna, and their daughter, Mary

Clarke, Richard

Cooke, Francis, and his son, John

Crakston, John, and his son, John

Doty, Edward, a servant of the Hopkins family

Eaton, Francis, his wife, Sarah, and their son, Samuel

English, Thomas, a seaman

Fletcher, Moses

Fuller, Edward, his wife, Ann, and their son, Samuel

Fuller, Samuel

Gardiner, Richard

Goodman, John

Holbeck, William, a servant to the White family

Hooke, John, boy servant to Isaac Allerton

Hopkins, Steven, and his wife, Elizabeth, and Steven's two
    children from a previous marriage, Giles and Constance,
    and two children with Elizabeth, Damaris and Oceanus*

Howland, John, a servant

Langemore, John, a servant to the Martin family

Latham, William, a boy servant

Leister, Edward, a servant of the Hopkins family

Margeson, Edward

Martin, Christopher, and his wife, Marie

Minter, Desire, a maid

More, Ellen, a little girl

More, Jasper, a boy

More, Richard, a boy

More, Mary

Mullins, William, his wife, Alice,
    and their two children, Joseph and Priscilla

Priest, Degory

Prower, Solomon, a servant to the Martin family

Rigdale, John, and his wife, Alice

Rogers, Thomas, and his son, Joseph

Soule, George, a servant of the Winslow family

Standish, Myles, and his wife, Rose

Story, Elias, a servant of the Winslow family

Thomson, Edward

Tilley, Edward, his wife, Anne, and two children who were
    their cousins, Henry Sampson and Humility Cooper

Tilley, John, his wife, Joan, and their daughter Elizabeth

Tinker, Thomas, his wife, and a son

Trevor, John

Turner, John, and two sons

Unidentified maid servant

Warren, Richard

White, William, and his wife, Susana,
    and their sons, Resolved and Peregrine

Wilder, Roger, a servant

Williams, Thomas

Winslow, Edward, and his wife, Elizabeth

Winslow, Gilbert

*born at sea **died at sea

Beginning in the 1840s, many families headed north and west following a path called the Oregon Trail. They weren't looking for instant riches—they wanted to settle their families in the fertile Oregon valleys. It's a good thing they were patient. The trek by covered wagon took anywhere from four to six months.

While the population began to move westward, the nation grew richer. Scientific advances like the cotton gin and the steam engine were turning the United States into an industrial power. American ships were sailing the seas and transporting goods everywhere.

Then, from 1861 to 1865, the bloody American Civil War was fought. At the end of that war, the rebellious southern states were defeated and the U.S. government ended the slavery that had trapped and abused millions of African people in this country.

Few immigrants entered the United States during these years. After the war between the states ended, however, immigration once again picked up.

Before the 1860s, most people came to the United

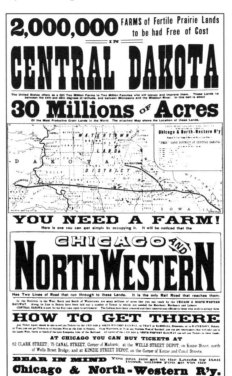

Go west! A railroad company ad tells settlers to move to Dakota.

States on sailing ships. A ship leaving Hamburg, Germany, might take eight weeks to arrive. But by the 1880s, steamships were traveling across the ocean in half the time, or less, than it had taken sailing ships. The trip was easier and healthier, and because steamships could travel more quickly, more trips could be made per ship.

By the 1890s, the arrival of a few thousand immigrants each year had turned into a mighty wave of millions. Some came from Mexico, Canada, and the Caribbean, and a good number came from northern Europe. But most immigrants came from the poorer lands of southern and eastern Europe.

The year 1907 marked the peak of immigration. An average of 3,000 people entered the United States every day of that year. By December 31, over 1,285,000 people had immigrated—a record that stands to this day.

Not everyone was happy about this latest wave of immigration. Before the 1880s, most immigrants had come from countries in northern and western Europe. Now these people were established here, and they didn't like the new immigrants from southern and eastern Europe because their customs and languages were so different.

American workers were also concerned. Would the newcomers work for less money and take jobs away from them? A debate about who should be admitted began in the 1880s and went on until the 1920s. In 1914, however, these arguments were put aside when war exploded in Europe. It was called the Great War because so many countries took part—including the United States, which entered in 1917. For four years, very few people sailed the seas or came to America.

But while the rest of the world stayed put, there was a giant movement inside America. Black Americans began leaving their homes in the rural South for the big cities in the North. This movement was known as the Great Migration. From 1916 through 1919, as many as 500,000 blacks moved to northern industrial cities such as Pittsburgh, Detroit, Philadelphia, Cleveland, and New York City. Like so many immigrants before and after them, they were looking for work, opportunity, and an escape from prejudice.

World War I ended in 1918. The wave of immigration began to rise again in mighty numbers. In 1921, more than 600,000 immigrants arrived.

And then the wave was stopped. Laws were passed by Congress to severely restrict entry into the United States and to fix quotas for each country. For the next 40 years, few immigrants were admitted. The terrible economic

Japanese immigrants arriving in San Francisco in 1920. Until 1965, restrictive laws put severe limits on the number of Asians entering the United States.

upheaval of the 1930s, which was called the Great Depression, played a role in that. So did the horribly destructive Second World War (1939–45), in which millions of young people from nearly every nation on earth fought and died. But even after World War II was over, American immigration laws kept out many who wanted to enter.

It wasn't until 1965 that things changed. In that year, President Lyndon Johnson signed a new immigration law. It made the quota system more evenly distributed for

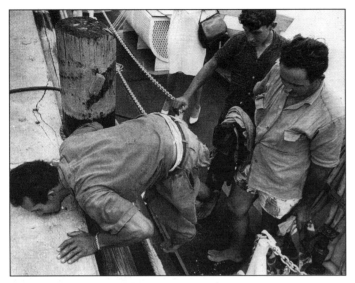

A Cuban refugee arriving in Miami shows his joy by kissing the ground, 1960.

all nations. Emphasis was also placed on uniting Americans with family members from overseas.

People still journeyed from countries that had been part of the great tide of immigration of the early 1900s. But now thousands were also coming from new lands. The greatest number left Latin America and the Caribbean. Their reasons were similar to those of earlier settlers: Some came fleeing harsh governments, hoping to find freedom; others came for economic opportunity; and many came for a combination of these reasons.

Thousands more arrived from Asia—from India, Pakistan, Taiwan, Korea, Cambodia, Laos, and Vietnam. They came because quotas no longer kept them out, and

because jet travel had cut dramatically the time it took to get here. But most of all, they came because their countries were poor and they wanted to reach for the same freedoms and economic opportunity that had attracted millions of immigrants before them.

Today's Immigration

At the end of the 20th century, immigration laws were changed again. In 1986, some people who had entered the United States illegally in prior years were given the chance to become legal citizens. A few years later, the laws were amended to make it easier for recent immigrants to bring their family members over from their home countries. The rules were also changed so people with skills that were needed in the United States could more easily gain entry.

As a result, the United States now welcomes as many as 1 million new immigrants a year from all over the world. Most new Americans now come from Asia—such countries as China, Taiwan, the Philippines, India, Vietnam, and Korea—and from Latin America (most come from Mexico, but many others come from the Dominican Republic, El Salvador, Colombia, and Peru). A large number of immigrants come from the Caribbean islands, such as Jamaica and Haiti, and many others come from Russia and other countries that were once part of the Soviet Union.

Once again the United States is a country that

welcomes, and is being changed by, immigrants. Immigrating to the United States is still difficult for many people; there are long waiting lists to get in. And there are still Americans who believe that the United States has admitted more than enough immigrants to our shores and that we should not encourage more to come.

But hundreds of thousands of immigrants from all over the world continue to arrive here every year. And they still bring with them their own customs, foods, cultures, skills, hopes, dreams, and history.

GOING TO A NEW WORLD
What Leaving Your Homeland Feels Like

You now know a bit about the history of American immigration. But how does it *feel* to be an immigrant? When you search for your family's "Coming to America" story, you will want to know not just the when and why, but the *how* and the *how it felt.*

If you or your parents immigrated to America, you may have come by jet plane. Your family story may be about airline terminals and visa worries and quotas and 10-hour or longer flights. Or perhaps your family was from Canada, or Mexico or one of the other countries of Latin America, and your relatives arrived by train, bus, private car, or even on foot.

Some of you will have ancestors who came on difficult journeys on slow, dangerous sailing ships

between 1620 and 1880. And if you are African-American, your ancestors may have been kidnapped and brought as slaves on inhumanely crowded, horrific "coffin ships."

From your family, you may hear several kinds of stories about coming to America. After all, you are made up of many families, and each one probably has a different arrival tale to tell.

Many new Americans now come from Asian countries.

Nearly half of all Americans can trace at least one of their ancestors' arrivals in this country back to the period 1892–1924, for that was the period of the biggest wave of immigration to this country. What would it have felt like to decide to leave your homeland and move to a new country around that time? Imagine . . .

You wake up one morning and say good-bye to everything you've known. Good-bye to your parents. Your friends. Good-bye to the familiar streets you have come to know so well. Good-bye to the music and food you have grown up with and even, in many ways, to the language you speak.

Involuntary Americans: The Africans

African people arrived in America before the *Mayflower* did. But unlike the *Mayflower* passengers—and nearly all other immigrants to America—they did not choose to come here. They were kidnapped.

In 1619, a ship arrived in Jamestown, Virginia, with 20 Africans in its hold. These first Africans to set foot in North America were slaves sold at auction to early settlers.

Over the next 200 years, British, Portuguese, Spanish, and other ships wandered up and down the coast of West Africa, capturing Africans who lived in what are today the nations of Senegal, Ghana, Gambia, Liberia, Benin (Dahomey), Togo, Nigeria, and the Ivory Coast. The tribes the slaves came from included the Ashanti, Bantu, Ibo, Mandingo, Efik, Kru, Dahomean, Hausa, and Fanti.

The youngest and strongest of these captives were stuffed into the slave ships' bottom—the dark, hot cargo hold. Although many immigrant groups traveled to America under terrible conditions, no other group faced the horrors that were routine for Africans. Some say as many as 40 million were brought to the Western Hemisphere in this fashion—and some say 20 million died on the trip over.

Africans were brought here primarily to work in the fields and great houses of the southeastern United States. They lived in small shacks on the grounds of the plantations.

African men and women were treated as property;

Saying your good-byes is painful. You might never see your loved ones again. That was the case for the father of Chinese-American writer Jade Snow Wong. He emigrated from Canton province, China, to San Francisco in 1903. "Many years later, when I was a grown woman, he told me with sadness that when he asked his mother, whom he adored, for permission to come to the United States, she expressed her reluctance," Ms. Wong wrote. When this only son insisted that he must leave, his mother scolded him: "Go! Go! You will have the life to go, but not the life to return!"

Throughout history, making the decision to emigrate has been only the first step. Most immigrants cannot just leave for America. Money has to be raised for the ticket; permits, passports, and visas have to be arranged; provisions have to be made for family members left behind.

In the 1800s and most of the 1900s, fathers often went to America first, worked to earn money, and then brought over their wives and children. Millions of immigrants, however, were single young men who came by

they could be bought and sold by their owners, who forced them to give up their names and identities. Families were broken up when the owner wished to sell a child or a parent to another owner.

When slavery was finally outlawed throughout the United States after the Civil War, African-Americans, though liberated, had few possessions or skills. Many stayed in the South. When millions moved to the cities of the North in the early years of the 20th century, they again encountered prejudice and discrimination. Years of struggle—including the famous civil rights movement of the 1950s and '60s—slowly eliminated laws that made discrimination legal. Attitudes, however, have changed far more slowly.

Slaves were *not* immigrants, and the way in which they were brought to America still echoes powerfully in the lives of their descendants. But like the groups that came to this land before and after them, African-Americans have struggled to make it in America, and they boast millions of success stories.

Millions of Americans of African descent worked in the cotton fields of the South, both during and after slavery.

themselves to earn a living. Some promised to bring over other family members when they raised enough money. Others intended to return to their homeland after making a fortune.

Children under 16 could not travel without their parents. Young women under 21 were not permitted to leave a country unless someone was waiting to meet them in America.

If an entire family was leaving, they probably sold just about everything they owned. Most immigrants took only what they could carry. They filled a trunk with clothing, bedsheets, pillows, some pieces of silverware, a framed photograph of the loved ones they left behind, and maybe a Bible or a set of candlesticks.

If there was room, women would wrap things like dishes and pots in the bedsheets. After all, these *would* be absolutely necessary in the New World. Men would often carry the tools of their trade: A barrel maker would bring along his special knife, for example. But families had to leave behind furniture, most kitchenware, and

(continued on page 90)

The Debate Over Closing the Door to America

Most Americans are proud of our reputation as the greatest immigrant nation in the world. But throughout U.S. history, heated debates have raged about immigration. Time and again, groups have mounted campaigns to have the doors to this country closed—if not to all immigrants, then at least to all of a certain group.

For the most part, these cries for exclusion came from two groups. One was American workers who were afraid of losing their jobs, believing that their bosses would fire them and hire new immigrants who would work for lower wages. This was the main reason that a law was passed in 1885 prohibiting immigrants from coming to America with a job already lined up.

The second anti-immigration group was made up of people who believed that newcomers were "inferior." They wanted to have immigrants excluded to "protect" American civilization.

Until the 1870s, there were no restrictions on immigration to this country. Over the next decade, barriers went up to exclude certain types of people, like convicts and people "likely to become a public charge" (those who looked like they would not be able to support themselves financially).

In 1882, the first law was passed banning people from a specific country. The Chinese Exclusion Act suspended the right of workers from China to come to the United States. This law was passed to satisfy white settlers who worried that the Chinese would take away their jobs by working for lower pay. The only Chinese people still eligible to enter were students, tourists, and businessmen—of whom there were very few.

The Chinese Exclusion Act marked the beginning of a new era in American history. Over the next 40 years, bill after bill was introduced in Congress to slow or stop the flow of immigrants.

These bills made their way into law slowly, almost piece by piece. In 1903, political radicals were excluded. In 1907, a "gentleman's agreement" between the United States and Japan barred Japanese immigration. In 1917, a bill that had been introduced many times over the previous 20 years—banning people who could not read or write—was finally passed over the veto of President Woodrow Wilson. By 1917, there were 33 categories of people who could not enter the United States.

The next step was to exclude poor immigrants from southern and eastern Europe. The anti-immigration forces suggested laws creating quotas, which would limit the number of people who could come to the United States from each country. In 1921, a law was passed that allowed more immigration from western Europe—which was no longer a source of many immigrants to this country—and severely limited immigration from southern and eastern Europe. Under the National Origins Act of 1924, even more severe quotas were established for those countries.

As many as 100,000 Italians had come in one year during the early 1900s. Now the quota was 5,802 a year. Millions had come from Russia, but the United States would now accept only 2,784 a year. Greeks had immigrated by the thousands. Under the new quota, only 307 could come yearly.

For the next 40 years, those quotas were in effect. Few western European countries ever met their quota; every eastern and southeastern European country exceeded its quota in normal years.

Finally, in 1965, the quota law was repealed and a new system was put into effect. It established more evenhanded numbers for countries from all over the world and made exceptions for political refugees and people who had relatives already in the United States.

Today, immigration is once again flourishing. The number of immigrants admitted to the United States

This was one of the many cartoons that tried to convince people that the U.S. should cut back on immigration.

today is comparable to the numbers that arrived during the high-tide years of the early 1900s. There are still restrictions and ongoing debates over who should be admitted. But the United States today continues to be a country that welcomes new arrivals from around the world.

probably most of their children's playthings (though a number of dolls and teddy bears did make the trip).

Many immigrants were afraid that they would never taste their favorite local foods again, so they stocked up for the trip. Greeks brought olives and figs. Eastern Europeans made sure to take their local sausages. Religious Jews brought kosher foods. Italians lugged bottles of wine, olive oil, fruits and nuts, and cheeses. "My mother . . . made a boxful of Italian biscuits," recalled Pasquale Forlinghieri. "She figured [the food] would last at least for eight or nine days: 'If I don't like their food, I'm not going to go hungry.'"

When someone left a small town, it was a big and sometimes sad event. "Half of Polotzk was at my uncle's gate in the morning to conduct us to the railway station, and the other half was there before we arrived," remembered Mary Antin, who was known as Maryashe when she left Russia in 1893. "The procession resembled both a funeral and a triumph. The women wept over us, reminding us eloquently of the perils of the sea, the bewilderment of a foreign land, and the torments of homesickness that awaited us. . . .

"The last I saw of Polotzk was a . . . mass of people, waving colored handkerchiefs . . . falling on each other's necks, gone wild altogether. Then the station became invisible, and the shining tracks spun out from sky to sky. I was in the middle of the great, great world, and the longest road was mine."

Steerage passengers on the ship *Westernland* come out onto their small deck for a few minutes of fresh air on the way to New York, 1901.

Aboard Ship in the Early 1900s

When the immigrants arrived at the departure seaport, they were examined by doctors, government officials, and steamship company officers before boarding ship. These inspections were used by the shipping companies to weed out those who were ill or ineligible to emigrate —because if a passenger was rejected in America, the company had to pay for his or her return trip to Europe.

For a lucky few—the wealthy—the trip would be a comfortable one. Steamships had fine first- and second-class cabin accommodations for those who could afford them. But most immigrants traveled third class—in steerage. This meant they found themselves on the lowest deck with hundreds of people and no assigned places. The next weeks were often awful. Conditions were unsanitary, and many fell ill. Some passengers spent entire weeks in their beds.

"The boat was . . . terrible, horrible," said Josephine Reale, who came from Italy to Philadelphia in 1920 when she was only five and a half years old. "We were like cows, all bunched up together. Of course we were seasick and we hated the food. . . . It was . . . terrible."

For some children, however, the steamer was a great new playground. "For 16 days the ship was our world," recalled Mary Antin. "I explored the ship, made friends with officers and crew, or pursued my thoughts in quiet nooks."

But the long days and nights slowly wore down even the children's enthusiasm. All there was to see was the vast blue-green water. Then, just as the trip seemed to be lasting forever, someone would spot land.

"Oh joyful sight! We saw the tops of two trees!" Mary Antin remembered. "What a shout there rose! Everyone pointed out the welcome sight to everyone else, as if they did not see it. All eyes were fixed on it as

if they saw a miracle. And this was only the beginning of the joys of the day!"

Soon all the passengers would crowd onto the top deck. Arrival—and America!—was drawing near.

ARRIVING IN AMERICA
What the Welcome Was Like

What people did when they arrived in the United States depends on when and where they arrived.

In the very early days of immigration, newcomers faced no examinations and were given no guidance when their ships entered ports like New York, Boston, or New Orleans. Those who survived the trip on crowded,

New arrivals, many of them holding their identification tags between their teeth, step off a ferryboat and onto Ellis Island.

Beware of Swindlers!

Polish immigrant Stanislaus Plzybischewski was a very happy young man in May 1913. He was 22 years old. He had just been accepted into the United States as an immigrant. And he had a $50 bill in his pocket.

As Stanislaus walked down the paths of Ellis Island on his way to the ferry that would take him to Manhattan, he must have been very excited.

Suddenly a red-faced man in a uniform stopped him in the hallway.

"What kind of money do you have?" the official asked.

The Polish boy showed his $50 bill.

"That money is no good," the man told him in German. He took the $50 bill and handed the boy a coin with a hole in the middle.

"Take this instead," the man said, then disappeared.

Stanislaus stood for a moment, confused. Then he realized what had happened: He'd been swindled.

The coin he held was from Argentina, and it was worth about four cents.

This story is one of hundreds told about how immigrants were cheated soon after arrival. Smooth talkers and con artists often gathered near immigration stations, waiting for a newcomer to wander by. These crooks knew that immigrants were dazed

filthy ships were very happy to disembark. They were free to head out on their own.

Two groups, of course, were exceptions: Slaves were held until they were sold at auction, and indentured servants had to wait until they were assigned families.

Soon after the Revolutionary War, in the early 1800s, the new federal government started paying attention to how people entered the country. Congress was concerned about unhealthy conditions on board ships bringing immigrants and about the people who died before they reached port. They were worried that

diseases were being brought into the United States.

In 1819, Congress passed the first law to improve conditions for immigrants. It limited the number of people a ship could carry, and it required captains to compile a list of passengers. This list was called a "ship's manifest." If anyone died aboard ship, his or her name had to be recorded. These lists were held by the official in charge of the port.

For the next four decades, records were kept—though not very carefully—by the states. In just about every state, from New York to Louisiana, doctors boarded ships to

and confused by their long trip, and unfamiliar with American ways.

Some pretended to be relatives of the immigrants. "Hello, I was sent for you. Let me carry your bag," one might say. Two seconds later, the crook would disappear with the bag.

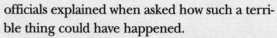

Others dressed as officials. In Stanislaus's case, the immigration officials on Ellis Island helped him look for the swindler, but they could not find him. "Men come to the island with caps and uniform jackets in their pockets, and it's hard to keep them out," one of the officials explained when asked how such a terrible thing could have happened.

Sometimes immigrants were cheated by the very people they were supposed to trust, including immigration officials, money changers, and restaurant help.

The U.S. government did try in a number of ways to protect the new immigrants from swindlers. Investigations were held and inspectors were hired. Most people got through the process without being hoodwinked. But there were a number of immigrants who had to learn the hard way that America was a land of opportunity—for crooks as well as for everyone else.

check for people with infectious diseases. Ill passengers were quarantined in hospitals, where they were supposed to be cured before setting foot in their new country.

As the flood of immigrants grew, it was obvious that a more organized system was needed. Finally, in 1855, the first official receiving station in the United States devoted solely to the processing of new immigrants was opened in New York City.

The station, called Castle Garden, had previously been a fort, an amusement hall, and an opera house. It was chosen because it could hold thousands of newcomers (10,000 people had jammed into it just a few years earlier to see the famous Swedish singer Jenny Lind).

For the next three decades, the state of New York ran Castle Garden as an overstuffed center for immigrant inspections. To Europeans, its name became a word—*Kasselgardena*—meaning "incredibly busy, noisy place." In this one great building, thousands of immigrants a day were inspected for disease, informed about jobs, and directed to their final destinations.

New York City was processing about 7 of every 10 immigrants who arrived in the United States. Castle

Hats are lifted and passengers cheer as the Statue of Liberty comes into view in New York Harbor. Soon these immigrants will arrive at Ellis Island.

Garden—once thought to be so huge—turned out to be too small. Then, in 1875, the government passed the first of what would be many laws denying admission to certain groups of people. As many people might be coming as before, but fewer would be let in. That meant inspectors had to spend more time examining arrivals. The need for a bigger building became crucial.

In 1890, a little island in New York Harbor, just north of the Statue of Liberty, was chosen as the location for a new processing center.

It was an unremarkable place, and over the years it had been known by a number of names: Gull Island, Oyster Island, Bucking Island, Gibbet Island. Soon, however, it would become one of the most famous—and feared—places in the world.

It was called Ellis Island.

The Isle of Hope and Tears

On January 1, 1892, a 15-year-old Irish girl named Annie Moore walked off a ferryboat and into history, becoming the first person ever processed at the new immigration station on Ellis Island.

Annie and her two younger brothers arrived in New York on the steamship *Nevada* to join their parents, who had come to New York in 1888. Federal officials presented her with a 10-dollar gold piece as a symbol of the great moment. Annie "had never seen a United States coin, and this was the largest sum of money she had ever possessed," the *New York Times* reported the next day.

The station opened just as the greatest wave of immigration in world history was about to begin. Over the next 30 years, nearly 20 million people, most of them from southern and eastern Europe, would enter the United States through many ports. (About as many new immigrants currently enter the United States annually, but the ratio of new immigrants to established population is much lower now.)

To the 12 million immigrants who followed in Annie's footsteps on Ellis Island during that time, the

Answer a Few Questions, Please

In the early 1900s, immigrants spent two hours or more a day at the immigration center. A series of questions had been asked on the ship, and now inspectors asked the same questions again to see if the answers matched. They asked questions like these:

1. What is your name?
2. How old are you?
3. Are you married or single?
4. What is your calling or occupation?
5. Are you able to read or write?
6. What is your nationality?
7. Where was your last residence?
8. Which U.S. seaport have you landed in?
9. What is your final destination?
10. Do you have a ticket to your final destination?
11. Did you pay for your passage over? If not, who did?
12. Do you have money with you? How much?
13. Are you going to join a relative? What relative? Name and address?
14. Have you ever been to the United States before? Where and when?
15. Have you ever been in prison, in a poorhouse, or supported by a charity?
16. Are you a polygamist (someone with more than one wife)?
17. Are you under contract, expressed or implied, to perform labor in the United States?
18. What is the condition of your health, mental and physical?
19. Are you deformed or crippled? By what cause?

processing center was far more than just a place where people were examined and their papers filled out. It was a place where lives were changed forever. Were you fit to be an American? Should you be allowed through the "Golden Door"? Was your life about to begin anew—or were you going to be sent back to the Old Country? These questions hung in the air for each immigrant as his or her steamship came into New York Harbor. Was that little island just beyond the Statue of Liberty the beginning—or the end—of a dream?

Ellis Island had not been built for everyone, however. Few first- or second-class passengers ever set foot on the island. It was for the steerage passengers that Ellis lay in wait.

(continued on page 98)

At right, dozens of immigrants sit down to a meal in the Ellis Island cafeteria. Josephine Reale, who was five when she arrived from Italy, remembers: "We were hungry . . . but we couldn't eat the bread. The Italian bread was so delicious. We couldn't understand this soft, mushy bread. It had a horrible taste. I like it now, but in those days, we hated it! We thought, 'Oh dear God, is this the kind of bread we're going to have to eat in America?'" Below, immigrant boys being examined by a health officer, 1911. Below right, an immigrant from Denmark holds his cane and considers his future.

What Is Your Final Destination?

An immigrant has just passed inspection at Ellis Island. He wants to know how to reach the city where his brother is waiting. So he approaches an inspector and says, "Excuse me. I go Tseekago. Where for train?"

The inspector, if he is friendly and understands the immigrant's accent, may say, "Oh, you mean *Chicago*. Let me write it down for you." But sometimes inspectors had difficulty deciphering the places that immigrants pronounced or wrote down. Usually, someone figured out the correct answer. But occasionally, immigrants ended up far from where they wanted to go.

Where, for example, was "Pringvilliamas"? A clever inspector figured out that it was Springfield, Massachusetts. Inspectors also had to decipher "Linkinbra" (Lincoln, Nebraska), "Neihork, Nugers" (Newark, New Jersey), and "Deas Moynes, Yova" (Des Moines, Iowa). And one bright immigration officer was able to translate "Szekeneveno Pillsburs" into "Second Avenue, Pittsburgh."

What about "Settlevash"? It was one immigrant's idea of how to say "Seattle, Washington." Jeanette Stirling, who came to the United States from Turkey in the early 1900s, took a train across the country to her new home in Washington State. "When we got to Seattle," she remembered, "we were all sitting together, a lot of immigrants with their bundles. A committee came to meet us. They said, 'Where are you going?'

"We said, 'We're going to Settlevash.'

"They said, 'Get off the train. This is Seattle, Washington.'

"And we said, 'No, we're going to Settlevash.' We wouldn't budge."

And there is the famous story about an immigrant who arrived at Ellis Island and wished to go to Houston. He was promptly put on a train to Texas. At some point, the big mistake was discovered; he really wanted to go to Houston *Street* in New York City. Legend says that at least one immigrant became a cowboy instead of a tailor because of an inspector's mistake.

Crossing the Border: Neighbors Who Came—and Come—to Stay

Until the 1950s, most immigrants came to America by boat and went through immigration procedures in cities like New York and San Francisco. Some immigrants, however, entered the United States by land. They came from Canada and Mexico, and their arrivals were—and still are—quite different.

For one thing, leaving home was not as difficult for Mexicans and Canadians as it was for Europeans and Asians. The trip was simpler, cheaper, and shorter. If things did not work out, they could go home far more easily.

This Mexican man was caught trying to enter the U.S. illegally in 1954 by an American immigration officer.

The whole immigration process was also less formal on land. There were no giant immigration centers, as there were for boat arrivals. Much of the processing was done quickly at the border. And in fact, millions of people probably immigrated without any processing at all.

Hundreds of thousands have come to the United States from Mexico. In the 1920s, when the flow of immigrants from Europe was stopped by American law, Mexican workers were in great demand. U.S. railroad companies needed them to lay tracks across the Southwest.

Where the Immigrants Were Processed

When Annie Moore arrived in 1892, all the buildings on Ellis Island were made of wood. There was a small hospital, a baggage area, a dormitory, and a power station. The biggest structure of all was the three-story reception building with four peaked towers at its corners. The building was huge—more than 5,000 people could pass through it at once.

For more than five years, these wooden buildings were filled with the sounds of nervous immigrants. Then around midnight on June 14, 1897, a fire broke out and quickly burned the entire station to the ground. No one died in the fire, but most of the records of those who had arrived in this country since 1855 disappeared with the buildings.

Many Mexicans came into the United States legally. Others sneaked across the border. They waded through shallow parts of the Rio Grande or hid in the trunks of cars driven in legally.

Today, Hispanic-Americans are the largest immigrant group in the nation. Hundreds of thousands of them are Mexican-Americans, and most of them live in California, Texas, Arizona, and New Mexico.

There is also a great deal of new immigration from Mexico—legal and illegal, temporary and permanent. The U.S. government attempts to crack down on illegal immigration, but as long as Mexico and the nations of Central America remain poorer than the United States, there will probably be more people who wish to come here than the law allows.

Our northern neighbor, Canada, is richer and has far fewer people than Mexico. Nevertheless, some Canadians have come to the United States because of economic problems in their country. Many were French-speaking residents of Québec province, who have come since the 1850s to work in the mills, stone quarries, and lumber industries of the midwestern and New England states.

Other Canadians were actually Europeans who had first immigrated to Canada in the hope that they would find it easier to be admitted into the United States. Some were then able to enter the United States; others were denied and had to remain in Canada.

Immigration works the other way, too. Over the years, a number of Americans have left the United States to live in Canada. Today, Canada and the United States still exchange citizens, and they are two of the most welcoming nations in the world for immigrants from everywhere.

Cars coming from Canada are inspected as they enter the United States.

Because Ellis Island had become so important, the U.S. Congress immediately set aside money for a new set of buildings to be constructed. These buildings were to be fireproof, made of stone and concrete. During the two and a half years it took to build the new processing center, all immigrants to New York were processed at the tiny Barge Office on nearby Manhattan Island.

Finally, on December 17, 1900, Ellis Island reopened. Its handsome new buildings were made of red brick trimmed with white limestone. There was a hospital, a post office, a customs house, a power house, staff housing, and offices.

Grandest of all was the Main Building. It was three stories tall in its center section, flanked by a couple of large two-story side pavilions. Four 100-foot-high towers, topped by copper domes that ended in sky-reaching spires, stood at the corners of its center section. At the main entrance, three tall archways guarded by stone eagles announced that this was a very important building.

The Long Arrival

The great steamships of the early 1900s that brought immigrants to America did not land at Ellis, however. In fact, the process of arrival in New York was a long one. For many immigrants, it must have been both exciting and frustrating.

These giant ocean liners, which carried as many as 2,000 passengers each, sailed into New York Harbor through a narrow passageway between Long Island and Staten Island, known as the Narrows. Shortly after the steamship pulled through the Narrows, a little immigration tugboat would come alongside it.

On the small boat were officers of the U.S. Immigration Service. They came on board and met with the steamship officers. The immigration officials had two jobs to do. The first was to learn if any passenger had a disease that might spread to other people—illnesses like typhus, smallpox, or diphtheria.

"Have there been any cases of contagious disease on board?" an immigration officer would ask the ship's doctor.

The Main Building at Ellis Island, sometime after 1900. In one year—1907—more than a million people came through this building.

"None at all," the doctor might respond.

In that case, the officials went on to their second job. They met with the immigrants in the expensive first- and second-class cabins, asking the "cabin" passengers a few questions and checking their passports. The ship's doctor then gave these immigrants a quick physical examination. If cabin passengers passed both exams, they were informed that they had been admitted to America and didn't have to visit Ellis Island. They would then leave the ship when it docked in New York or New Jersey.

Occasionally the ship's captain told the immigration officials, "Yes, we've discovered contagious disease among our passengers." In those cases, all passengers who might be infected were taken off the ship and put into isolation. Those who were ill were sent to a hospital on Hoffman Island, a dot of land close to Staten Island; they would stay there until they recovered.

Passengers who had been exposed to the illness but had not come down with it were sent to nearby Swinburne Island. They were kept under observation in a clinic until doctors were certain that they had not caught the disease.

In most cases, the ship was free of contagious disease. Immigration officials finished their job and left, allowing the ship to complete the last leg of its long voyage.

Shortly after the cabin passenger inspections were over, the Statue of Liberty came into view. As the steerage passengers crowded on deck to get a look at the famous

They made it! These immigrants passed their tests on Ellis Island and have been admitted to the United States. Next stop: their new homes in America.

"Lady with the Lamp," how many of them noticed that just a few hundred yards beyond the statue were the red-brick buildings of Ellis Island? This was where the steerage passengers would undergo their immigration processing.

Finally, the ship pulled into its final destination,
(continued on page 104)

The Lamp Beside the Golden Door

Millions of Americans will never forget the first American woman they met. She stood 151 feet tall and wore a spiky crown and a long green robe.

Beneath her feet were broken chains. In her right hand, thrust high into the sky, was a glowing torch. In her left hand was a book with "July 4, 1776" inscribed on its cover.

Lady Liberty arrived in pieces, before she was assembled on an island in New York Harbor.

Their first view of her came as they crowded onto the deck of a ship entering New York Harbor. Many stood and silently stared. Some cheered. And more than a few cried when they looked up at this great symbol of freedom welcoming them to their new home.

The statue of *Liberty Enlightening the World* was a gift to Americans from the French people. It symbolized the friendship between the two countries. Its cost was raised by contributions from the French, just as the cost of the pedestal on which it stands was raised by American donations.

The statue was born at an 1865 dinner party. French professor and writer Edouard de Laboulaye,

the host, talked about giving a monument that would celebrate American liberty and promote democracy in France. Sculptor Frédéric-Auguste Bartholdi, a guest at the party, was excited by the concept, and for the next 20 years he worked on it. Bartholdi visited the United States in 1871 and identified a site for the great statue—tiny Bedloe's Island, which is now known as Liberty Island, in the heart of New York Harbor.

Fund-raising in France began in 1875. At first, Bartholdi wanted the statue ready for the American Centennial (100th anniversary) in 1876. As it turned out, he was able to finish only the arm and the torch by that time, so those pieces were sent to Philadelphia for the celebration.

The arm and torch were transferred to a park in New York City in 1877. They remained there for eight

years, a reminder to Americans that *we* had to raise money for the place where the statue would stand—the pedestal.

The statue was completed in 1884. A year later it was taken apart, placed in 214 boxes, sent on

Enormous toes and a piece of torch.

the steamship *Isère* to New York, and stored on Bedloe's Island until the pedestal was completed. Finally, with money raised by millions of contributors—including American schoolchildren who donated pennies and nickels—the pedestal was finished and the statue raised. It was unveiled at a huge dedication ceremony on October 28, 1886.

At the time, little was said about a poem called "The New Colossus," written three years earlier to help raise funds for the pedestal. The author, a young Jewish woman named Emma Lazarus, was not even invited to the dedication ceremony. In her poem, Lazarus called the statue "Mother of Exiles" and focused not on the abstract idea of "freedom" but on the people coming to win that freedom. Lazarus's words have become world famous:

> *Give me your tired, your poor,*
> *Your huddled masses yearning to breathe free,*
> *The wretched refuse of your teeming shore,*
> *Send these, the homeless, tempest-tost to me,*
> *I lift my lamp beside the golden door!*

In 1903, Emma Lazarus's poem was placed on a plaque and attached, permanently, to the Statue of Liberty's base.

The Statue has lifted her lamp to greet many immigrants since 1886. In the background, the coast of New Jersey.

a pier on the New York or New Jersey coastline. The first- and second-class passengers would leave, free to start their new lives. Steerage passengers, meanwhile, remained on board. Eventually they were brought off the ship, lined up, divided into small groups, and then led to a ferry or barge. Hundreds of them, all carrying their luggage, were crowded onto the boats. They were taken to Ellis Island and quickly led into the Main Building.

Inside the Main Building

Inside that imposing building were many rooms, large and small. The immigrants' first stop was the baggage room on

The Ellis Island maze: From 1900 till 1911, the Great Hall inside the Main Building was broken into tiny sections by a jumble of iron railings.

the ground floor, where they were expected to leave their luggage. Up the stairs were the immigration offices, a cafeteria, a place to exchange foreign money for American dollars, and a railroad ticket office. Also on this floor were the galleries where physical and mental tests were given.

At the center of the building was the greatest space of all—the Registry Room, better known as the Great Hall. This huge space, more than 50 feet high and filled with light and noise, was a place that millions of immigrants would never forget.

It had a wraparound balcony looking down on the main floor. Light streamed through enormous windows. New York City, with its fabled skyscrapers, was framed in some windows; in others, the Statue of Liberty loomed.

For the first 11 years it was open, the Great Hall looked like a maze. It was divided into sections by railings, and confused immigrants were jammed in tightly as they waited their turn for processing. After 1911, the railings were taken down, and rows of more comfortable benches were placed throughout the hall.

On the third floor of the Main Building were hearing rooms, where some immigrants were sent to appear before "Boards of Special Inquiry." A special inquiry was a kind of mini-trial in which a group of inspectors asked a newcomer questions and determined whether or not he or she should be admitted. Many immigrants appeared before a board of inquiry; most of them were found acceptable.

PORTS OF ENTRY

Seattle

WASHINGTON

MONTANA

NORTH DAKOTA

MINNESOTA

OREGON

IDAHO

SOUTH DAKOTA

WISCONSIN

WYOMING

MICHIGAN

NEW YORK

St. Albans

MAINE

Bangor
Bath
Kennebunk
Marblehead
Boston
Barnstable
New Bedford
Nantucket
Bristol
Newport

Plymouth
Warren
Providence

VT.

N.H.

MASS.

CONN.

R.I.

San Francisco

UTAH

NEBRASKA

IOWA

ILLINOIS

INDIANA

OHIO

PENNSYLVANIA

New York
Philadelphia
Baltimore
Annapolis
Alexandria
Richmond

N.J.

DEL.

MD.

WEST VIRGINIA

VIRGINIA

COLORADO

KANSAS

MISSOURI

KENTUCKY

Los Angeles

ARIZONA

NEW MEXICO

OKLAHOMA

ARKANSAS

TENNESSEE

NORTH CAROLINA

SOUTH CAROLINA

Charleston

Savannah

TEXAS

LOUISIANA

MISSISSIPPI

ALABAMA

GEORGIA

FLORIDA

Jacksonville
St. Augustine

Mobile

New Orleans

Galveston

Miami

Key West

Between 1892 and 1924, immigrants entered the United States through all the cities above, though very few people were processed in some places. Copies of passenger lists for these places are in the National Archives in Washington, D.C., or its regional offices.

If for any reason they were found ineligible to enter the United States—because of a physical handicap or illness or because they did not strike the officers as someone likely to be able to support themselves in this country—they could be rejected and deported. This meant they would be held until the steamship they had arrived on could return them to the port from which they had come.

For the majority of immigrants, a visit to Ellis Island took no more than three or four hours. Most left happily—98 percent passed all inspections and were sent on to their final destinations. A few were detained,

Internet Links

For these and other clickable links, go to *www.workman.com/familytree*.

There are hundreds of websites about immigration and the immigrant groups who came to America. Here is a sampling of some of them.

African-American

AfriGeneas: African Ancestored Genealogy
afrigeneas.com

British

United Kingdom and Ireland Genealogy/GENUKI
www.genuki.org.uk

Eastern European

Federation of East European Family History Societies
feefhs.org

French

The National Huguenot Society
huguenot.netnation.com

German

German Genealogy Home Page
www.genealogienetz.de

Irish

Fianna Guide to Irish Genealogy
rootsweb.com/~fianna/

Italian

The Italian Genealogy Home Page
italgen.com

Jewish

JewishGen: The Official Home of Jewish Genealogy
jewishgen.org

some waiting for relatives to pick them up, others confined to the hospital until their infectious diseases were cured. Only 2 out of 100 arrivals were rejected and deported.

For millions, Ellis Island was only a stop on the way to a new home somewhere in America. Two out of every three Ellis Island immigrants left the New York area. They converted their foreign money to American dollars at the island's exchange, then bought a ticket at the Ellis Island railroad office.

Many took a ferry to New Jersey, where they caught trains chugging into the heartland of America. For some, this could be a short ride—a day, perhaps, to Pennsylvania or Maryland. For others,

The sites below contain immigration resources, ships' passenger lists, historical information, and more.

Angel Island Association

angelisland.org
Information about this West Coast entry station, at which many Asian (especially Chinese) immigrants were detained, from 1910 to 1940.

The American Family Immigration History Center

ellisislandrecords.org
This site has a database with more than 16 million names extracted from ships' passenger lists from the Port of New York between the years 1892 and 1924. (For more information on how to make the most of this important website, see Chapter Eight.)

Cyndi's List—Immigration & Naturalization

cyndislist.com/immigrat.htm
A huge list of links to sites dealing with immigration to the United States.

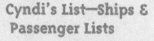

Cyndi's List—Ships & Passenger Lists

cyndislist.com/ships.htm
Great resource for information about ships' passenger lists.

Immigration and Ships' Passenger List Research Guide

home.att.net/~arnielang/shipgide.html
An excellent guide to finding your ancestor on passenger lists.

however, the train ride was a long journey. Many Swedes and Norwegians headed for the Great Plains, Germans to Pennsylvania, Poles to the cities of the Midwest, Greeks or Spaniards to Washington State or Nevada.

Other immigrants leaving the area took a ferry from Ellis Island to New York City. There they caught trains to their final destinations in the Northeast or upstate New York.

But no matter how long they stayed there, everyone who stepped onto the "Isle of Tears"—as Ellis Island soon came to be known around the world because of the deportations and tearful family separations—remembered it well.

The Wall of Honor on Ellis Island lists thousands of immigrants. Are any of these your ancestors?

DOORS TO AMERICA

Where did your ancestors enter the United States? If you know the answer to that question, there's a good chance that you can find a copy of their records.

For a huge number of Americans, the answer is Ellis Island—it's estimated that more than one out of every three Americans can trace at least one ancestor back to there.

But more than 100 other U.S. cities and towns could have also served as an entry place for your ancestors. If you know where and approximately when your family arrived, finding their records will be much easier.

For the first 300 years of immigration, most people came by boat. Besides New York, a few other East Coast cities received a sizable number of immigrants. Boston was a major landing spot for Irish immigrants. Baltimore took in lots of Germans. Philadelphia was a destination for many Italians and eastern Europeans.

In the 1880s, Charleston, South Carolina, and New Orleans, Louisiana, had busy years as immigration ports. Galveston, Texas, was an unusual but important destination for immigrants from eastern Europe in the early 1900s. San Francisco was the busiest boat arrival point for immigrants from Asia and the Pacific islands. Seattle and Los Angeles also received newcomers.

Not everyone came by boat, of course. Cities on the Mexican border—like El Paso, Texas, and Nogales,

Outside the U.S.A.

During the 19th and early 20th centuries, more than 60 million people left their homelands for other countries. One out of every four did *not* come to the United States. They went instead to other countries. Argentina, Australia, Brazil, and Canada took almost 15 million people.

So when you're trying to trace your family members from overseas, ask if any immigrated to other countries.

Arizona—were entry points for Mexicans and Latin Americans who walked, drove, or rode into the United States. Up north, St. Albans, Vermont, and Detroit, Michigan, were among the checkpoints for those coming through Canada.

In some ways, immigration has changed a great deal over the past 50 years. If your family came to the United States after the 1950s, most of the paperwork (including the medical examination) was done in the country of origin. If your family arrived by plane, the trip took hours, not days. And they could have entered the United States in any of a hundred airports.

There are, however, three major cities that attract most immigrants today. The first is Miami, Florida. This tropical city on the Atlantic Ocean has become *the* major entryway for immigrants from South America and the Caribbean, and they have given Miami a new identity as an international city. More than half of all Miamians today were born outside the United States.

Los Angeles, California, is the second big arrival port for immigrants arriving here today. Hundreds of thousands of immigrants have poured into this city, the greatest number from Central America, especially Mexico. Many others are from Russia, China, India, Korea, and the Philippines.

New York City is still probably the greatest entryway for immigrants. Tens of thousands arrive from Asia, South America, Europe, and Africa every year. Many settle in the New York area and become United States citizens.

So, where did *your* family enter the U.S.? When you start researching that question, consider the date when your family members arrived. Ask questions and seek out clues. Then look in the most likely place for that period of history.

Detector's To-Do List

❑ Ask about the immigrant ancestors or relatives in your family. Approximately what years did they arrive here? What countries did they leave from?

❑ If you can find information easily about your family's immigrants, try to get specifics: Did they come by ship? If so, from which port? Which port did they arrive at?

❑ Look back at your family history interviews. Did you get any immigration stories? Share the information in this chapter with relatives who have immigrated. Ask how their experiences compare.

❑ Research the websites that offer information about your family's entry points, such as *ellisislandrecords.org* (see Chapter Eight for more information).

CHAPTER SIX

Becoming an American

Immigrants Make a New Life in a New Land

In this chapter, you will learn:
- What life is like for newly arrived immigrants
- Where different immigrant groups have settled
- How newly arrived immigrants help each other
- How immigrants become U.S. citizens

No one stays an immigrant forever. At some point, newcomers to this country become Americans.

The process can take a long time. For adults who arrive here after years in their native land, learning new ways may feel very slow. Many have to learn a new language. All have to get used to new customs, new foods, new ways of doing business, and new ways of living.

For kids, the process is often easier. Children usually adapt quickly to new homes. That's why many kids who come from other countries end up speaking English without a foreign accent, while adults who arrive here

often carry with them, for their entire lives, the sounds of their native lands.

Regardless of when your family arrived here from another country, they had to choose *where* to live. Throughout history, one way that many immigrants have made their adjustment easier has been by living in American communities where other relatives and countrymen have already settled.

This was true for immigrants in years past. It is true today. And it will surely be true for many years to come.

It was true for Harry Raskolenko in the early 1900s. Harry was the son of Polish Jewish immigrants. He grew up in one of the world's most crowded immigrant neighborhoods, New York City's Lower East Side. Packed together in that one small community in 1907 were many families from Russia, Poland, Italy, and Ireland. Jews, Roman Catholics, and Russian Orthodox lived side by side. And yet . . .

"All of us had our special places, dictated to us by our faces, our speech, our jobs, our music, dances, and books—and, of course, our religion and country of origin," Raskolenko recalled. "Each one lived in a ghetto within a ghetto. . . . We wanted to be among our own people, our own languages, our own religion, and to be ourselves down to our last Jewish roots."

The drive to share "immigrant roots" created many new communities in the massive wave of immigration from 1892 to 1924. "Little Italys" and "Irishtowns" sprang up in cities across the Northeast. Thousands of Dutch newcomers settled in cities in southwestern Michigan. A Norwegian immigrant who wanted to farm in the Great Plains would head toward Iowa or Minnesota because both those states had large Norwegian populations.

Living with countrymen and women made it easier to socialize and to feel a part of a community. In those

Above, New York City's Lower East Side around 1900.

neighborhoods, it was simpler to meet a prospective husband or wife or to shop for familiar foods. You could be sure there would be a place to buy newspapers written in your language and that you'd find a church, temple, mosque, or synagogue much like the one you'd left on the other side of the ocean.

For immigrants who felt nervous in their new

(continued on page 114)

Where They Settled

In looking for your ancestors, it may be helpful to keep in mind where different national groups settled. Here is a listing of some of the many groups who came to the U.S. and some of the places where they tended to live.

Africans: Southeast; later, big cities of mid-Atlantic and midwestern states

Arabs: New York; Los Angeles; Detroit

Armenians: New York; Massachusetts; Rhode Island; California

Basques: Nevada; southeast Oregon; southwest Idaho

Belgians: Detroit; eastern Wisconsin

Chinese: San Francisco; Los Angeles; New York City; Honolulu

Cubans: Miami and south Florida; New York City area

Czechs and Slovaks: Prairie populations in Wisconsin, Nebraska, and Texas; urban populations in New York, Chicago, Cleveland, St. Louis, Pittsburgh

Dominicans: New York City; also Chicago, Massachusetts, Florida

In 1892, immigrant shopkeepers posed in front of their store in San Francisco's Chinatown.

Dutch: Hudson Valley, New York, and New Jersey coast; later many moved to California and to Michigan (especially Grand Rapids and Holland)

English: Atlantic seaboard, north and south

Filipinos: San Francisco; Los Angeles; Seattle; New York City

Finns: Midwest, especially Michigan and Minnesota; California; New York

French Canadians: Mill and factory towns of New England

French Huguenots: South Carolina; New Rochelle, New York; Rhode Island

Germans: Northeast; Midwest, especially Wisconsin, Illinois, Indiana, Iowa

Greeks: Northeastern and midwestern cities, particularly New York and Chicago

Haitians: New York City

Hungarians: Pennsylvania; industrial midwestern cities like Chicago, Akron, Toledo, Milwaukee, Detroit

Indians (from India): New York; California

Irish: Northeastern big cities, especially New York and Boston

Italians: Northeastern and mid-Atlantic cities, especially New York and Philadelphia; California

Japanese: Hawaii; California; Washington; Oregon

Koreans: California; New York; Hawaii; Washington

Mexicans: California; Texas; Arizona; New Mexico

Norwegians: Midwest, especially rural areas

Poles: Midwestern cities, especially Chicago, Cleveland, Pittsburgh, Buffalo

Portuguese: New England states, especially Massachusetts, New Jersey

Russians: New York; Pennsylvania; Illinois; New England

Russian (eastern European) Jews: East Coast cities, with especially large numbers in New York City area

Swedes: New York State; Minnesota; Illinois; Washington; California

Swiss: California's famous Swiss colony; northern and central Ohio

Vietnamese: California

Welsh: Mining towns in Pennsylvania and Ohio

Many immigrants from India have settled in and around New York City and in California.

country, these neighborhoods also offered protection. The Chinese who immigrated to America during the 1850s and '60s encountered a great deal of prejudice from white Americans. Living together in "Chinatowns" not only made for an easier life but also gave the inhabitants a greater sense of security.

Because these neighborhoods were so filled with

Immigrant children pledge allegiance to the flag in 1889. Kids often become "Americanized" more quickly than their parents.

the flavor of their homeland, people could spend their whole lives in America and never really become Americanized. There are many stories of immigrants from Italy or Puerto Rico or Russia who came to the United States when they were young, lived here for 40, 50, or 60 years, and after all that time could speak almost no English! They didn't need to—just about everything could be done in their neighborhood using the old language.

That way of life appeals to some immigrants, especially those who feel lonely and homesick for the old way of life. To many, however, the Old World is the past. By coming to America, they have entered the future. Now it is time to become something new and different: an "American."

In 1908, the English playwright Israel Zangwill called America "the great Melting Pot, where all the races of Europe are melting and reforming." Zangwill believed that America was the place where all the peoples of the Old World would lose their hatreds and their rivalries. He hoped that coming to America would change things, that prejudice and old feuds would disappear. "These are the fires of God," he wrote in his play, also called *The Melting Pot*. "Germans and Frenchmen, Irishmen and Englishmen, Jews and Russians—into the Crucible with you all! God is making the American."

The idea of the melting pot was irresistible to many people. Immigrants saw it promising acceptance: I am an

American, someone who belongs here, not just someone living here from a country across the sea. Many U.S. citizens liked the melting-pot idea, too: It promised an end to the confusing and strange differences the newly arrived immigrants brought with them.

The melting-pot notion sounded good, but it had an important flaw. Many of these immigrants didn't want their past simply to melt away. Although they had left their homelands, they were still proud of their cultures, their customs, and their religions—and were not about to throw away long-held traditions. Instead, immigrants combined their original cultures with American customs and created their own mixture. They became Americans, but Americans with a past as well as a future.

Above: A view of the cramped tenement life of an immigrant family in Chicago, around 1910. Below, left: An immigrant boy takes a bath and washes his underwear at the same time.

Making the Adjustment

In the late 1800s and early 1900s, few people could afford, or wanted, to spend all their time in their neighborhoods. Adults went to work. Kids went to school. They made new friends and learned new ways, and most learned to speak and read English. Over time, they began to understand how America worked. But it wasn't easy.

Many children didn't go to school in the Old Country because they had to work. In America, children *had* to go to school—it was required by law.

A Countryman's Helping Hand: Immigrant Aid Societies

In the late 19th and early 20th centuries, where could new immigrants go when they needed financial assistance? Banks were often nervous about lending money to these poor new arrivals. And besides, banks charged a lot of interest.

Family members, of course, helped each other, and so did friends. But sometimes a new American needed more assistance than family or friends could give. In these cases, many newcomers turned to a group of countrymen: self-help groups known as "immigrant aid societies."

These aid societies were run *by* immigrants *for* immigrants. Most offered financial assistance and job-hunting advice. Others collected and forwarded mail for their members, arranged social events like dances and parties, or helped immigrants find apartments. Some ran summer camps for their members' children.

Many societies were large organizations open to anyone who came from the Old Country. They carried names like the Danish Brotherhood in America or the Ukrainian Alliance of America. One group, the Russian Orthodox Catholic Mutual Aid Society, had 138 branches in 17 states and Canada. Other groups were smaller, made up of people who emigrated from the same city, town, or village. The Chmielniker Sick and Benevolent Society, for example, was a *landsmanshaft* organized in 1929 by Jewish immigrants from the tiny Polish village of Chmielnik to offer aid to any "landsmen" (persons from the same community) who needed it. Chinese *hui* and Japanese *kenjinkan* were self-help groups usually organized by immigrants from the same home province.

These groups recruited members on the streets of immigrant neighborhoods or in the churches or

"I went to public school and . . . I had a miserable time. I would come home and cry and say, 'I don't understand them and they don't understand me,'" remembered Josephine Reale, who spoke only Italian when she arrived in Philadelphia at age five. "I learned very fast, though. Before I knew it I could speak as well as the other kids," she added, with a laugh. "And we got along fine. . . . I began to like this country."

The new immigrants expected life in the United States to be very different from life in their homeland, but nothing could have prepared them for many of the changes.

synagogues of the community. Each member paid dues to the group. Although each individual amount was small, it turned into a mighty sum when multiplied by the number of members. The total was a kind of community insurance policy, enough to help members in need.

When Nils needed money to start a business, he might ask the Sons of Norway for a loan. If Giuseppe's wife died, he might be given a grant by the Calabrian Emigrants Organization to pay for the funeral. Heinrich might buy life insurance through the Order of the Sons of Herman in the State of Texas; and if Blima were looking for a

nice boy to go out with, she might attend the dances organized by the Jewish *Arbeiter Ring* (Workmen's Circle).

There were thousands of these groups in the early 20th century, when so many immigrants arrived in America. But they are not a thing of the past. Today, many new groups have been formed as the latest groups of immigrants have created their own self-help organizations. The nationalities are now Vietnamese, East Indian, and Latin American, among others, but the help they're offering would be familiar to any former member of a *kenjinkan* or a *landsmanshaft*.

A "fancy dress ball" was sponsored by an immigrant self-help group.

In the late 1800s and early 1900s, most European immigrants came from small villages and farms. Now they were learning what it was like to live in cramped apartment buildings in noisy, crowded, and dirty cities.

In the Old Country, most people worked long hours just to feed their families. Many worked in the

fields. In this new world, the people worked long hours in factories, mines, or mills, doing exhausting, dangerous work.

In the big American cities like New York, Philadelphia, Boston, and Chicago, male and female immigrants working in the clothing industry were

Internet Links

For these and other clickable links, go to www.workman.com/familytree.

Here are some sites dedicated to different nationalities that came to America:

Society of Acadian Descendants
acadian.org

The Society of Hispanic Historical and Ancestral Research (SHHAR)
members.aol.com/shhar/index.htm
users.aol.com/mrosado007/
home.att.net~Alsosa/

Ancient Order of Hibernians in America
aoh.com

Lithuanian Global Society
www.lithuaniangenealogy.org

Polish Genealogical Society of America
pgsa.org

Sons of Norway
www.sofn.com

Ukrainian Genealogical Society
rootsweb.com/ukrgs

Swedish Colonial Society
colonialswedes.org

---

packed into small, crowded rooms for 10 or 12 hours every day. The conditions in these rooms were so terrible that the word *sweatshop* was invented to describe them.

As they worked, these immigrants learned more "American" ways. Their clothing began to change. The colorful costumes of European farmers and peasants soon disappeared, replaced by the more functional coat and jacket of the workingman. In the early 1900s, beards began to disappear, too. American men were mostly clean-shaven, and soon many European-born men were also. For European-born women, mass-produced dresses and stylish hats replaced the handmade outfits and shawls that they once wore.

Children brought many changes into their homes. Often parents learned English more slowly than their kids, who picked up "Americanisms" right away in school. Kids were also quick to copy American dress styles and to pick up American games. Soon the sons of Italian fishermen and Russian farmers were practicing baseball

New York City's Lower East Side neighborhood has been home to many waves of immigrants. In this 1970s photo, neighborhood kids are about to beat the summer heat with some cool ices.

and basketball on city streets, and the daughters were playing jacks and jump rope.

Food was another great Americanizer. When European-born immigrants sat down to eat, they discovered the *real* melting pot. At first, of course, all families ate only what they had eaten in the Old Country. They were suspicious of other types of food.

But slowly they began to experiment. Mary Antin, who arrived in America from Russia in 1893, wrote about her very first American meal: "My father produced several kinds of food, ready to eat, without any cooking, from little tin cans that had printing all over them. He attempted to introduce us to a queer, slippery kind of fruit, which he called 'banana.'" The family refused to eat this strange new fruit, however, and Mary's dad finally gave up his experiment.

Over time, "foreign" foods turned familiar. Italians sampled something called a bagel. Kids whose parents were born in Bristol or Olso or Dublin or Kiev gobbled up a flat baked bread with cheese and tomato on it. Soon there were pizza parlors on city street corners. The children of Chinese immigrants learned to like German delicacies called frankfurters.

The power of the immigrant neighborhoods of the late 1800s and early 1900s lasted for many years. But ever so slowly things changed. The children of immigrants went on to get a better education than their parents had. They became businesspeople, doctors, lawyers, and teachers, and they moved out of the old neighborhood. In many cases, their parents moved with them. In other cases, the parents kept the old neighborhood alive.

Things have constantly been changing in Harry Raskolenko's Lower East Side. In the 1850s, it was filled with German and Irish newcomers. When they moved out by the 1880s, Italian and eastern European Jewish families moved in, along with Romanians, Hungarians, Greeks, Poles, Turks, and Slovaks. In the 1940s, the Jews and Italians began leaving and large numbers of Hispanic immigrants starting making the area their home. Then, in the last two decades, the newest groups—thousands of Chinese, Vietnamese, and Koreans—began moving in.

The cycle repeats itself over and over. A poor immigrant group comes into a neighborhood, works and saves its money, and eventually moves to a more prestigious area. As that group leaves, another group moves in.

The Lower East Side today is filled with more different languages, foods, and houses of worship than it was 150, 100, 50, or even 25 years ago. Most of the residents are immigrants or the children of immigrants, and the neighborhood in many ways has remained the same—bustling, noisy, and crowded with the sights and smells of far-off lands. It remains an "entry community," a spectacular mirror of 150 years of immigrant history.

There are Lower East Side–type neighborhoods in big cities all over the United States. Each is a kind of launching pad, a place where people on the way up live while they work to better themselves and their families. As long as they serve as doors for people moving on up, these neighborhoods will continue to be a vital part of the American immigrant experience.

BEYOND IMMIGRANT: BECOMING A CITIZEN

Whether they lived in immigrant neighborhoods or not, newcomers did want to get the rights American citizens had. To do that, they had to apply for citizenship.

"I hereby declare, on oath, that I absolutely and entirely renounce and abjure all allegiance and fidelity to any state or sovereignty, and particularly to Russia or any independent state within the bounds of the former Russian empire, of whom I have heretofore been a subject; that I will support and defend the Constitution and laws of the United States against all enemies, foreign and domestic; and that I will bear true faith and allegiance to the same."

By signing that wordy pledge on June 9, 1920, my grandfather, Hymen Perlo, became a citizen of the United States of America.

Immigrants are not required to become American citizens, but most want to do so. Being a citizen means you are a real American: You're entitled to vote in elections. You can have a say in who runs your town, your city, your state—even your country! For millions of immigrants who had no voice at all in the governing of the countries they came from, being an American citizen is a privilege, one they were eager to attain.

Anyone born in the United States or born to parents who are American citizens is automatically a U.S. citizen. All others must apply to be accepted for citizenship. That process is called "naturalization."

In order to become a naturalized citizen, immigrants must formally apply to do so, must learn to speak English, and must become familiar with American government and history. The procedure has changed over the years, but these standards generally have applied.

In the early 1900s, applying for citizenship was a three-step process. No sooner than three years after being legally admitted to the United States, the immigrant had to go to a federal courthouse and file a document called the "Declaration of Intention," which was sometimes called "First Papers." On this form, applicants usually gave their home address and information about where and when they were born and when and how they arrived in the United States.

A year or more later, immigrants filed a second application, the "Petition for Naturalization," which was

A great moment in an immigrant's life: becoming a U.S. citizen.

While the certificate was the most important piece of paper as far as the immigrant was concerned, it is the Declaration and Petition that are of most use and interest to genealogists.

Paolo Gamarello, born in Italy, became a U.S. citizen in 1925.

sometimes referred to as "Second Papers" or "Final Papers." On this document, immigrants repeated the information on the First Papers and perhaps added the name of a husband or wife and children.

Shortly thereafter, if the application was accepted (there was an investigation to ensure that there was no good reason to deny the request), the immigrant received a "Certificate of Naturalization." It was this document that the immigrant received with great pride. It meant that the immigrant was now a full-fledged U.S. citizen. Many immigrants framed or in some other way displayed their citizenship certificate.

Detector's To-Do List

Here are some steps to take to learn more about your immigrant relatives and/or ancestors:

❑ Find out about their experiences adjusting to life in the United States.

❑ Find out if anyone in your family became a naturalized citizen. Can you locate information about his or her naturalization?

❑ On a United States map, indicate where different branches of your family live. Find out why people chose to move to particular locations.

❑ Ask if any relatives are or were members of ethnic self-help societies.

❑ Were any of your relatives the children of immigrants? Ask them about their experiences growing up with parents who had come from another country.

CHAPTER SEVEN

The Great Record Hunt

How to Find—and Use—Documents About Your Family

In this chapter, you will learn how to:
- Gather information to help you find documents
- Identify which documents you are most interested in
- Send away for and get copies of those documents
- Begin to search the Internet for transcriptions of documents

Whenever I played at my grandparents' house as a child, two very serious people watched me in silence. No matter what I did, they never spoke, but they were always there, observing me.

They were portraits—large hand-colored portraits—of a man and a woman, and they hung on the walls of my father's parents' living room.

The man had a stern, solemn look. His beard was long and straight and white, and he wore a dark jacket and black hat. The woman was serious-looking, too. She had high cheekbones and deep dark eyes, and she wore a black shawl around her head. Something about her was tough, strong, and proud. I wasn't surprised to learn they were my great-grandparents—my grandfather's mother and father.

When I became interested in genealogy, I started to ask more about these stern faces that now hung on the wall of my parents' den. What were their names? Had they ever come to America?

We'd always known Great-grandpa's full name, but Great-grandma's was a mystery until we found a document.

No, my father told me, they never came to America; they lived and died in Russia. The man's name was the same as my father's: Dad had been named after his grandfather. But my father didn't know his grandmother's full name, and no one else did, either. In fact, no one remembered anything about her.

That seemed to be the end of it. No one knew her name, and I guessed I never would, either. But one day I did find it out—with the help of the city of New York. In an office in lower Manhattan was a copy of a wedding license that my grandfather and grandmother had filled out in 1909. And there, on the license, were the names of the parents of the bride and groom—including that of my great-grandmother, Slava Shapiro.

It felt good to read those two words. Now the proud face on the wall had a name.

This is one small example of the importance of learning how to use public documents.

Facts about *your* family are just sitting on shelves and in file cabinets and desk drawers, waiting for you to find them. As a genealogist, one of your jobs will be to figure out how to get at those facts.

There are hundreds of places where information about your family may be found, because from the moment your ancestors set foot in America, someone was writing down their names. Did they arrive on a ship, by bus, or by plane? There's probably a record of this somewhere. Did they get married, divorced, have children, die? Forms had to be filled out, and those forms are on file in some office. Did they apply for American citizenship, a passport, Social Security? Did they ever vote? Somewhere in the United States, there are records of all of that. And the information on these records can help you find out a great deal about the people in your past.

The most important documents for genealogists are:

- Cemetery records
- Census records
- Citizenship papers
- Land records
- Military records
- Passenger ship lists
- Religious records
- School records
- Vital records (birth, marriage, and death certificates)
- Wills

You'll want to track down these records, because they often have information that no one remembers. A copy of your grandmother's birth certificate, for example, might give you information about her parents—your great-grandparents—that Grandma herself has forgotten. A copy of a long-gone ancestor's marriage license may hold clues to relatives even further back.

Your family may be able to provide you with some of these documents. For copies of many other records, however, you will have to conduct a search.

Until recently, genealogists had to write to or visit records centers, libraries, government offices, and courthouses to find many of their family records. The Internet, however, has changed all that. Over the past few years, millions of records have been entered into digital databases—and now you can find at least some of these records through the Net.

In this chapter, you will find a lot of information about where different kinds of records can be found. Whenever it is possible to go online for the records, you will find a website listed.

For greater in-depth directions about web surfing for records, see Chapter Eight, "Catching Your Ancestors with a Net."

Even with the wonderful web at your fingertips, you will often find that you still must go to a records center

in person to find what you need. In some cases, you will be able to look at the documents yourself. In other cases, you will have to pay a small fee and let other people look for you.

This crucial process of tracking down the records that reveal your ancestors' life stories is called a "document search." You'll be surprised at how many different kinds of documents there are. You may also

This certificate of naturalization was the proof that an immigrant was now a citizen of the United States.

be astonished at how many places you may have to search to find the ones you're seeking.

Some original genealogical records no longer exist; some may have been put on microfilm or microfiche. In other cases, you may actually get to hold the original document and see a signature that was put down on paper by one of your ancestors long ago.

Old postcards make your ancestors' hometowns come alive. This is a view of Albany, New York, in the early 1900s.

10 THINGS YOU MUST KNOW BEFORE YOU START YOUR DOCUMENT SEARCH

So now you're excited and ready to find those documents. Not so fast! Before you turn on your computer or call your local library or records center, read these 10 tips. You almost certainly won't find out much about your family if you start searching without some crucial information:

1. Know approximately when something happened. In order to find anyone's personal records, you need to know *where* that person was and approximately *when* an important event (birth, marriage, death, etc.) happened. This is true whether you're searching online or offline.

You can go online and look for your ancestor in any number of databases, but if you don't know anything about where and when he or she lived, how can you be sure that you're on the track for *your* ancestor?

The same is true if you are looking for records offline. Documents are generally kept near the location of an event. Birth certificates are usually on file in the city where the birth took place. Many immigration papers are kept in the city where the immigrant

Checklist:
Before You Go to a Records Center

Many records searches can be done through the mail or online, but sometimes you will have to go to a records center in person. Call first and ask every possible question. It is better to spend five minutes on the phone than to waste an hour going somewhere only to be told you can't use the records.

Here are the key questions to ask:

* What's your exact address? How do I get there?
* What days and what hours are you open?
* What's the latest you'll let someone enter?
* Is there a photocopy machine there?
* If not, is there any way I can get the documents copied?
* Do I need any kind of identification to look at records?
* I'm (say your age) years old. Can I look at the documents by myself?
* Do I have to pay for anything? Can I pay you in cash? If not, how can I pay for the documents?
* Does the center have a website? What is the URL?
* Is there an information packet you could send me?
* Is there anything else I should know?

landed. Know something about where and when each event happened—or you will have difficulty finding the records.

2. Know your ancestor's name. This may sound funny, but without your ancestor's name—the complete and original name—you may waste your time. If you're looking for an immigrant relative, for example, don't assume the name you've heard is the original one. I knew my grandmother Edna Burstein came to America through Ellis Island sometime after 1900. But when I went to *ellisislandrecords.org*, I couldn't find Edna Burstein anywhere. I had to poke around awhile until I found someone named Etty Burstein (which, it turned out, was the name she was born with and went by in her small town of Zambrow, which is now in Poland). Since this Etty came from Zambrow and was the age my grandmother would have been, I was finally sure I had found the right person.

But even knowing the complete, correct name may not be enough. If your ancestor's name was a common one—Mary Jones or William Rogers, Hermann Schwartz

Old passports may include photos of your ancestors; this Greek passport dates from 1916.

3. Use the clues you find on documents. Sometimes information on one document can point you to an earlier one. My grandfather's citizenship papers, which I found fairly easily, told me what boat he arrived on and when. This information made it much simpler for me to track down his boat manifest information.

The same principle works on many other documents: Your grandmother's birth certificate may tell you the date of your great-grandparents' marriage, which can lead you to their marriage license.

4. Make it easy for people to reply. When you send a request by mail, include a self-addressed, stamped envelope. This will make it easier for the person to respond, which means you'll probably get a response faster.

5. Give only relevant facts. This is true in person or by mail. Don't talk about your entire family history. Just explain exactly what you are looking for and offer only

or Maria Russo—then you'd better know a lot more. If you know that John Smith was born in Brooklyn in 1906, you don't know enough. You'll have to have an address, an exact birth date, and/or both of his parents' names, including his mother's maiden name (let's hope his parents weren't John and Mary Smith!).

enough information to make this clear. Here's an example of a letter you might send to a city bureau of records:

> *Hello:*
>
> *I would like a copy of the birth certificate of John Robert Jones, who was born in Kansas City sometime in June 1876. His parents were Joseph and Elvira Jones. Enclosed is a self-addressed, stamped envelope. Thank you.*
>
> *Sincerely yours,*

6. Keep a research calendar. Keeping a research log will help you stay on top of what you've done and what you need to do. For example, "John Robert Jones: Wrote to Kansas City Bureau of Records requesting his birth certificate, 15 June 2001," will tell you what you did and when. If you get a reply, note that, too. In this way, you won't look for the same thing two or three times. (The same idea applies to web searches; see the next chapter for more information about tracking your Internet activities.)

7. Call before making a genealogical visit. Whether you are going to a records center, a library, a museum, or even a relative's home, call before going and make sure they have the type of document you are looking for. Find out what the office hours are, if the records you are interested in are available on the day you are planning to come, and if you will be allowed in. Nothing

Helen Rabkin's birth certificate tells how old her parents were, what work they did, and where they lived.

is more frustrating than going to the wrong place—or the right place at the wrong time. Some places may have minimum age requirements for looking at documents; ask about that. Find out what kind of copying is permitted, how much each copy costs, and if there is a money-changing machine on the premises. (See "Checklist: Before You Go to a Records Center," on page 127.)

8. Handle everything carefully. If you are allowed to examine original records, you may come across fragile old books that could chip, flake, or even fall apart. These records are precious to many people besides you, so

The Mystery of the Missing Days

In 1752, something very odd happened in the British Isles and all English colonies, including America. People went to sleep on September 2, 1752. When they woke up the next morning, the date was September 14, 1752. Eleven days—September 3 through 13—disappeared.

These are the famous "missing days" that keep genealogists on their toes. They vanished in British lands in 1752, but a number of days have disappeared in other countries, too, at other times.

As a result of this mystery, you may find dates in the 18th century written with two numbers: 11 Feb. 1731 O.S./22 Feb. 1732 N.S. *O.S.* means "old style"; *N.S.* means—what else?—"new style."

What's this all about? Here's what happened. The British were among the last people in the world to accept the fact that the calendar they were using was flawed. The "Julian" calendar—named after Julius Caesar, who adopted it around 45 B.C.—called March 25 New Year's Day and said the year was 365 days and 6 hours long. The length was very close—wrong by only a few minutes. But after nearly 2,000 years, those

---

handle them as gently as you can. Work hard to leave them in the same condition as you found them.

9. Make a photocopy of the record. If you can't, write down ("extract") the important information. Some records cannot be photocopied. They may be too old, or a photocopier may not be available.

Don't think that you have to copy every word. Many documents are very long and filled with legal jargon and unimportant phrases. The best thing to do in these cases is to read the document slowly and thoroughly. Then carefully write down all identifying numbers and important information.

If you end up looking at the same kind of document—like citizenship papers or land deeds—very often, you may want to make up an "abstract" of that kind of document. An abstract is like a shopping list—it will help you remember what you're looking for when you do a document search. Write down the information you expect to see, leaving blank spaces for filling in the specific information you discover on each document. You'll find an abstract for citizenship papers in the Appendix.

10. Don't blindly trust the document. It's exciting to find an ancestor's old records. You may discover some

few minutes added up to an error of 10 days. Most of the world adopted a new calendar (advocated by Pope Gregory XIII), called the "Gregorian" calendar, sometime after 1582, when they jumped forward by 10 days and October 5 became October 15.

The British refused to go along until the middle of the 18th century, and by then the difference had grown to 11 days. Finally, on September 2, 1752, the British joined most of the world and changed their calendar. In all British lands (with the exception of Scotland, which had changed 100 years before), September 2 was followed by September 14. And 1753 began on January 1, not on March 25.

All this means is that you have to double-check the dates you find in English-speaking countries between 1582 and 1752. Are they listed as O.S. or N.S.? Do you see a date listed for 1750/51? That would probably be a date between January 1 and March 24—which means that 1750 is the old-style notation and 1751 is the one we now use.

Here is when the date changes took place in some other countries:
Austria: January 7, 1584, became January 17, 1584
France: December 10, 1582, became December 20, 1582
Norway: February 19, 1700, became March 1, 1700
Sweden: February 18, 1753, became March 1, 1753

new and interesting information. But as in all your ancestor detector work, don't assume that because a piece of data is in print, it's accurate. You've got to evaluate what's in front of you. Who filled out the form? (It's usually more trustworthy if the person himself wrote the information down.) Does it match other information you have? Are there "facts" that contradict what you already know? Which "fact" is more accurate?

You play judge and jury here. Weigh the evidence and decide what you can trust. Then take the information from the document and transfer it to your Family Group Sheets and Pedigree Charts, noting carefully where each bit of information comes from. (If you're not sure of the accuracy of something, put a question mark next to that fact.)

THE BEST SOURCES FOR ANCESTORS' RECORDS

Now you're ready to search for the records your ancestors have left behind. The first place to go is to your relatives. Ask them to look for any official records they may have. Carefully look over the documents. Have you found new names? Addresses? Dates of important events? Some of this information will help you find other documents.

When you're ready to go outside the family, begin with the most common documents: vital records.

Vital Records: Birth, Marriage, and Death Certificates; Divorce Decrees

Everyone is born, and everyone dies. That's one reason why birth and death certificates are among the easiest and best places to begin searching for family documents.

These records are called "vital" because they come from the Latin word *vita,* which means "life." They are also vital—important—because they are filled with lots of information. These certificates often are an excellent source for hard-to-locate data like women's maiden names and family addresses.

Birth certificates include many facts about a child's parents. Death certificates, filled out by relatives of the person who died, are good sources of information about the surviving family members.

When you start to look for your family's vital records, begin with your parents' birth and marriage certificates. Then start looking for your grandparents' documents. Move slowly backward in time.

Where to look: Vital records are local records. They are usually kept in the capital of the country where someone lived, though some states keep them in their capital cities.

If your ancestors lived in the same state as you, your parents may be able to tell you where to write for records. If not, your best bet is to get your hands on the information contained in a U.S. government booklet called *Where to Write for Vital Records.* This booklet shows where to find birth, marriage, divorce, and death records for every state. You can order a copy from the Superintendent of Documents, U.S. Government Printing Office, Washington, DC 20402. There is a small charge. *Note:* If you're able to get online, you can find *all* of this information on the Internet for free (see "Web tips," below).

When you find out where the records are kept, send for them by indicating the name of the person whose records you are looking for and the actual or approximate date (have at least a probable year) you believe an event happened. Send a self-addressed, stamped envelope. The clerk will conduct a search, and if the records exist, they will be sent to you—after you pay a fee—within a few weeks.

Web tips: You can pick up all the information for every state found in *Where to Write for Vital Records* by going to the website *vitalrec.com.* This website also has links to many other sites, including places to get information about vital records centers in many other countries.

Several Internet sites offer some of the information contained in the vital records themselves. The LDS church site, *familysearch.com,* is a good place to look for this. Try running a general search on the family member you are seeking in their Vital Records Index area. A more targeted approach would be to go to *usgenweb.org,* a volunteer-run website that specializes in making U.S. records available to all. When you get to the *usgenweb.org* homepage, click to the page for the state in which your ancestor lived. Look for the vital records section there, then enter your family member's name.

In many cases, special-interest websites (ethnic groups, religious groups, etc.; see pages 106, 118, and 184) also have either transcriptions of vital records or index information for ordering the vital records through LDS centers.

Census Records

Every 10 years since 1790, the United States has commissioned a head count of every inhabitant of the country. This "Federal Census" is done for many reasons. One of the most important is to determine how many representatives each state will have in Congress. The census also helps the U.S. government keep on top of the ways the country is changing. The nationwide census completed in 2000 was the 22nd in American history.

These counts take place across the United States on one specific day set by Congress. During the last few censuses, forms with questions about the people who lived there were mailed to every known household. Recipients were requested to answer the questions and mail the forms in before a set date. If a household did not respond, a census taker (or "enumerator") was sent to that address. In 2000, people were also encouraged, for the first time, to send their census information in via the Internet.

A census taker pays a visit in 1930. You can use old census records to fill in blanks on your family tree.

In the years before mail-in forms became common, the census was a kind of national counting party. Census takers went door to door in every community in the United States. They didn't just count people; they also gathered a lot of information, such as the person's age, place of birth, and occupation. Census records before

Keeping Dates Straight:
Calendar Watching for Genealogists

Can someone be born three times? My grandfather was. According to his tombstone, Morris Wolfman was born on November 16, 1879; his death certificate clearly states November 25, 1882; and his citizenship papers say November 25, 1881.

Obviously, they can't all be correct. In fact, it's pretty obvious which date is the most reliable. The information on the tombstone and death certificate came from other people. Only the citizenship papers date came straight from my grandfather.

You will find, as you do your research, that this kind of confusion is not uncommon. While all facts in genealogy have to be checked, dates turn out to be the trickiest of all. There are a lot of reasons for this:

• **Americans write dates differently from** most other people in the world. You probably use the American style of month-day-year. You write October 7, 1950, as 10/7/50. When you begin to look into records of other countries, you will find that most places use a different style: day-month-year. They write 7 October 1950, or 7/10/50.

If you are not careful, you may end up wrongly assuming

1900 have less information. Until 1850, only the name of the head of the household was listed, and almost all of the records of the 1890 census were lost in a fire.

To protect people's privacy, census records are off-limits to the general public for 72 years. In 2002, the 1930 census became available for general viewing. In 2012, the 1940 census will be made available.

Therefore, if you know where your ancestor lived in a year ending in "0" from 1930 back (excluding 1890), you can relatively easily access information about them. You will be able to look at copies of the actual pages of the census and see—in the census taker's own handwriting—what the census taker found out about your family.

By looking up a family across two or three censuses, you can learn about changes in the family, discover people you never knew existed, or learn the names of people you knew about but could not identify.

Where to look: Copies of the U.S. Federal Census

that 7/10/50 is July 10, not October 7. Be sure to double-check all your sources for how they make notations. The proper way to write dates for all genealogical research is day/spelled out month/full year.

• **People were sometimes listed as younger** than they really were. For example, immigrant ship tickets for children under a certain age (sometimes 14, sometimes 12) were cheaper than adult tickets. So, many parents subtracted several years from their children's ages.

Occasionally people made themselves younger. They didn't like being 52, so they became 50. Simple—but confusing for the genealogist who follows their path. (In cases like these and the next one, the best thing to do is to look for records made close to the time of birth, like birth certificates or christening records.)

• **Some people made themselves older than** they really were. If a 16-year-old boy wanted to emigrate to America but wasn't allowed to leave by himself until he was 18, he might figure out a way to gain two years in a hurry.

• **Some people really didn't know exactly** when they were born. No birth records were kept in many American states until after 1900. In other countries, records were often incomplete or nonexistent. And in some religions, dates were kept by a different calendar. These people were never 100 percent sure how "Tammuz" or "Ramadan" translated to our calendar, so they made something up.

• **Several countries changed their calendar.** Days disappeared and years were renumbered all around the world between 1582 and 1923 (see "The Mystery of the Missing Days" on page 130).

results are kept on microfilm at the National Archives in Washington, D.C., and in branch offices in other cities around the country (see Chapter Nine, pages 174–175). In addition, major research and genealogical libraries often have copies of the census on microfilm.

Web tips: You can also find transcriptions of censuses online and even on some CD-ROMs offered for sale by commercial genealogy sites.

Websites where you can check for census records, or for information about tracking down those records, include:

• Census Online—Census Sites on the Web: *census-online.com*
• Clues in Census Records, 1850–1920: *www.nara.gov/genealogy/cenclues.html*

The USGenWeb Archives Census Project was started in February 1997. Its mission is to transcribe every U.S.

That Old-Time Handwriting

Old documents were handwritten, and old-time script can make your eyes swim. But don't give up! If you've found an old handwritten record, you're probably looking at valuable information.

Take extra time to read the document carefully. The best way to tackle an older document is to study the writer's style, the way the letters are written. Here are other suggestions to make that task easier:

• **Use the known to take you to the unknown.** Legal documents are loaded with terms like "Whereas" and "Therefore," and you usually can spot your ancestor's name. Make a note of the way the letters are written in those names and other words, and try to find the same letters in other, less obvious words.

Federal Census and upload it to the USGenWeb Archives. There are people working on this project who will look up one or two records for you. Check these websites for more information: *www.rootsweb.com/~census* or *www.us-census.org.*

Citizenship Papers

Most immigrants, once they arrive here, want to become American citizens, and many of them quickly file applications. These citizenship applications are filled with information. If your family members arrived after 1906, you will probably find out from these papers what ship they arrived on and when; you may also find their photographs.

Where to look: If your ancestors became citizens after September 26, 1906, you may track down their immigration papers by sending form G-639 to the Immigration and Naturalization Service, FIOA/PA Office, Washington, DC 20536. (You'll find a copy of this form in the Appendix; photocopy it, fill it out, and

- **In early American documents, be on the lookout** for what is known as the "long s" (f). This letter looks a lot like today's "f," but it was often used in colonial times as the first "s" when two appeared together: Congre$f$s, progre$f$s, ble$f$sing. For some good examples of this, see if you can find a copy of the handwritten Declaration of Independence.

- **Watch for common abbreviations.** Many words were shortened, with the second letter raised. Some examples of this include J^r for "Junior," s^d for "said," and afs^d for "the aforesaid," which means the person previously mentioned. Often names were written this way also: Abra^m stood for Abraham, W^m or Willm for William, Marg^t for Margaret.

- **Take special care with capital letters;** they can be especially hard to figure out. L and T often look the same; M and N, I and J, L and S, and U and V all can be difficult to differentiate.

If you are stumped on a letter, make a list of all the letters it could possibly be and then search for them in the document. By process of elimination, you may be able to determine what letter you are looking at.

- **In English-language documents, read** through a sentence and make guesses at what a difficult word could be. You can sometimes fill in a missing word just by figuring out the meaning of the sentence.

- **In libraries, ask for help.** There may be a handwriting style card for the period you are researching. At a Latter-day Saints Family History Center, I came across a helpful full-page chart of Polish handwriting, showing a variety of styles for every letter.

---

send it in. You can also download this form at *www.ins.usdoj.gov/graphics/formsfree/forms.*) Tell them you want to find your ancestors' naturalization papers and that you are applying under the Freedom of Information Act. If you don't have all the information that's required, include what you do have and send in the form anyway. There is no fee unless the papers can be found.

This process may take a long time. There is a shortcut, however, *if* you know which court your ancestor was naturalized in. See if anyone has a copy of the citizenship certificate your ancestor received; that has the name of the court on it. If your ancestor lived primarily in one county, there's a chance he or she was naturalized in that county's federal court.

If you find out which court handled an ancestor's naturalization, contact that court. Say you want to know how to obtain copies of your relative's naturalization papers. Then either mail in your money or do the search in person.

Passenger Ship Lists: Hidden Treasures

Ship manifests, like many other documents, contain extra information that seems hidden at first. If you find a ship manifest that includes one of your ancestors, look for the following:

How many categories stretch across the sheet? For many years, there was no set number—maybe 5 or 6 on a sheet. Starting in 1893, the U.S. government required 21 different categories. In 1903, "race or people" was added. In 1906, "height," "complexion," "eye color," "hair color," and "place of birth" were added. And in 1907, "name and address of relative" in the country from which they had come was added, making for a total of 29 categories.

Are there markings handwritten on the numbers 1 through 30 on the manifest's far left-hand side? You may see "X" marks on some, and "SI" on others. These notations were added to the list by U.S. government inspectors when the passengers arrived.

***SI* stood for "Board of Special Inquiry"**—a hearing that had to be held in front of immigration officers before the individual was admitted to the United States. This designation could result if an individual was carrying only a small amount of money or if immigration officials had other concerns about him or her.

***X* meant that the inspector was worried that** the person was "likely to become a public charge." The concern was that these people could not earn a living and support themselves. Women and children traveling by themselves—usually being met by a husband, father, or other male relative—received these marks and were held until the male relative picked them up.

Did you find an *SI* or *X* by your ancestor's name? Then be sure to check the entire ship manifest and go to the very end of the document when you finish reading. You will quite probably find more information about that ancestor (What happened in

Be forewarned, however, that finding an ancestor's naturalization records may be very frustrating, especially if he or she applied before 1906. Up until that year, an applicant could apply at any federal, state, or local court, and the records were held *only* by the court to which he or she applied.

Web tips: Check out the USGenWeb page (*usgenweb.org*) for your state to see if any naturalization data has been put on the Internet. Also take a look at the National Archives and Records Administration (NARA) page on naturalization records (*www.nara.gov/genealogy/ natural.html*) for more background and information.

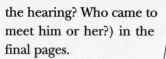

the hearing? Who came to meet him or her?) in the final pages.

How much money did your ancestor bring? The minimum amount required changed from year to year. In 1902, it was $30. By 1913, it had gone up to $50. Did your ancestor meet the requirement? If not, how much less did he or she have? If it was a particularly low amount, check the far left-hand side of the document to see if, as a result, your ancestor was sent to a special inquiry.

Is there information about "Going to join a relative"? (In later years, "or friend" was added to this category.) What you find here may give you not only the name of a family member who was already in the United States but also that person's address.

Does the manifest ask for the name of a relative in the country from which the immigrant left? Often there will be a name and an address, which gives you valuable information about where your family lived in the Old Country.

Official records may be filled with errors: Note how Alexander Rabkin's name is spelled on line 30 of this ship's manifest.

Passenger Ship Lists

One of the great finds for an American genealogist is the passenger ship list with his or her ancestor's name on it. Until recently, these lists were difficult to find and required a lot of legwork. But with the opening of the Ellis Island site, *ellisislandrecords.org*, on April 17, 2001, it became much simpler to trace an ancestor for the millions of Americans whose family came through Ellis Island (see "Web tips," below).

A ship's manifest with your ancestors' names on it is a kind of short story. It tells you which ship they arrived on and when they arrived—and usually a lot more. To find the ship's manifest, you need a great deal of information.

The first and most important piece of information is the name under which your ancestor arrived. Remember that many names—both first and last—were changed in the United States. This was especially true for eastern European immigrants, whose names were often long and hard to pronounce (hard for Americans, anyway).

Where to look: Once you have an original name, what you do next depends upon the date you are researching. If your ancestors came to America *before 1820,* your task may be complicated. From the 1600s until 1819, no specific government group was paying close attention to who immigrated. The only records you can count on are local ones, and finding them may require some ingenuity (see "Locating 'Early Bird' Ancestors" on page 171; for African-American ancestors, see page 191).

But if your ancestors arrived in America by ship *between 1820 and 1950,* things may be easier. Starting in 1820, the Immigration Act required ships' captains to report to the government the name, age, sex, occupation, and country of origin of each passenger. These lists contained a surprising amount of information about their passengers, and fortunately, many of them still exist today. They are stored on microfilm at the National Archives building in Washington, D.C., and in 12 branch offices around the United States (see pages 174–175). Of course, if your ancestors arrived at Ellis Island or at a

number of other ports, you should definitely try to search the Ellis Island database now on the Internet (see "Web tips," below).

The staff of the National Archives will search for the documents for you. If the only information you have is your ancestors' names, where they arrived, and the month and year of arrival, the staff will search their index for you and let you know the name of the ship. If you already have the name of the ship, plus the arrivals' names, port, and month and year, the staff will send you a copy of the ship's manifest. Write to the National Archives, General Reference Branch, NNRG, 8th and Pennsylvania Avenue, NW, Washington, DC 20408. Ask for the NATF Form 81. There is a small charge.

You can do the search yourself, of course, by going to any branch offices or to one of the great genealogical libraries (see Chapter Nine), or searching other online databases (see "Web tips," below). If you do your own research, you do not need to know the month of arrival or the ship's name. But naturally, if you have this information, your job will be much easier.

There is always a chance you will not find your ancestors in these records. Many ships' manifests between 1820 and the early 1880s are incomplete. Some passengers were left off lists and some manifests have been lost.

Web tips: A wonderful thing happened in 2001: The Ellis Island website opened up an enormous database with more than 20 million names of immigrants to the United States. That made it possible to find the names of people who came through Ellis Island between 1892 and 1924. If you go to *ellisislandrecords.org* and register, you will be able to enter your ancestors' names and see if you can find them. (For more tips about searching the Ellis Island site, see "Great Starter Sites" on page 161.)

Of course, millions and millions of Americans did not enter through Ellis Island. And manifests from ships landing at other ports will be slow in coming to

the Internet. That's because of the enormous amount of time and energy required to input the information from the manifests into a database. There are, nevertheless, many other small lists that are also online or will be shortly.

In looking for ancestors' ship information on the Internet, follow all the clues in the general advice above so you have as much information as possible about when and where your ancestors entered. One good place to look after you've come up with some information is Cyndi's List's general information page about passenger ship

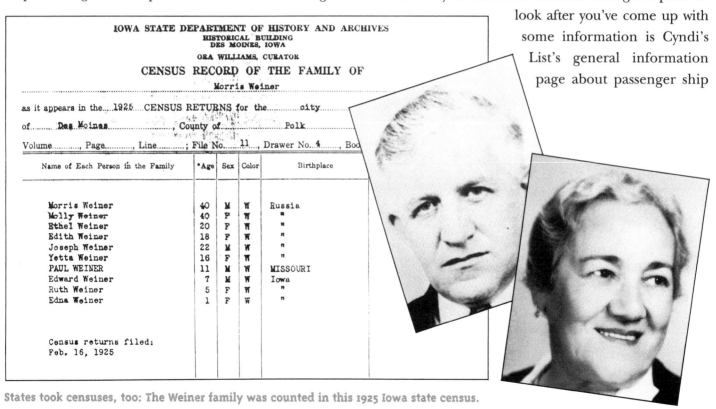

States took censuses, too: The Weiner family was counted in this 1925 Iowa state census.

lists, *cyndislist.com/ships.htm#lists.* Here you'll find a listing of the many sites online that offer information or specific data about immigrant ships.

One extensive online ship database that already exists holds 130,000 names of immigrants who came through Galveston, Texas, between 1846 and 1948. If you think your ancestors may have arrived through Galveston at this time, check out *tsm-elissa.org/immigration-main.htm.*

You might also want to try logging on to the National Archives web page on immigration records, *www.nara.gov/genealogy/immigration/immigrat.html,* for general information and updates.

Cemetery Records

Cemeteries are not the first place you'd think of to look for records. But if you know where your ancestors are buried, you may find a good source of family information.

Where to look: Relatives often know where ancestors are buried. If they don't, look for the individual's death certificate. These certificates generally give the name of a cemetery.

When you have located the proper cemetery, call or write to their office. Tell them you are working on a genealogical project and explain that your ancestors are buried there. Give the ancestors' names and dates of death and ask if the cemetery has any records that you might get copies of (or look at). If you live nearby, you may want to go with your parents to pay a visit to the cemetery. Ask for directions, hours, and specific locations of your ancestors' graves.

The main reason to visit a cemetery is to look at tombstones. Many tombstones list genealogies, such as "Beloved father, devoted husband, cherished grandfather." Older stones frequently list

Is a cemetery any place for a genealogist? Absolutely! Find out where your ancestors are buried. By reading tombstones and checking cemetery records, you may learn a great deal about your family's history.

(continued on page 146)

Alternative places to look for information

To find out a birth date, you can look at a birth certificate. But what if you can't find a birth certificate? You might try to locate a death certificate, because one of the items commonly listed on a death certificate is "date of birth."

This chart cites common bits of information that genealogists need and suggests alternative places where you may find them. It just may help you uncover some particularly hard-to-locate facts.

What You Want to Find Out	Where to Look
Date of birth	Marriage license, death certificate, children's birth certificates, census records
A woman's maiden name	Her marriage or death certificate, any of her children's vital records
Children's names	Census records, wills
Date of arrival in the United States	Naturalization records
Name of ship, port of entry	Naturalization records
Line of work, business address	Local directories, census records
Family addresses	Local directories, phone books, naturalization records, vital records
Earlier ancestors' names	Birth and death records of their descendants, cemetery inscriptions
Where someone is buried	Death certificate

Finding Your Family's Name with SOUNDEX

As you search for your ancestors' records, you will discover a very confusing fact: Your family name, or surname, can be spelled many different ways.

Your grandfather's surname may be Smith, Smyth, and Smythe on three different documents. Two brothers may spell their surnames differently: one named Li, the other Lee.

There are a number of reasons why there is so much confusion about surnames. For many years, names were not standardized. Sometimes people didn't know how to write, so officials interviewing them made up letters to fit what they heard. In addition, many people changed the spelling of their names to fit the country they were in.

These changeable names can make your research difficult. That is one reason why the U.S. government adopted a special indexing code called SOUNDEX. Under the SOUNDEX system, names are grouped together by sound rather than letter, which makes it possible to find names with the same sound—no matter how they are spelled. In fact, immigration records, some U.S. Federal Census records, and many other documents are indexed by SOUNDEX.

Every SOUNDEX code has a letter and *three* numbers. The first letter of SOUNDEX is always the same as the first letter in the surname. For example, people named Fedelovicz, no matter what spelling they used (like Faitelovicz, Fudelovich, or Feydalovich), could find their records under the heading F341.

Before you search, make sure you know the *original* name of the person you're looking for. Then, figure out your SOUNDEX code. You can find "SOUNDEX machines" that do the work for you on the Internet (see "Web tips," below). But here's how to do it by yourself:

1. Take the name Johannson. The first letter of the name always remains the same. So the first SOUNDEX space in this case is filled with J.

   NAME: J O H A N N S O N
   SOUNDEX: J _ _ _

2. Now look at the SOUNDEX code:

Letter	Number
B P F V	1
C S K G J Q X Z	2
D T	3
L	4
M N	5
R	6

   Ignore the letters A, E, I, O, U, W, Y, and H.

3. Go through the name, crossing out those letters SOUNDEX tells you to ignore:

NAME: J Ø Ħ Á N N S Ø N

4. If you have any double letters, treat them as one letter. For example, cross out one N in Johannson.

NAME: J Ø Ħ Á Ń N S Ø N

5. Finally, fill in the other three SOUNDEX spaces with the numbers that represent the remaining letters:

NAME: J Ø Ħ Á Ń N S Ø N
SOUNDEX: J 5 2 5

6. No matter how many letters there are in the name, every SOUNDEX code is made up of one letter and three numbers. So J525 is the number you will use to look through the SOUNDEX index for the name Johannson. This code would also work for Johanson, Johnson, and Johnsson, among other names.

7. If different letters that are side by side have the same number—as they would in JACKSON (C, K, and S are all number 2)—use the number only once.

8. Every SOUNDEX code must have one letter and three numbers. If your code ends up shorter than that, add zeroes to the code. For example, Lee, which translates to L, would become L000.

9. If there is a prefix in your name—such as de Mornay—figure out your SOUNDEX code both with and without it. Try "Mornay" and "deMornay." Your documents may be filed under either name. (MAC and MC are *not* considered prefixes, so those names will be coded only as M _ _ _.)

10. Finally, here's how you use the index. If you are looking up Johannson, go to the J525 names and begin searching alphabetically by *first name*. Alice Johnson will be listed among the first J525s. Zachary Johanson will be among the last J525s.

Now spell out your own name:

– – – – – – – – – – – – – –

And code it into SOUNDEX:

– – – –

Double-check your results. It's important to be sure you've got the right code. Now you're ready to look through federal SOUNDEX indexes.

Here are some other names in SOUNDEX :

R O G E R S	R262
L E W I S	L200
R U S S E L L	R240
K O V A L C H I C K	K142

Web tips: The National Archives site, *www.nara.gov/genealogy/soundex/soundex.html*, has a "SOUNDEX machine" that will quickly translate names into numbers for you. You could also try going to *www.familytreemagazine.com/soundex.html*, or *pa-roots.com/soundex.html*.

several names, including infant children. Jewish tombstones usually have inscribed, in Hebrew, the name of the father of the deceased.

On many stones, you may find an epitaph, a few lines that tell how someone wished to be remembered. Many are straightforward: "An honest man, a loving husband" could be all you find. Others poke a little fun:

"Here lies a man of good repute
Who wore a No. 16 boot.
'Tis not recorded how he died,
But sure it is, that open wide,
The gates of heaven must have been
To let such monstrous feet within."

If you visit a cemetery, make a note of inscriptions and any decorative stonework. Take a camera and photograph the stones.

Mark the dates on the tombstones, but absolutely do *not* assume they are correct without proof. Because tombstone dates were secondhand information, taken in a time of grief and difficult to correct if inaccurate, they are among the most suspect of records.

When you are visiting a family grave, be sure to look over the neighboring plots. If your ancestors were immigrants, they may be buried in a fraternal organization's section of a cemetery. Other family members may also be buried nearby. Sketch out the location of the stone and its relationship to other stones of significance to your family. If you have located the grave of a distant ancestor, ask at the office who is paying the upkeep fee. You may discover a lost relative this way.

Web tips: Cemetery records can be found at *interment.net.* This site collects searchable information about cemeteries. In 2002, it had nearly 3 million records from more than 4,500 cemeteries!

Land Records

If your family owned land at any time in American history, you might be able to trace the history of that land in official documents. You may be able to find out how much the land cost, what was built on it, from whom it was bought, and to whom it was sold. You might even be able to take a trip to see it one day.

Most land records—often called "deeds"—are kept in the seat, or capital, of the county where the property is located. Someone in your family may have a copy of an old deed that proved an ancestor's ownership of land. If so, you can contact the office that holds the records and ask them for more information about the land. They may discover old maps, records of sale, or other information.

You may even hear stories about an ancestor who was given land by the federal government. These "land grants" took place in 30 states, most of them in the Midwest and West. If you have reason to believe your ancestor obtained land in this way, you may want to write

When land was for sale in the American West, millions responded. The records of their purchases can be found in courts across the United States. Many other settlers got their land for free; the Homestead Act of the 1860s offered a farm to anyone who worked the land for five years and became a citizen in that time.

the National Archives for more information. Include your ancestor's full name, the state in which he or she possessed the land, and whether it was granted before or after 1908. Write to the National Archives, Reference Branch, NNRR, Washington, DC 20409.

Web tips: You can find a surprising amount of information about land records on the Internet, especially land granted by the federal government. Here are some sites to check:

The Bureau of Land Management: Eastern States, General Land Office *glorecords.blm.gov*
This site allows you to search more than 2 million federal land title records issued between 1820 and 1908. Despite the name "eastern," the database does not cover the original 13 states. In fact, most data is about midwestern states. Records are continually being added, so anyone with federal land history should check this site occasionally.

Where to Obtain Land Patents/Warrants

homepages.rootsweb.com/~haas/
learningcenter/patentlocations.html
A regularly updated site that explains what's happening with these records of who owned what land and when, and where to go to find them.

Retracing the Trails of Your Ancestors Using Deed Records *www.ultranet.com/~deeds/deeds.htm*
A long, interesting article about why and how these records are valuable.

Military Records

Is there a family story about the heroic actions your ancestor took during a famous battle? Was Great-grandpa a soldier in World War I, or did a great-great-great ancestor distinguish himself in the U.S. Civil War?

War stories turn into legends very quickly. But if anyone in your family was in the U.S. military, there are ways to verify his service. And these records may hold interesting information.

In addition to records that tell if your ancestors served in the armed forces, there are also pension records. "Pensions" are payments made to veterans as a reward for service years after the serviceman retires from the military. Pension records are usually more interesting for genealogists than military records are, as they may contain facts about the pensioner after his service days:

Was Great-grandpa in the U.S. Army? His records might still exist. These Civil War soldiers came from Michigan.

where he lived, what type of work he did, whom he married, and information about the children he had.

Even if your ancestor did not serve in the army, there may be some draft registration records under his name. If your relative was living in the United States between June 1917 and September 12, 1918, and was between the ages of 18 and 45 during those years, the United States required him to fill our a registration form. Copies of all those records have been kept and indexed by the U.S. government.

Where to look: If your ancestor served in the military before 1917, check the National Archives in Washington, D.C. You must know your ancestor's full name, the approximate dates during which he served, and the state or territory from which he entered the military. If you would like the archives staff to search for your ancestor's file, write to the National Archives, Reference Services Branch, General Services Administration, Washington, DC 20408.

If you are interested in the 1917 draft registration records, write to the National Archives, Atlanta Branch, 1557 St. Joseph Avenue, East Point, GA 30344, and ask for a World War I Registration Card request form.

And if you want to search for military records after 1917, write to the National Personnel Records Center (Military Records), NARA, 9700 Page Boulevard, St. Louis, MO 63132.

Web tips: There are a number of places to look on the Internet for information about military records—and for transcriptions of the records themselves. Here are two:

Family History SourceGuide/U.S. Military Records
familysearch.com/sg/Military.html
You'll find lots of specific information here about how to trace military records.

Military & Pension Records for Union Civil War Veterans
oz.net/~cyndihow/pensions.htm
This site offers a first-person account of how to get these records from the National Archives.

Religious Records

Many churches and synagogues kept notations about their members' births, christenings, marriages, and deaths.

Where to look: This may take some detective work. If you know your ancestors' religious affiliation, check to see if there are any institutions

(continued on page 152)

There are hundreds of documents that hold facts about your family, and you can get copies of many of them. This registration card, for example, is the kind that was filled out by millions of American men during World War II.

Back to the Old Country:
Tips on Tracing Your Family Across the Ocean

Many genealogists call it "crossing the water." That's what you do when you begin to trace your ancestors back to their country of origin.

America is a land of immigrants, and many people have family lines that lead back overseas. The good news is that it is possible to research your ancestors' lives in their original nation even without leaving the United States.

Before you attempt to go international, however, get everything you can about your ancestors from American documents (naturalization papers, ships' manifests, and such) that could be of help to you in tracing your ancestors overseas. Such documents may, for example, list your ancestors' last address in their country of origin or the names and addresses of relatives they left behind.

Techniques and rules are different for each

country. If you are seriously interested in researching overseas, you should look for a good genealogical guide to international research (see the list of books in the Appendix).

There are, however, four tips that apply to researching your foreign roots no matter where your ancestors hailed from.

1. From family and official records, get as much information as you can about your ancestors' lives prior to immigration. Absolutely crucial are the names of the village and the province they came from. Add to that any addresses you can discover and any copies of documents.

2. Check with LDS. The best place for any American to start a search for overseas information is with the Church of Jesus Christ of Latter-day Saints (Mormon) Family History Library (see page 175). The LDS collection of genealogical material includes vital records from dozens of nations. There is a good chance that you will find something of interest to you there. In addition, the LDS main library and its thousands of branches have excellent materials to help you in finding, translating, or deciphering records.

To find an LDS office near you, log on to their website at *familysearch.com,* look in the phone book under "Church of Jesus Christ of Latter-day Saints," or write to LDS Genealogical Library, 35 North West Temple Street, Salt Lake City, UT 84150.

3. Learn a bit of your ancestors' original language. In searching foreign records, you do not have to be fluent in another language (though it certainly wouldn't hurt if you were). But if you can pronounce and understand a few words, it may make your work go a lot faster.

4. Go online. You can find lots of information about your ancestors' homelands on the Internet. *Cyndislist.com* is a great place to begin your search for information about foreign-country websites. Other good sites include *genealogy.com*'s site finder and *www.genealogytoolbox.com/places.html.* You can also find a huge collection of electronic mailing lists on *lists.rootsweb.com.*

5. Look for genealogical societies that specialize in the country you're interested in. Genealogists tracing foreign-born ancestors have created groups that offer support and information to others with the same interest. Ask your local librarian for ideas on finding these groups. One good resource is the Federation of Genealogical Societies (FGS), which has a listing of over 500 different genealogy organizations. You can find the FGS list by going to *family history.com/societyhall/main.asp.* You can also write for this information at FGS, P.O. Box 220, Davenport, IA 52805 (include a self-addressed, stamped envelope).

of that type in the place where they lived.

If you are able to find the place where your ancestors worshipped, write to the office there. Explain that you are conducting a family history search, and list the names you are researching, the dates of their lives, and the years you believe they might have belonged to the church or synagogue. "If you have any records of my ancestors, I would be most interested in seeing them. Please let me know if there is any fee." As always, enclose a self-addressed, stamped envelope.

Web tips: Many religious groups maintain their own websites, which at the very least will have information about their practices and history. In some cases, you may actually find information about baptismal records or other vital documents. Check at one of the major Internet search engines (*yahoo.com, google.com, lycos.com,* or others) for information about the specific group in which you are interested.

Wills

Wills are another interesting resource you may want to explore. These are legal documents that record what people want to have happen to their property after they die. Wills tell you which people and which possessions were important to the writer. Notice how people were referred to and how the property was distributed. Be on the lookout for unfamiliar names—you may discover a new ancestor or two.

If you want to find an ancestor's will, you need to know where he or she died and the year of death. The best way to proceed is to contact the local civil court in the county where your ancestor died and ask if you can see a copy of that will. You should also ask about probate records. If there were questions or problems with your ancestor's will, legal hearings called "probates" might have been held. These records are often full of valuable information.

Web tips: You won't find information online about individual wills. But an interesting article, "Analyzing Wills for Useful Clues," taken from the website of the Board for Certification of Genealogists, talks about what genealogical information you can get from looking at a will . . . carefully. You can find the article at this URL:*www.bcgcertification.org/ skillbuilders/skbld955.html.*

School Records

Schools keep student records for a long time; you might even be able to find your great-grandmother's report

Tough grader: Old report cards offer a window on an ancestor's childhood.

card. (Imagine someone finding your own report card 100 years from now!) You can write to the schools your family member attended, give them the name and dates when he or she was in school, and ask if they can send you any of his or her records. These records can give you a peek at your ancestor's younger years.

PRESERVING THOSE DOCUMENTS

Documents are more than just sources of information. They are bits of living history, snapshots of your ancestors' lives. So treat them with great care. Every time you locate a document, make a copy of it—either a photocopy or your own extract of the information. In fact, make a number of copies so you can share them with other family members.

And don't let these copies sit in a drawer, accumulating dust. One good idea is to put them in a record book, like your loose-leaf binder. Try not to cut or otherwise mark these copies; keep them safe under clear plastic sheets. After a while, you will have accumulated an ancestor scrapbook—a record of the people who make up your heritage. That's something you can proudly share with the rest of your family.

Detector's To-Do List

❑ Choose the document categories you are most interested in.

❑ Gather all information to help you find those documents.

❑ Set up a research calendar.

❑ Write and/or visit local records centers.

❑ If you find original documents, handle with great care.

❑ Make copies of all records; place one copy in your loose-leaf binder. Enter the information onto your family charts and records.

❑ Go online to look for indexes, transcriptions, and original documents. To get the most out of your web surfing, read the next chapter, "Catching Your Ancestors with a Net," before you go online.

CHAPTER EIGHT

Catching Your Ancestors with a Net

. . . The Internet, That Is!

In this chapter, you will learn:

- How the Internet can help you find your family
  - How to get the most out of your time on the Internet
  - What kinds of sites you should be visiting
  - How to use the Internet to hook up to other genealogists and to family members
  - Which are the best sites on which to start your search

Until a few years ago, ancestor detecting was a daytime project. Sure, you could meet and interview relatives at night. And yes, weekends were good for writing letters to faraway archives or libraries. But in general, everything had to be done during working hours. And much of it was very slow.

When I wanted to find a document, I had to find out which archive held it and whom to contact there.

Then I'd write a letter and drop it in a mailbox, hoping it would be answered quickly, or I'd schedule a trip to the records center.

Now, however, that process is much faster. I can find documents listing my family members, past and present, at any time of day or night! I've found lots of terrific information about my ancestors, the places they lived,

and the times they lived in—all without ever having to leave my home.

None of this could have happened without the help of that international information highway we call the Internet. For example:

• In the early 1990s, it took me weeks to uncover my grandparents' wedding information. But when I visited the database of birth, marriage, and death records on *familysearch.com*, I was able to locate those records within minutes.

• My ancestors lived in Poland and Belarus, countries I never knew much about. But by visiting web pages filled with Polish, Russian, and Belarussian history (and very nicely indexed!) on *jewishgen.org*, I've learned a great deal about the places where my grandparents and great-grandparents lived.

• When I want to know how common a name is in the United States, I go to *hamrick.com/names*. There I search for any of 50,000 last names, including many of my family's surnames. I watch as a colorful map displays how many people with that name live in each of the 50 states.

• I've found lists of dozens of great websites that were important to my research at *cyndislist.com*.

• I've found all four of my grandparents' names on ship manifests—the lists of who came to America on what boat—by visiting the *ellisislandrecords.org* website.

On that site, I found other family members on boat lists. Some of the "new" people I found I had never even heard of before!

• Where and when did my grandfather Hymen Perlo become a citizen? The answer was Brooklyn, New York, in 1915. I found that information through a local Brooklyn index that had been put together on *jgsny.org*.

The Internet doesn't just help me find information. It also connects me to people. I've discovered groups of people interested in the same kinds of research as I am. Through e-mail, they've helped me find new relatives and information about the towns my ancestors came from.

You, too, can benefit from the Internet. Using your computer for family research is easy and fun—as long as you know what to expect and how to make the most of the particular riches of this new tool. That's what you'll discover in this chapter.

Make a Plan Before You Go Online

Clearly the Internet can be a great tool for your family history research. But don't rush online to find your family—because you'll end up frustrated.

Going online is like taking a train trip. Would you jump on a train without knowing where it's going—or where you want to go? No way! You might see interesting things, but you'd waste a lot of time. And you'd probably end up someplace you didn't really want to be.

It's the same with genealogical web surfing: If you don't know where you're going, you'll waste time. If you haven't got the right information, you won't accomplish anything. So it's important to do research before you go online. Draw up a list of all the names in your family that you want to research—and be sure to ask if each name was changed at any time. Also, ask people to tell you when anything important happened (births, marriages, immigration, etc.). Get the names of the places where these events happened (the town or city, the county, the state, the country).

Got the answers? You're almost ready for genealogical surfing. But first, plan your time by doing this:

Identify a goal. What are you after? Information about a particular person? Background on a place where an ancestor lived? Connecting with other people who are researching a last name?

If you don't know what you're looking for, you're not ready to conduct an online ancestor hunt. But if you do, and you know which websites you want to visit and have the information about the ancestor you are researching at hand, then boot up the computer and start the search!

Be realistic. Don't expect to come back from a trip online with a fistful of original records. Finding one bit of new information about an ancestor after one session online is a great achievement! (If you get more than that, consider yourself very lucky.)

Set a time limit each time you log on. It is easy to get caught up in websites or online conversations and lose track of time. So choose a finish time or even set a timer to remind you to leave cyberspace and go back to the real world.

Try to learn about just one or two ancestors. Usually the best plan is to visit a particular website for information about just a few people on your "most wanted" list. You might visit the Ellis Island site to search for your great-great-grandparents who came from Italy in the 1920s. Log on knowing their original first and last names, the approximate year they arrived, and approximately how old they were when they got here. If you search with that much information, you stand a good chance of finding your great-great-grandma or -grandpa . . . if, of course, they did come to the United States through Ellis Island.

Try a few searches for general information about your family. Pick a good general genealogical website that has a database you know. Enter one of your family (last) names and see what comes up. You might find ancestors you don't know anything about. *However,* you can do this kind of search only if you are looking into an unusual last name. Names such as Wolfman or Schpoont or Kovalchik may yield interesting results. But if you search for Johnson or Jones or Miller on almost any English-language website, you may end up with thousands of possibilities. That won't help you at all!

Be prepared to try more than one spelling of a name. Our ancestors came to the United States from all over the world. Often their names were translated from another language (and even another alphabet) into English. That means that you may find their records under many different spellings. The SOUNDEX system can help you with this. SOUNDEX arranges names by a code rather than by a letter, so by using it you stand a better chance of finding a name spelled in different ways. For example, someone named Weber (who pronounced his name Vay-ber) can be searched under a code that would find both "W" and "V" spellings of his name. (For more on SOUNDEX, see Chapter Seven, page 144.)

What Kind of Site Are You Looking For?

A plan isn't enough. You need to know *where* to go. Cyberspace is a huge place, and certain kinds of places and information are most helpful. Below are the general kinds of places and information that you can find online. (Unless indicated otherwise, access to the information on any of the sites is available free of charge.)

Indexes and databases. These are long lists with names you are looking for—and that you can search through quickly. You type in a name. Within seconds, the computer lists any records that exactly match that name. In many cases, you can click on that name and go to more information about it.

It's easy to waste time online. Have a plan before you log on.

EXAMPLE: *familysearch.com*. The International Genealogical Index of this site includes names on hundreds of millions of birth and marriage records—from around the world!

In addition, if you go to any of the larger genealogy sites, such as *rootsweb.com, ancestry.com, genealogy.com,* or *www.genealogytoolbox.com*, you will find information on how to use any of a number of common indexes.

Sites with pictures of the original records (rare, but becoming more common online). In some cases, records have been scanned or photographed and converted into digital information that can be shown online. When this has been done, you may see a photograph of an ancestor's actual birth certificate. Other

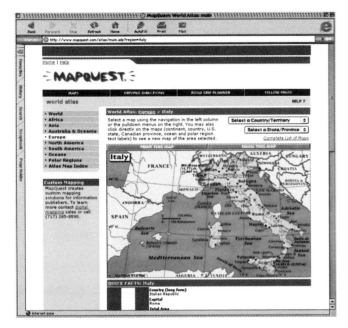

Go to *www.mapquest.com* to search for good maps of your ancestor's homeland.

photos might show a ship manifest or census records that include your ancestor.

EXAMPLE: At *ellisislandrecords.org*, you will find photographs of hundreds of ship manifests with the names of immigrants who came to America through Ellis Island. At this site, you'll also find a typed database with those names and millions more (see "Great Starter Sites," later in this chapter.).

Sites that link you to other websites. These are a terrific resource for online researchers. At links sites, you will find carefully organized lists of other websites that could be helpful. All you have to do is choose the website that sounds most useful, then click on its name. You will be sent directly to that website.

EXAMPLE: *cyndislist.com*. This is a great weblinks site. Genealogist Cyndi Howells has organized a huge number of websites into more than 150 categories. Some of the categories are African-American, Catholic, Finland, etc. At last count, she had over 120,000 different pages you could click on and visit!

Sites offering maps and other geographic information. Say your great-grandmother came from a small town in Ecuador, and you'd like to know where it is. The Internet can help! Many geography-oriented sites now make it possible to find little-known places.

EXAMPLE: At *mapquest.com*, you can type in more than 150 country names and see where a particular city is on maps of those countries.

Sites that help you get records you can't find online. Millions of records are not yet online. And many records may never be available at the click of a mouse. But the web can still help because there are even websites that offer tips for finding the information offline.

EXAMPLE: Looking for an American birth certificate? At *vitalrec.com*, for example, you can find an enormous amount of information about where to send an application for your ancestors' birth, marriage, death, or divorce records. Some sites even help you create an application letter that you can print out and send to the center.

Sites of groups (or individuals) with whom you have something in common.

EXAMPLE: By visiting *italgen.com*, the official site of English-language Italian genealogists, you may find listings of others who are searching for the same name that you are. That may lead you to someone who has ancestors in common with you. Even if you don't discover a cousin, you may find useful information on these more specialized websites.

There are even websites for specific families—like the Schmulewitz family or the Capuletti family. You can find them by running a search on a search engine site (a site where you enter a few words and then—with a click of your mouse—get a list of web pages with those words).

Newsgroups and mailing lists (listservs).

These are mailing lists for people with specific interests. Listserv subscribers send e-mails to the entire group about anything they think their fellow subscribers will be interested in. They share tips, ask questions, and offer new ways to find information.

There are thousands of genealogy listservs. Many of them are devoted to a specific area of genealogy—Irish or early American; African or Jewish; and so on. There are two ways to join a listserv: You can ask for a one-a-day digest note, which sends you a list of the topics of that day's discussion (and some information about those topics), or you can get every piece of e-mail any listserv member sent that day, which could be 100 or more messages per day! Most people don't want that much mail, so choose that only if you are really, really interested in the subject.

To get your name onto these kinds of lists, you must sign up at a website.

EXAMPLE: The biggest, most current genealogy mailing-list directory online is *rootsweb.com/~jfuller/gen_mail.html*. You can also find a good list of newsgroup and mailing list sites at *cyndislist.com/mailing.htm*.

Advice and articles from professional genealogists.

Much of this information is available free of charge. You can find tips on a wide range of genealogical subjects, from conducting overseas research to tracing female ancestors; from using census records to translating foreign documents.

EXAMPLE: If you'd like help deciphering old-time handwriting, go to *amberskyline.com/treasuremaps/oldhand.html*. Here you'll find an article by genealogist Sabina J. Murray that includes lots of examples of old-time letters and a handwriting mystery that you can try to solve at the end to see how much you've learned.

In addition, at any of the larger genealogical sites (*www.genealogytoolbox.com, rootsweb.com, ancestry.com, genealogy.com*), you'll find many other helpful articles.

Genealogical shops.

Need a hard-to-find book about African-American genealogy? Looking for software that you can't find elsewhere? Searching for forms that no one seems to have? Commercial genealogy websites

Protecting Your Privacy—and Your Family's—on the Internet

Genealogy is all about finding information and sharing it. It's great fun to bring a family tree to a family party or to share newly found documents at a reunion.

Sharing information with your family, though, is different from making it available on the Internet. That's why almost all genealogists believe that you should *never* include information about *living* people in Pedigree Charts or other family records that are posted on any public website.

For kids, online safety and privacy are even more important. Here are a few commonsense rules for kids using the Internet:

- DON'T include your home address or phone number in your e-mails.
- DON'T give personal information to people you've met only through the Internet.
- NEVER agree to meet anyone you've communicated with on the Internet without your parents' participation.

will sell—to an adult with a credit card—lots of materials that can help you with your research.

EXAMPLE: *ancestry.com, www.lineages.com, everton.com.* For a fee, these sites give you access to genealogy databases, research services, and mailing lists. They also offer some free information. To see what a genealogy shop is like, take a look at *genealogy.com/storemain.html.*

Now that you know the types of sites you can search, visit a few and learn how to use them.

Throughout this book, we have already given you many sites to check out. You may now want to go back and take a closer look at those sites. There are also many

more. The following section contains the web addresses of important genealogical sites and in-depth information about them. Happy surfing!

GREAT STARTER SITES

The websites and databases listed below offer an enormous amount of information. If you're looking for an ancestor who fits into any of their areas of focus, they're great places to do your research.

Familysearch.com—The LDS Storehouse This huge source of information is the official website of the Church of Jesus Christ of Latter-day Saints (known popularly as the Mormon Church). The Mormon Church has, over the years, accumulated billions of names on millions of records from all over the world. Neither you nor anyone in your family needs to be a Mormon in order to access these files or to be in them.

By going to the Mormon Church home page of *familysearch.com*, you can explore its many databases at once and see what comes up on any one ancestor. (Do *not* try to search any common last name unless you have lots of information—original first name, date of birth, and such.)

When you click on "Search for ancestors" and then click on a search of "All Records," the computer will search through the International Genealogical Index, Vital Records Index, U.S. Social Security Death Index (see more about this index on page 166), and many others.

The LDS church's website also holds the key to many documents that are *not* available online but that you can look at if you get them through the church's huge genealogical library system. (For more about the LDS libraries, see Chapter Nine.)

Ellisislandrecords.org—Millions of Immigrants

Did any of your ancestors come to America through Ellis Island? If so, this is a site you must not miss. At *ellisislandrecords.org*, you might find your ancestors' names, their exact date of arrival, and lots of other

A genealogy treasurehouse: The LDS church has collected billions of records, and placed them in a vault in the side of a mountain near Salt Lake City, Utah. You can gain access to many of the records through *familysearch.com*.

information. You might find a picture of the ship the family came on. You might learn what town they came from, whom they might have been visiting, and how much money they had with them. You might even get to see a photograph of the original ship passenger list . . . and the page that has your ancestors' names on it!

This website was created by the Statue of Liberty/Ellis Island Foundation—the same group that helped restore both the Statue of Liberty and Ellis Island—

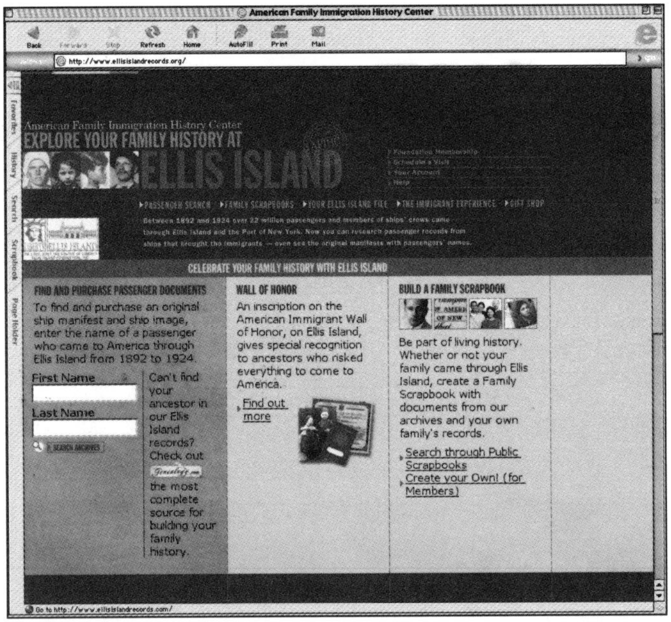

Ellisislandrecords.org **offers a wealth of information about immigrants who arrived in New York.**

working with volunteers from the LDS church. The volunteers spent three million hours reading passenger ship lists and entering the information they found into a computer database. The information was then put online on April 17, 2001. It quickly became one of the most popular websites on the Internet!

Finding your ancestors here will depend on what you already know. *Before* going to the site, it's important at least to know your ancestors' original names, the years they arrived at Ellis Island, and the names of their hometowns. Don't bother searching this site unless you think you have an ancestor who arrived in the United States between 1892 and 1924.

Have with you all the information you can when you come to the site. If you have an unusual last name, you might try indicating only that last name the first time you conduct your search. This way you can see how many full names come up. If it's fewer than 50 or so, you can go through them individually, looking for your ancestors.

The Ellis Island records site, with its 16 million names, is a great place to find immigrant ancestors. If you can't find anyone on the site, check and recheck your information. Work with your parents as well to see if you can get more information.

Rootsweb.com—Great Databases Rootsweb is an amazing site that was built by volunteers—ancestor detectors who wanted to help others find *their* families, too. It includes many databases (such as a giant surname list), search engines, mailing lists, online genealogy magazines, and a lot more. Volunteers maintain the site's computers, gather new information, transcribe records, create new databases, write newsletters, maintain message boards, and do a whole lot more. The Rootsweb volunteers hope to eventually put millions of records online for everyone to use.

If you think you have an unusual last name, be sure to make time to visit Rootsweb's "Search Everything" page at *searches.rootsweb.com.* This site will search through dozens and dozens of databases. You will then

Dot-What?
What Those Internet Address Endings (com, org, edu) Mean

Website and e-mail addresses (also called URLs) use a special code: two or three letters that help you understand what their background is. These letters are usually, though not always, at the end of the address.

You've surely seen dot-com addresses—*amazon.com, priceline.com, genealogy.com,* etc. But that's only one of the codes you'll come across. Here are common three-letter codes and what they mean:

.biz — business site
.com — commercial account (also businesses)
.edu — educational institution
   (college or school)
.gov — government

.net — a network computer organization with its own server
.org — an organization (usually not-for-profit)

Two-letter endings tell you that the e-mail comes from another country. (Email from the United States does not require a country identification within the U.S.) Here are just a few examples:

.au — Australia
.br — Brazil
.fr — France
.jp — Japan
.mx — Mexico
.za — South Africa

receive a list of all the databases that contain the name.

There are some interesting features at Rootsweb that you might want to explore just for fun. For example, you can find the genealogy of every U.S. president at *rootsweb.com/~rwguide/presidents/*. Click there and see which presidents were related! Or check out the Notable Kin area, where you may find the family trees of rock 'n' roll legend Elvis Presley, *Little House on the Prairie* author Laura Ingalls Wilder, or other famous folk. And if you know anything about the infamous Salem witch trials, look for the connection of Mickey Mouse's creator, Walt Disney, to a minister tried and hanged at Salem because of his supposed acts of wizardry, at *www.genealogy.com/famousfolks/waltd/*.

Genealogy Software

Software programs can really help as you compile your family history. They allow you to print out multiple copies easily, to make corrections quickly, and to share what you've learned with other people— all at the click of a mouse!

Software programs often come with good graphic features, which may enable you to print out complicated family trees and arrange your information in a number of inventive ways. Most popular programs are available only for computers with a Windows-compatible operating system. (One or two can be used with Macintosh computers.)

Below is a list of a few leading programs. You can learn about these programs by calling the toll-free numbers or visiting the websites. To discover even more, read reviews in genealogical magazines such as *Family Tree*, or ask other genealogists.

To find out more about new software packages, you can also check *cyndislist.com/software.htm*.

Ancestral Quest
(Windows)
800-825-8864
ancquest.com

Legacy Family Tree
(Windows)
800-753-3453
legacyfamilytree.com

Family Tree Maker
(Windows)
800-315-0672
familytreemaker.com

Personal Ancestry File
(Windows)
familysearch.org

Generations
(Windows)
800-757-7707
*sierra.com/sierrahome/
familytree/*

Reunion
(Macintosh)
717-697-1378
leisterpro.com

Through Rootsweb you can also subscribe to an e-mail newsletter or join a listserv of genealogists, all of whom are researching the same thing you are. Rootsweb boasts of having more than 21,000 mailing lists. Every month the site receives about 180 *million* e-mail messages.

Cyndislist.com—Lots of Links! Once you know the kinds of sites you are looking for online, *cyndislist.com* is the place to look. Genealogist Cyndi Howells has put together a listing of more than 120,000 web pages that are related to genealogy.

Cyndi's List gives you lots to choose from. For example, the list of "F" topics includes countries such as Finland and France; it also includes links about family Bibles, famous people, and female ancestors. (In 2002, there were 109 links to sites about family Bibles; 140 links to information about famous people; and 140 links to sites about female ancestors.)

This is the perfect place to explore your special category more deeply. For example, if you are researching your Italian family roots, Cyndi's List includes nearly 200 different links related to Italian research. You can find translation sites, Italian library sites, research in specific area sites, Italian map sites, links to church records, Italian-genealogy mailing-list sites, message-board sites, places that offer you information about Italian culture and history, and more.

Cyndi has hundreds of categories to choose from,

Cyndi Howells started with a little list of genealogy websites. Today her site indexes more than 120,000 genealogy links!

and all of the sources you find there are just a click away!

Ancestry.com and Genealogy.com—Free Lessons! These are among the top genealogy sites on the Internet. Both websites offer a lot of information and databases for free. They also have "subscription services" that are interesting to advanced searchers who are willing to pay for the right to read the information.

Among the indexes and databases on *ancestry.com* are the Ancestry World Tree, which is made up of thousands of "family charts" put onto the site by visitors. *Ancestry.com* estimated that there were over 83 billion names in this collection in 2001; by now the number is surely much higher!

Both *ancestry.com* and *genealogy.com* offer some free census records, vital records, military records, and the Social Security Death Index. You can also find lots of helpful information for beginners and free e-mail newsletters.

Genealogy.com is part of the company that owns the popular genealogical software program Family Tree Maker. The website offers visitors a free, simplified version of Family Tree Maker to store their information online. It features easy links to *historychannel.com* and *biography.com*—also owned by the same company.

The Social Security Death Index—65 Million Names. No, the name doesn't sound friendly. And this is a database, not a site, so it can be found on lots of different websites. But if you're looking for your American ancestors born after 1880 or so, this is a good place to check. The list contains more than 65 million American names!

The Social Security Administration (SSA) was created in the 1930s to help ensure that older people would have some money saved after they stopped working. Beginning around 1933, people signed up to be covered by Social Security. When they applied, they had to indicate their home address, the name of the company where they worked and its address, and their parents' names on an application card. Those cards

are what is covered in this index—and all of that information can be valuable to your research.

The Social Security Death Index (SSDI) contains the names of people who are no longer alive, had a Social Security number, and whose death was reported to the Social Security Administration. You can find the SSDI at any number of websites, including *genealogy.com, ancestry.com,* and *familysearch.com.* Some sites may have more up-to-date versions than other sites.

If you find your ancestor when you search the list—be sure it's not just someone with the same name—you can send away for a copy of his or her application to get a Social Security card. In fact, most websites that carry the SSDI also help you write the letter to ask for a copy of the application.

You have to use the U.S. mail to send away for these forms, and you also have to pay a fee.

USGenWeb and USGenWeb Kidz—Great States of Data These sites show the power of people's love for genealogy. They are worth visiting for a lot of state and local information that may help you when you're doing your U.S.-based research. And the Web Kidz site has activities that you should definitely look over.

UsGenWeb *(usgenweb.org)* began as a volunteer project to make available online genealogical information about every state in the United States.

Internet Links

For these and other clickable links, go to *www.workman.com/familytree.*

E-NEWSLETTERS

You can subscribe to any of thousands of e-mail newsletters about genealogy—for free. A newsletter may specialize in a type of genealogy, a geographical area, or a family name. These newsletters keep you informed about new things in the world of online genealogy. Here are a few that are well known.

Eastman's Online Genealogy Newsletter
rootsforum.com/newsletter/index.htm

Heritage Quest Magazine Online
heritagequest.com/magonline

Missing Links: A Magazine for Genealogists
petuniapress.com

RootsWeb Review
rootsweb.com/~review/e-zine.html

MESSAGE BOARDS

Some websites set aside space where you can post questions and answers about genealogical research. Here are a few places to check out:

AOL Keyword: Roots
In the Genealogy Forum, choose "Messages."

RootsWeb Ancestry and Message Boards
http://boards.ancestry.com

FamilyHistory.com—Online Genealogy Community
familyhistory.com

Genealogy.com Genforum
genforum.genealogy.com

CyndisList Queries & Message Boards
cyndislist.com/queries.htm

Each state has its own home page. To visit yours, go to the link map at this URL: *usgenweb.org/statelinks.html* —and click on your state. When you get to your state homepage, you'll find information about state history and geography. You can locate hard-to-find towns and check out county maps of those towns.

USGenWeb Kidz (*rootsweb.com/~usgwkidz/*) offers beginners some introductory links to click on. The site aims to be solely for kids ages 18 and younger. You'll also find a beginners' forum where you can ask questions about genealogy in general or post a query about someone you are researching.

WorldGenWeb and WorldGenWeb for Kids—The World a Click Away

Similar to the USGenWeb site, WorldGenWeb *(worldgenweb.org)* is a world-connected website. It, too, has a kid-specific area that is a little more grown up and perhaps a little more useful than the USGenWeb Kidz project.

The volunteers running WorldGenWeb pull together genealogical information from all over the world. Many countries have sites, overseen by volunteers who have often put up their own genealogies plus any databases or information sites they can find. On the WorldGenWeb for Kids' pages *(www.rootsweb.com/~wgwkids/)*, you will find a page of links to many information sites for Africa, Asia, the Caribbean, Europe, the Middle East, the Pacific Islands, and South America.

As on USGenWeb's kids' pages, there is a surname mailing list sign-up page solely for kids ages 18 and younger.

Detector's To-Do List

Prepare for genealogical web hunts by doing the following:

❑ Gather information about one or more ancestors.

❑ Decide both where you want to look online for your ancestors and how long you want to be online.

❑ Carefully type in the URLs, or go to *www.workman.com/familytree* and look for them in the "Links" area under the correct chapter number.

❑ Conduct your search. Use computer "bookmarking" to remember any sites that you want to return to.

❑ Print out copies of any documents you want to keep.

❑ If you've found your ancestor in an index or abstract of records, find information about where to write for copies of original documents. Then write and mail your request.

CHAPTER NINE

Where the Records Are

Libraries, Archives, and Other Resources

In this chapter, you will learn:
- How to begin researching your community's history
- What kinds of records are available at the National Archives and its 13 regional branches
- About some of the vast resources available through the LDS (Mormon) Family History Libraries

here's one great genealogical resource we haven't talked about yet: libraries. Whether big or small, libraries have maps, directories, local histories, even published genealogies—all of which can help you in your research.

Even in the Internet age, libraries are invaluable resources. You'll find books and indexes there that can really help in your research. And many libraries also offer Internet access.

The key to getting the most out of any library is to know what's in it. This is as true of your small local branch as it is of the biggest libraries in the world.

Local Libraries

Let's say your great-grandparents lived in the same town you do now, and you are looking for details of their lives. Visit your local library and tell the librarian, "I'm doing research on my family's life in this town in the 1880s and 1890s." Then politely ask some questions:

- Is there a local history section? What kind of materials does it have? Are there newspaper clippings? Old phone or city directories? Business listings? Local maps? Family histories?

- What kind of indexes or card catalogs will help me use the materials?

- Do you have any special materials that are helpful to people doing family history research?

- Does the library have any indexes to larger genealogical collections? Does it have Internet access?

Books of general interest to genealogists are filed under call numbers 929.1 in the Dewey decimal code. You may want to browse through that section to see if anything interests you. You should also look at genealogical magazines and newsletters if the library subscribes to them.

But your major interest here is in local materials. You might find a history of your town or county that was

written to commemorate the community's special anniversary. Check the index; your ancestors or their businesses may be mentioned. Or maybe there's some information about schools they attended or an event you've heard about at family get-togethers. Even if you don't find anything personal, these histories are worth a glance for local color.

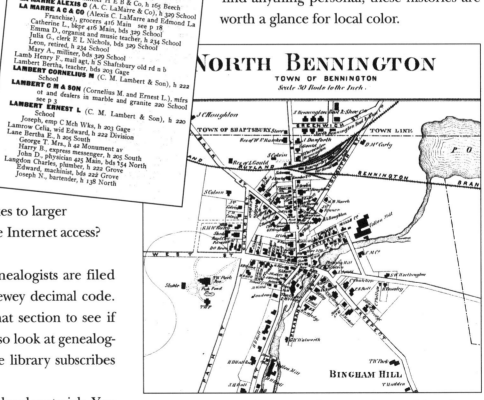

Old local directories (above, left) and local maps (above) may be filled with clues and news about your ancestors.

Locating "Early Bird" Ancestors

Passenger lists before 1820 are not in the National Archives except for a small, incomplete collection for the port of Philadelphia. But they may be on file at the actual port of entry or in the archives of the state where the port is located.

If you know where your ancestor arrived in America before 1820, begin your search by examining some of the many guides to records of those years. Two starting points are *Passenger and Immigration List Index: A Guide to Published Arrival Records,* by P. William Filby, and *A Bibliography of Ship Passenger Lists, 1583–1825,* by Harold Lancour.

Many colonial and U.S. ports filed copies of manifests as a requirement of clearance. These records are incomplete and rarely indexed but are helpful when there are no other records.

Many ships' logs have been collected by museums. Notable collections are at U.S. Mariner's Museum, Newport News, Virginia; Mystic Seaport, Mystic, Connecticut; National Maritime Museum, San Francisco, California; Newport Historical Society,

Newport, Rhode Island; Peabody Museum, Salem, Massachusetts; Great Lakes Historical Society, Vermillion, Ohio; Great Lakes Maritime Museum, Detroit, Michigan; and Bernice P. Bishop Museum, Honolulu, Hawaii.

An early view of Boston Harbor.

If your ancestors entered at any of these ports, it may be worthwhile to examine these logs. This is especially true if you know the name of the boat they arrived on.

Web tip: Check *cyndislist.com/ships.htm#lists* for shiplist website information.

Genealogical libraries can be great places for ancestor detectors—if you're prepared. It's best to call ahead and go looking for something specific.

Speaking of local color, you should definitely look for a collection of local newspapers. In addition to town news, you might find information about your family members in the birth, wedding, or death announcements. (If you know when someone in your family was married, for example, check that day and two or three days after the event took place.)

Old local city directories can be another very valuable resource. They were like telephone books in the age before telephones (almost no one had a phone before about 1910). These books listed everyone— or nearly everyone—who lived in town and included business addresses and often home addresses. In some cities and towns, the directories were published as far back as the early 1800s. If you find one, check for your ancestors' addresses. Old phone books can be helpful in the same way, giving you more addresses for your records.

Finding an address may—in the great tradition of genealogical hunting—lead you to more information. For example, if the library has old town maps, you may be able to find your ancestors' homes on them.

If you find something of interest, don't just scribble it down. Write legibly and with care. Probably the greatest frustration researchers have is trying to read their own handwriting a few weeks later. Also be sure to make a clear note of where you find information. Write down the library you are in, the complete title of the book, its author, the date of publication, and the page number.

If there's a call number on the book, write that down, too. Whenever you photocopy a page, note all the source information on the back of the copy. It's very easy to forget which book a page comes from.

As for those indexes to larger collections, check them out. If you find anything of interest, ask your librarian how to best go about getting the materials. Your branch may be able to borrow books for you through interlibrary loan programs.

Historical and Genealogical Libraries

You may find your town has a historical society or even a genealogical society with a library. These places have many more books on local history, but be careful. It's easy to get lost and waste time in big libraries if you don't narrow down your search. Before you go to such a library, determine what it is you want to find. Then call ahead and see if the library can help you.

These libraries may have hundreds of family histories, complete collections of local publications (including directories and local histories), local vital records, books of passenger arrival lists, and/or old census records.

The paper and online indexes, electronic catalogs, and other research aids are even more important here than in smaller libraries. If you have any questions about how to use them, ask the librarian.

The National Archives and Records Administration (NARA)

Some people have given the National Archives the nickname "the Nation's Attic" because this records center holds so many of America's precious old possessions—

The National Archives building in Washington, D.C., holds the nation's most important documents.

including originals of the Declaration of Independence, the Constitution, and the Bill of Rights. But NARA is also an enormously valuable resource for genealogists.

NARA has its main branch in Washington, D.C., and many regional offices around the United States. Among the many documents of special interest to genealogists in its collections are the following:

- Passenger ship records
- Military records
- Census records
- Naturalization records
- American Indian records
- African-American records

The 13 branches are located in or near major U.S. cities, including New York, Chicago, Philadelphia, Boston, Fort Worth, Seattle, Denver, and Kansas City (for a complete list, see the following page).

Many researchers go to these centers to search for microfilm copies of documents naming their ancestors. I did my first genealogical search ever at the Washington, D.C., building and found my paternal grandfather's name on his boat manifest (as I discussed in Chapter One). A great advantage to doing research at one of the NARA centers is that the staff is extremely knowledgeable about genealogical research.

You can get any of a number of free publications from NARA to help you plan your research. *Using Records in the National Archives for Genealogical Research* and *Military Service Records in the National Archives* are two of the many useful booklets available. To request those or others, write or call the Archives or log on to their website *(www.nara.gov)*. You can also read many of these documents online.

Web tips: Happily for genealogists, NARA intends to make as much of its information available on the Internet as it possibly can. This is, of course, a slow process, but some real progress has been made.

You can find a NARA web page specifically aimed at genealogists *(www.nara.gov/genealogy)*. On that page is not only a list of new information available to researchers, but also links to some of the genealogical databases themselves.

NARA has also created an experimental online catalog called NAIL (for NARA Archival Information Locator). NAIL contains the first records and descriptions of records that NARA has been able to put online. However, at the time this book was published, no census records or passenger ship manifest information was yet available online at the NARA site.

If you decide to visit a branch of the Archives, take advantage of the "microfilm locator" on the NARA website before you go. Check it out to ensure that the branch nearest you does in fact have the film you wish to view.

National Archives Branches

To get a complete list of all of the National Archives and Records Administration regional branches, including addresses, hours, and general information, go to *www.nara.gov/regional/nrmenu.html*. You will also find clickable links to all the regional offices at this site.

If you want to go directly to a regional page, here are the URLs:

National Archives–Northeast Region (Boston)
www.nara.gov/regional/boston.html

National Archives–Northeast Region (Pittsfield)
www.nara.gov/regional/pittsfie.html

National Archives–Northeast Region (New York)
www.nara.gov/regional/newyork.html

National Archives–Mid-Atlantic Region (Philadelphia)
www.nara.gov/regional/philacc.html

National Archives–Southeast Region (Atlanta)
www.nara.gov/regional/atlanta.html

National Archives–Great Lakes Region (Chicago)
www.nara.gov/regional/chicago.html

National Archives–Central Plains Region (Kansas City)
www.nara.gov/regional/kansas.html

National Archives–Southwest Region (Fort Worth)
www.nara.gov/regional/ftworth.html

National Archives–Rocky Mountain Region (Denver)
www.nara.gov/regional/denver.html

National Archives–Pacific Region (Laguna Niguel)
www.nara.gov/regional/laguna.html

National Archives–Pacific Region (San Bruno)
www.nara.gov/regional/sanfranc.html

National Archives–Pacific Alaska Region (Seattle)
www.nara.gov/regional/seattle.html

National Archives–Pacific Alaska Region (Anchorage)
www.nara.gov/regional/anchorag.html

The Greatest Genealogical Library in the World

There is one place every genealogist turns to eventually: the Family History Library in Salt Lake City, Utah. This giant records center has more genealogical documents than any library on earth. It even has copies of records more than 700 years old!

The LDS Family History Library in Salt Lake City, Utah.

The library is run by the Church of Jesus Christ of Latter-day Saints (LDS), otherwise known as the Mormons. The materials in it are open to the public, free of charge.

You've already read about the amazing LDS website, *familysearch.com*. All the incredible resources found on the site—and many more, including the microfilmed original records you've discovered indexed online—are available through the Family History Library and its many branches. In fact, the LDS runs more than 3,400 branches of its library across the United States and in more than 100 countries around the world.

At these branches, called Family History Centers, you can order copies of the records kept in Salt Lake City. They will be sent to the local branch, where you can use them for months on end at a minimal charge.

The LDS libraries have extraordinary microfilmed records. You can find millions of copies of documents from the United States, including every census through 1930, immigrant arrival records, wills, probate records, records from many religious institutions, and birth, marriage, and death records prior to 1900.

The Family History Centers also have access to copies of records from just about every European country, plus records from Asia, Africa, Australia, and South America.

The list of available materials goes on and on: hundreds of thousands of books about genealogy; computer access to *familysearch.com*, with its International Genealogical Index, U.S. Social Security Death Index, and Military Records Index; research aids like translation and handwriting guides; and so on.

You can easily find the Family History Library branch nearest you. Just go to *familysearch.com* and click on "Family History Library System." In no time at all, you should have the address, phone number, and hours at any number of centers in your state. Or you can look in the White Pages under "Church of Jesus Christ of Latter-day Saints" or write to the Family History Library, 35 North West Temple Street, Salt Lake City, UT 84150, and ask for a list of the centers in your area.

The main reason the Latter-day Saints have done all of this is that genealogy is a part of their religion. Mormons believe that by locating their ancestors, they can save their souls and reunite them with their families after death. It is fortunate for the rest of the world's genealogists that Mormon researchers have been willing to share their findings.

Other Great Libraries

Many other libraries around the United States have wonderful genealogy collections. Listed below are 15 of them, with addresses (and websites, when available):

California: Los Angeles Public Library, 630 West Fifth Street, Los Angeles, CA 90071
lapl.org/central/history.html

The Library of Congress has a great genealogy collection.

District of Columbia: Library of Congress, Thomas Jefferson Building, 10 First Street SE, Washington, DC 20540

lcweb.loc.gov/rr/genealogy/

Library, National Society of the Daughters of the American Revolution, 1776 D Street NW, Washington, DC 20006

dar.org/library/library.html

Illinois: Newberry Library, 60 West Walton Street, Chicago, IL 60610

newberry.org/nl/genealogy/genealogyhome.htm/

Indiana: Allen County Public Library, 900 Webster Street, Fort Wayne, IN 46802

ww.acpl.lib.in.us/genealogy/genealogy.html

Maryland: The George Peabody Library of the Johns Hopkins University, 17 East Mount Vernon Place, Baltmore, MD 21202

Massachusetts: New England Historical Genealogical Society, 101 Newbury Street, Boston, MA 02116

www.newenglandancestors.org

Michigan: Burton Collection, Detroit Public Library, 5201 Woodward Avenue, Detroit, MI 48202

www.detroit.lib.mi.us/burton/index.htm

Missouri: St. Louis County Library, Special Collections, 1640 South Lindbergh Boulevard, St. Louis, MO 63131

www.slcl.lib.mo.us/slcl/sc/sc-genpg.htm

New York: New York Public Library, Fifth Avenue and 42nd Street, New York, NY 10018

nypl.org and *catnyp.nypl.org/*

New York Genealogical & Biographical Society, 122 East 58th Street, New York, NY 10022

www.nygbs.org

One of the imposing lions outside the main building of the New York Public Library, which houses an impressive genealogy collection.

Ohio: Western Reserve Historical Society, 10825 East Boulevard, Cleveland, OH 44106
www.wrhs.org

Texas: Dallas Public Library, 1515 Young Street, Dallas, TX 75201
www.dallaslibrary.org

Virginia: National Genealogical Society Library, 4527 17 Street N, Arlington, VA 22207

Wisconsin: State Historical Society of Wisconsin, 816 State Street, Madison, WI 53706
www.wisconsinhistory.org

Web tips: To find out more about genealogical libraries, go to LIBDEX, the library index that connects you to more than 17,000 libraries, at *www.libdex.com.* Also check out these other online resources for library information:

Cyndi's List—Libraries, Archives, and Museums
cyndislist.com/libes.htm

Houston Public Library, Texas
http://www.hpl.lib.tx.us/clayton/

Library of Virginia
www.lva.lib.va.us

Detector's To-Do List

❑ Identify an area of local history that is most interesting to your research. Go to a local library and investigate it.

❑ Look for listings for your family in old city directories.

❑ Ask if your town has a historical or genealogical library where you can research. Find out hours and requirements for researching.

❑ Go online or call to find the LDS Family History Center closest to you.

CHAPTER TEN

"My Story's a Little Different"

Strategies and Suggestions for Ancestor Detectors with Special Situations

In this chapter, you will learn:

- How to trace your family history if you were adopted
- How to trace your family history if you are in a stepfamily, blended family, or other nontraditional family situation
- Special genealogical research strategies to find African-American, American Indian, and Jewish ancestors
- How to trace your family history if your family recently immigrated to the United States

When it comes to tracking down ancestors, your family may present special challenges. Almost every family does.

Few, if any, family histories are neat and simple. As you gather information, you may come across surprising facts that make your research more difficult than you expected. Or you may know from the beginning that some aspect of your story—your ethnic group or your family structure—is going to make it harder for you to move easily through the past.

I wrote this chapter to help you and anyone who thinks that his or her family's special circumstances make the genealogical hunt more difficult. Here you'll find special strategies for getting your particular genealogical work done. You'll also find examples of the tricky

questions that genealogy may raise for you and suggestions for how you might deal with those questions.

If you were adopted, you may feel awkward being asked to trace your family history. Or you may feel uncomfortable because you live in a family that doesn't resemble the typical "Mom, Dad, and the kids" structure.

If your family recently immigrated, you may be unsure about how to proceed with your research. Or maybe you're from an ethnic group—say, African-American or American Indian—that has some tragic history that you may not know how to explore.

It was *never* true that everyone lived in a "Mom, Dad, and the kids" type of household. And that kind of family is even rarer today than it was years ago. In addition, the United States is a far more ethnically diverse country today than it was years ago.

It's my hope that this chapter will show you how you can participate in ancestor detecting and enjoy the process, rather than feel hurt or diminished by it. I invite anyone who has a special story, or a particular problem or question with his or her family tree, to write to me at *climbingyourfamilytree@yahoo.com*.

Adoption: When "My Family" Is More Than One

Adoption is more common than most people realize: More than 6 million adopted people live in the United States today. And American families adopt over 100,000

Like all kids, children who have been adopted are the product of many families.

children each year. Some kids are adopted from foreign countries, while others are born here. But no matter how adoptive families came together, it was the parents' desire to love and raise a child that created them.

When asked to research a family tree, adopted children may have mixed feelings. They may ask, "Which tree is mine—the family I am a part of biologically or the one I am growing up in? How do I deal with having two different families?"

This is a real, and complicated, question. It's a good one to discuss with your parents, of course. Part of the answer, however, is obvious (and very genealogical!): You are a product of *all* of your families. You began as the fruit of a tree—you were brought into the world by your birth parents, with their family histories and their biological characteristics. You inherited eye color, skin color, hair color, and other aspects of what you look like and feel like from your birth parents.

You now have become attached to another tree. Your parents' love and care over the years have become a part of you. Many aspects of who you are today were shaped by the parents who have raised you, day by day, in their hearts and their home. When you begin your family research, therefore, it makes sense to start with the people some might call your adoptive parents—but who are, in the end, simply your parents.

Your mother and father have carried forward the gifts and traditions of their families. You trace their history by asking your parents the same questions any other ancestor detector would—for example, How did they meet? What do they know about your family history? Of course, you can also ask questions that pertain to your story alone, such as, Why did you decide to adopt a child? When did you first see me? What were you feeling? What did I look like? How did you get me home?

You might also want to trace the history of your birth family. Your adoptive parents may have information they wish to share with you. If they do, you can discuss what the information means and how you might incorporate it into your family history research.

If you were born overseas or to a family of a different ethnic group, you may be very interested in researching that culture, too. Your original culture may have been incorporated into your upbringing already, or it may be something you can seek out.

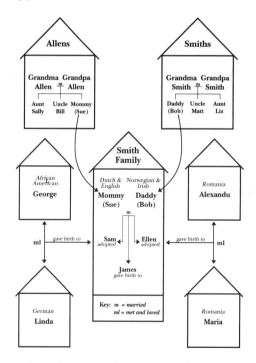

Adoption Option: This Home Chart shows a family with adopted children—and includes both the biological and adoptive parents. Each house represents a family, with a list of the people in it.

Beyond that, you might not be able to learn much more about your birth family. This may feel frustrating, but in this circumstance you are not alone. In the end, every genealogist arrives at a closed door, for there is only so far anyone can trace his or her family history. At some point, record keeping disappears, and our ancestors are beyond our reach.

If you are very interested in issues of adoption, there are places to turn. *Cyndislist.com* offers more that 100 links related to adoption. *Rootsweb.com* maintains mailing lists dealing with all aspects of adoption, birth parents, adoptive parents, and biological/adopted children. If this interests you, go to this site: *rootsweb.com/~jfuller/gen_mail_adoption.html.*

At some point, you may want to get in touch with an organization called the Adoptees Liberty Movement Association (ALMA). ALMA works with people 18 years and over who were adopted and wish to find their birth parents. If you want more information, write to ALMA, P.O. Box 727, Radio City Station, New York, NY 10101. You can also find them on the web at *www.almanet.org.*

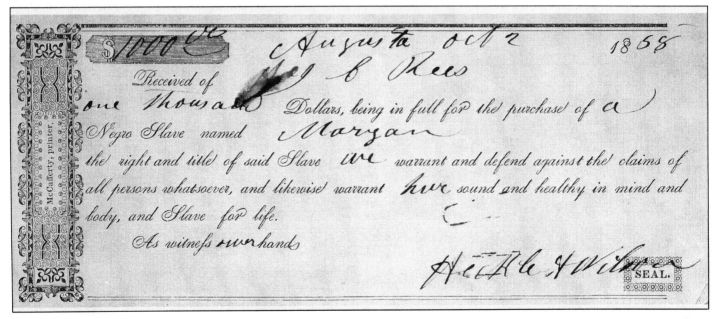

Documents can tell tragic stories—as does this 1858 receipt for the purchase "for life" of a girl named Maryan, a "Negro Slave."

African-American Ancestors

In the beginning, researching an African-American family is no different from researching any other family. You take down oral histories, fill out family charts, and search the same records and databases as do other Americans.

But if your research gets back to the 1860s, you will probably hit a huge roadblock: slavery. Unless you are descended from one of the relatively tiny number of people who were freed from slavery before the Civil War, you will find no information about your ancestors before 1870 in censuses or other records. African-American slaves were counted, but not named, in U.S. censuses until 1870.

You can, however, find information about your slave ancestors. Many good sources now exist to help you trace those roots. A website called *afrigeneas.com* is an excellent starting point. There are good books as well that go into specifics about the African-American search. *How to Trace Your African American Roots*, by Barbara Thompson Howell (Citadel Press, 1999), is one, and there are many others. A good beginning book for researching slave ancestors is *Slave Genealogy, A Research Guide with Case Studies*, by David H. Streets (Heritage Books, 1986).

You can also find records in the National Archives about African-Americans who served in the military from the 1860s on. These archives *(www.nara.gov)* and the LDS libraries *(familysearch.com)* are excellent places to check for African-American records.

Some of your ancestors' history may be tinged with sorrow. In this photograph, steamboats are taking Native American Sioux Indians away from their Montana homeland.

American Indian Ancestors

Are there branches of your family tree that include American Indian relatives or ancestors? If so, your roots extend as far back as anyone's in the United States. But this may also make it more difficult for you to find out about your ancestors.

At some point in your research, you will need to know the nation (or "tribe") that your family member

Internet Links

For these and other clickable links, go to *www.workman.com/familytree*.

There are many ethnic group websites that offer help and information to family researchers. Here are a few of them:

Interracial Families

rootsweb.com

To be included on a mailing list for anyone who is researching his or her interracial ancestry, go to *rootsweb.com* and click through on mailing lists. Additional information can be found on the Interracial-Genealogy Mailing List home page.

Asian Families

rootsweb.com/~asiagw

Resources are growing on the Internet for families from all over Asia. Asiagenweb is a project of WorldGenWeb with information and links to many countries.

Latino Families

users.aol.com/mrosado007/

This is the Internet page for an AOL special-interest group site for Hispanic research. The discussions are for AOL members, but the links and information are available to all on the World Wide Web.

elanillo.com/recursos.htm

This Spanish-language site is filled with links and useful information for Latino genealogists.

Ethnic Groups

cyndislist.com

Members of every major ethnic group in America and many smaller groups can find information about genealogically oriented websites by searching *cyndislist.com* for their nationality or ethnic group.

belonged to. You'll also have to find out where that nation settled—which may be tricky. Many American Indian nations did not stay in one place. Some moved on their own. Others were forced to move by the United States government.

Learning about the nation your ancestors belonged to will help you understand and trace your family history. A good place to start is with the United States government's National Archives and Records Administration (NARA). NARA has a collection of many useful documents, including Indian tribe censuses, wills, records of land transactions (especially for families living on reservations), and even some school records. Also look for *A Guide to Records in the National Archives Relating to American Indians*, which is available in genealogical libraries. You can find out how to order it through the NARA website *(www.nara.gov)* or by writing to the U.S. Government Printing Office, Washington, DC 20402.

You might also find useful information about American Indian families on *accessgenealogy.com/native*, the LDS (Mormon) website, *familysearch.com*; or at the LDS Family History Library centers. Another source of good information is *Native American Genealogical Sourcebook,* edited by Paula K. Byers (Gale Research, 1995).

Jewish Ancestors

The special problems of Jewish family research come up on the other side of the ocean. Most Jewish immigrants came to the United States from eastern Europe between 1880 and 1924. Nearly all of the communities those immigrants came from were virtually destroyed and the inhabitants murdered by the Nazis during World War II, a period and a disaster known now as the Holocaust.

But while the communities were destroyed, many of their records were not. Large numbers of Jewish birth, marriage, and death records—along with other information—were preserved and can be found in

numerous places. Probably the most important one is the volunteer-run website *jewishgen.org*. Jewishgen has worked with the LDS (Mormon) church and with other organizations on genealogical records. It now offers rich resources, including databases with hundreds of thousands of names of Jews and their communities around the world. There are also mailing lists and special-interest groups that link Jewish researchers to one another.

In addition, there are memorial books to hundreds of the communities that were destroyed during the war. Called *Yizkor* books, they include photographs, reminiscences, and obituaries for many of the people killed between 1938 and 1945. The books were usually written

Family history often connects with world history. For many Jewish genealogists, the giant shadow of the Holocaust—the deaths of 6 million Jews at the hands of the Nazis during World War II—becomes far darker when they discover how many of their own ancestors were killed. Above, distant cousins of the author, all of whom are believed to have died in the Holocaust.

in Yiddish or Hebrew, but many of them have sections written in English. They can be found in libraries with large collections of Jewish materials. The *Yizkor* books are slowly being translated and made available on the Internet. If your research has found that you had ancestors in one of these communities, check with *jewishgen.org* for information about it.

Newly Arrived Immigrant Families

We talk a lot in this book about the importance and richness of the huge immigration to the United States that has taken place over time. If your parents and you have come to the United States from another country, you are the most recent chapter in this story. This is something to be very proud of, even if it makes tracing your family history a little more complex.

Interviewing your parents is, of course, very important. Here are some suggested questions for them:

- What made you decide to emigrate?
- How long had you been thinking about it?
- Was the United States the only country you considered? If not, where else? What made you choose this country?
- How difficult was leaving?
- Do you think you will remain in the United States permanently?
- Have you applied for citizenship? Why or why not?

- How does life in America compare to life in your original country? What do you miss here? What do you think is wonderful here?

Ask your parents if you can see any documents relating to the process of coming to America. Try looking at visas, passports, and applications.

Talk with any other family members you can find—in the United States *and* around the world (e-mail can come in very handy here).

With all family members, attempt to get as much information as you can about your parents' home country. Ask for the full names of ancestors and relatives; the full names of the places they live and lived; and even addresses and approximate dates of when they lived there. All of this may come in handy if and when records in that country are made available. Of course, if your family is from a country where English is not spoken, surnames and place names may have a variety of spellings in English. Take what you think is the best approximation of the sound of the names.

As the world becomes more closely linked through the Internet, increasing amounts of genealogical information will be available online. In particular, WorldGenWeb *(worldgenweb.org)* and WorldGenWebkids *(rootsweb.com/~wgwkids)* will offer you useful information about specific countries and regions of the world (see page 168).

We are family! Parents and kids make a family—no matter the shape, color, or size.

If You Live in a Blended Family

Kids who grow up in blended families face another kind of genealogical challenge. In these families, a mom or dad remarries to someone who is not the biological parent of his or her child. Often there are other kids in the family—children from the other spouse's previous marriage or children who are then born to both of the parents together. This, too, can create questions and dilemmas for your research.

Where does my stepdad go on a family chart? Does he belong there at all? How about my stepbrothers? And how do I fit with children of the parent with whom I don't live? Are they part of my family charts? And what about my baby brother—whom some people call "half-brother." How do you make a tree with a half-relative?

Technically, there is a way to reflect all of this—by creating a second Family Group Sheet for the newly created family. But the answer that is closer to the heart of things is that family trees and genealogical record-keeping reflect the people you share your life with. On page 181, you'll find one example of a creative family tree that encompasses a family with numerous different current branches. As always, making up your own is as good as using anything you might find in a book or a store or a software package.

Families of Gay and Lesbian Parents

A family can be created by two same-sex parents. If your family came about in this way, you will quickly face the same question that adopted children do: How did our family come to be?

Your research should start with your parents, of course. They will tell you the story of your arrival in their lives. They can also share the history of their families. Then you can take that information and create a chart that reflects your family.

When a Parent Has Died

If your mother or father has died, tracing your genealogy may be painful. One of the key steps—interviewing both of your parents—is now impossible. Wonderful details you might have filled in during a personal interview with that parent are lost to you.

One consoling thought, perhaps, remains: When the time is right, you may find it comforting to research the line of the parent who has died. Doing so can be very valuable for you. You will be preserving memories of that parent, keeping alive his or her name and those of all your other relatives who are no longer living. You may also learn things you never knew about your parent—a sad but nonetheless valuable way to keep a kind of "conversation" alive between you and that parent.

When a Parent Is Unknown

In a few families, the identity of a parent—usually the father—simply may not be known. There are probably as many reasons for this as there are people in this situation. If this is what you are dealing with, your research obviously can only be through one parent.

That can leave a large gap on one side of the family tree or Pedigree Charts. But here again, you should feel free to create your own version. Some of the examples in this book—flower, tree, fan, pyramid, house, etc.—may work well. You can also devise a shape or format of your own.

The important thing to keep in mind in every one of these cases is that your family, like every other, has its own history and glories. Whatever shape your family chart takes, it reveals a chain of love and connection that is uniquely yours. And that is something to cherish throughout your life.

Detector's To-Do List

❑ Look for those special resources that will help you research your family's history and its more complicated ancestry stories.

❑ Talk with your parents if you have questions or uneasiness about tracing your family history.

❑ Create a version of a family tree that you think reflects your own family situation. Use any shape or approach that works for you.

CHAPTER 11

Getting Connected

Sharing All You've Discovered with Your Family

In this chapter, you will learn to:
- Put together a genealogical scrapbook
- Send out a family newsletter
- Compile a family roster
- Help plan and run a family reunion
- Organize a family club
- Create a family website
- Write a family book

Share the results of your research! This is an important rule for ancestor detectors. Genealogy isn't only about the past; it should enlighten people in the present and preserve both past and present for the future.

It's important, therefore, that you don't leave all the

information you've uncovered sitting in a file drawer, a loose-leaf notebook, or in your computer. Spread your knowledge around. Let your relatives in on all the wonderful things you've learned. By doing this, you will spread joy *and* get back information to help you continue your research.

There are a number of ways to share the wealth: creating a family display book; putting out a newsletter; creating and distributing a master list of family names and addresses; helping to put together a family reunion; forming a family club; even publishing a book about your family. (Remember Dafna's book in Chapter One? It can be done!) You might even create a family web page online. All of these projects require help from

an adult, although some are simpler than others. Tackle the one that suits you best or make up one of your own.

Family Show: Display Books

After you've done some research, you'll probably have a small collection of family documents, maps, and photos. One of the easiest ways to share your findings is to put them together in a family display book.

Celebrate your family by sharing what you discover with your relatives.

A loose-leaf notebook and some clear plastic display pages—sold in stationery and art-supply stores—will make a fine display book. Gather all your copies of documents: birth, marriage, and death certificates, immigration papers, passenger ship lists, and so on. Also include old letters, family photographs, and maps of your family's hometowns showing the places where they lived. Then arrange each set of papers by family. Put them in the display pages, beginning with the oldest documents and moving to the newest. In that way, you'll be able to leaf through the pages and see your family's history develop.

Keep adding documents as you find them, and show your book to relatives. It will be fun to share your discoveries—and it may even inspire other family members to help you with your research.

Drop Me a Line: Family Newsletters

One great way to keep family members informed about your research is to produce a family newsletter. You could do a print version and mail it out. E-mail, however, makes this project much easier—and is the fastest way to get the information to everyone (well, at least everyone in your family who's online!).

A newsletter is the perfect place for family news—births, weddings, and deaths, as well as graduations, christenings, confirmations, bar and bat mitzvahs, family relocations, and other special events. A copy of the family tree will interest readers, as will scanned-in pictures you've discovered, or old documents like a ship's manifest with an ancestor's name on it. (Of course, if you don't have a scanner, you can include the URL of the page where you discovered your document or information. Or, if you are making a print version of your newsletter, you can include photocopies of pictures or documents.) You might include profiles of interesting family members, artwork, summaries of research, and even jokes.

The lifeline of any newsletter is the reaction of its readers. Encourage your subscribers to send you notes, announcements, stories, drawings, and photographs. With a little bit of help from friendly relatives, you may find yourself a big-time family publisher.

Somewhere in Minnesota in 1905, members of this family posed in their Sunday best. What stories do your old family photos tell?

Gather 'Round: The Fun of Family Reunions

One of the liveliest ways to share and celebrate your common heritage is to attend a family reunion.

What could be more entertaining or exciting or *fun* than a great gathering of all your relatives? Imagine a party with visits from family no one has seen in years, plus sharing and laughing and eating and singing.

"Anyone who holds a family reunion has got to be crazy," says Eileen Lyons Polakoff, a New York City genealogist who has organized numerous family reunions. "It's an enormous amount of hard work, and you'll end up doing all of it."

But even though she knows how time-consuming a reunion is, Eileen says it's worth it. "You create a very special connection for people at a family reunion," she notes. "Older relatives get to relive a part of their life when they see family they haven't seen in years. For younger people, it's a kind of proof: 'Hey, I've got a past. I've got something to connect to.' And for kids, it's a great opportunity to make friends and play with relatives their own age."

Reunions can be anything from a small gathering at your family's house to a giant party at a football stadium. At the first reunion that Cecelia Kailaa Freeman organized for her family in Hawaii, about 50 people showed up. But after 13 years of reunions, the Kauaua clan had a party that attracted 5,000 relatives! "Our family reunions have created one unit out of many, many strangers," says Hoaliku Drake, one of Cecelia's nieces. "They have been a wonderful force for good."

Here are some pointers to help you put together a reunion.

Family reunions enable cousins from all over to meet and get to know each other.

Plan in advance. Even a small party requires a lot of notice. With the help of your parents, pick the date and the place well in advance, and aim for convenience for other family members (summer weekends are often a good bet). Three to six months beforehand is best; that gives you time to recruit other family members to help. And whatever date you choose, remember that it is 100 percent impossible to pick a date that will satisfy everyone.

Mail out a packet of information. The invitation should promise a special family gathering and may include a list of the people you've invited. Ask people to tell you if they'd be interested in attending and if they

know of other family members who should attend. It's also a good idea to ask relatives if they have any photographs or other memorabilia that they could send ahead so you can prepare it for viewing by all the family.

Remember that it will cost money to run the reunion. You have to pay for mailings and phone calls, feed everybody, and maybe even hire a hall or provide entertainment. Discuss with your parents how best to handle this. Many family reunions have some kind of price per person to cover food, drink, and other costs.

Plan events for the party. Most reunion time is spent sitting and talking, but it's nice to have a few events

Family Meeting Places . . . Online

The most exciting reunions take place in person, of course. But you may also be able to create a kind of family reunion online.

Even if you aren't a computer whiz, you can create a members-only website for your family's private use. These sites help relatives keep in touch, share stories and photographs, and make announcements about family events. Many genealogy software programs help you create this kind of website with a few clicks on the keyboard.

On a family site, you can share what you've discovered with other relatives, even those who aren't interested in doing genealogy themselves. And it's all private: Only family members can access the information, because a password is required to come onto the site.

Despite the security, however, it's probably still smart to honor the online privacy rule: When you post public family trees and pedigrees, don't include any personal information—birth dates or wedding dates —about people who are alive.

Are you interested in setting up a site? Two places where you can construct these family meeting places are *myfamily.com* and *familybuzz.com*. And here are two sites where you can learn more about why, and how, to put together a family website:

Cyndi's Genealogy Home Page Construction Kit
cyndislist.com/construc.htm

Publishing Your Family History on the Internet
compuology.com/book2.htm

planned. You could have a recitation of the family history, a few speeches from the family elders, or a special event like a dance contest.

The Galloway clan of North Carolina, Philadelphia, and other points east and south is descended from a slave named William Henry Brinkley. The Galloways have held reunions at a different family location every year since 1969. One year the New Jersey branch hosted 150 guests. They sponsored a dinner at a local hotel. All

entertainment was provided by family members. A raffle, dancing to records, a family talent show, a limbo contest, and a mother-daughter fashion show topped the bill.

A speech of general welcome was given and then Rosa Galloway, the family historian, recited the entire six-generation family tree. The event was videotaped, and copies were made for those who wanted to buy one.

Reunions don't have to be formal. A Wolfman family reunion was a barbecue in cousin Michael's backyard.

The entertainment consisted of conversation, kids chasing each other around the yard, and the Wolfman brothers reciting the family's old phone numbers. A great time was had by all!

Get things in place as the event draws near. When the reunion is just a few weeks away, send out a one-page reminder or call relatives who said they might come. "This is one of the best times to ask for information," says Eileen Polakoff. "No one wants wrong information published about them."

Be sure that all your materials are ready. Name tags are important; you could color-code them so everyone knows which side of the family everyone else is from. Mount documents like marriage licenses, high-school diplomas, and maps of the old neighborhood or town.

Old photographs are probably the most popular of all attractions. Mount them (use copies when possible) carefully, and identify as many people, dates, and places as you can. If you've got photos you can't identify, mount them and ask, "Who is this?" underneath. You might even create a "wanted" poster of relatives you can't identify or those you've lost contact with. Leave room for people to write down information.

Family trees are a must. At the Schwartz reunion, Eileen had a huge family tree—with more than 800 names!—prominently posted and covered in clear plastic. This allowed people to study their branches and make corrections or additions.

A very popular family reunion activity: Can you find *your* branch on the family tree?

Have an evaluation sheet at the reunion. This will allow everyone who attends to get in their two cents and tell you what worked and what didn't. It also can let you know who'd be willing to work with you on other family projects.

Join In: A Family Club

In spite of all the hard work, one family reunion usually inspires another. These events remind people of how much they have in common, and they usually want at least one more chance to share before they lose touch again. (And there are many cases in which

Who's at the reunion? Uncles and cousins, aunts and grandparents—and even a pet or two.

or family association. The group may simply agree to get together on holidays, or to send cards to one another. They may sponsor family research, or plan the next family reunion.

Some families go beyond the purely social and turn into true organizations that charge dues and hire an accountant to keep track of their money. "I know of families in which this kind of organization leads to a fund to help the younger people," explained Alex Haley. "In fact, I know of one black family that had such a fund, and one member of that family had an idea in which he believed. The family fund lent him $700 back about 30 years ago," Haley noted. "His name is Berry Gordy, and the idea he had such faith in back then was a record company called Motown." It went on to be a gigantic success, making Gordy a multimillionaire—money he might never have made without his family club's help.

families become closer, and stay closer, as a result of a reunion.)

"What tends to happen," recalled *Roots* author Alex Haley, "is that the first little group is chuckled at by other family members. 'Ha, imagine, a family reunion.' But when they hear about the good time had by our first group, they end up going to the second one. Something starts to take hold in these people, and once they gather again, they turn into something bigger than a family—they become a clan. A sense of soul, of *us,* starts to develop."

One way to keep the family in touch is to start a club

Family Bestsellers: Preserve Your History

After you've done a lot of research, you might consider assembling all the information into a "complicated genealogy," or family book.

You could simply produce it on a computer, scan in some photos, and use a loose-leaf or other simple binder to create a relatively inexpensive keepsake. If you don't have a scanner, you could make photocopies of your photos.

Try to include the following:

• An introduction that explains which families are covered. A good place to begin is with your furthest-back ancestors, telling who they were, what you know about them, and who their descendants were.

• A history that follows the generations from the past forward: descriptions of your ancestors' towns, their occupations, and any details about their lives and profiles of the more interesting or colorful people in your family. There is a place for family folklore here, but be sure to label a story "family myth" or "legend" if you cannot prove it really happened.

• A description of how your family came to this country.

• A family tree listing everyone you have found and whatever details you may have (dates and places).

• Any photographs, documents, or maps that help tell your story.

• An index listing the pages on which each ancestor's name can be found.

• A family roster.

• A source list, telling where your information comes from. (This makes your book more authoritative.)

A father shows off his large family tree to his sons and a friend.

There is one crucial rule: Be accurate. If you do not know which date is right or if you are not sure of any fact, make that uncertainty clear in the book. There's nothing wrong with including questionable information, as long as it is *clearly labeled* as such. But passing down misinformation is a disservice to everyone.

At the beginning of your research, you should check to see if anyone else has written a book about a branch of your family. Ask your local librarians if they know where you can locate one of the many catalogs that include lists of published family histories. (And ask them about *Genealogies in the Library of Congress: A Bibliography,* and its supplements, edited by Marion J. Kaminkow.)

Photos from family reunions show the passage of time. The little boy in the picture on top is the man at top left in the photo below!

If one has been done on your family, try—through interlibrary loan or other means—to read through it. It may save you time and give you information you haven't seen before. Just double check the facts; many compiled histories, especially early ones, are known to have been inaccurate in places.

When you have finished writing your story, have someone read it over for grammatical and typographical errors. If you're going to share this with your family members—and with the future—you want everything to be correct and readable. Typos that change Jan into Jane or Tate into Tote will drive everyone crazy years from now.

Family books make wonderful gifts at reunions or holiday time. No matter how small your book is, relatives will be pleased to receive it. (Some people ask for a small contribution to cover costs; that's up to you.)

Don't assume that no one else is interested in your family besides your family, however. If your history is substantial—carefully researched, and more than 60 to 70 pages—you should consider contacting your local library and offering them a copy. In fact, you could even write the Library of Congress and suggest that you send them one to add to their collection of compiled genealogies. Write to the Library of Congress, Genealogy Division, Washington, DC 20540, or contact them on the web at *lcweb.loc.gov/rr/genealogy*. Your future will thank you.

Detector's To-Do List

❑ Organize all your documents so you can share them with your family.

❑ Put together some kind of family list or newsletter.

❑ Go online to learn about private family-only websites.

❑ Think about planning a family reunion.

Appendix

A Dictionary of American Last Names

The following list includes translations and origins of almost 400 family names found in the United States. American family names come from all nationalities and cultures—so this list is made up of names from every part of the earth. Much of the information is adapted from a wonderful book, *The New Dictionary of American Family Names,* by Elsdon C. Smith.

The following code is used to explain the origin of the names:

(Ar) Arabic
(Arm) Armenian
(Chi) Chinese
(Cz) Czech
(Cz-Sl) Czecho-Slovakian
(Dan) Danish
(Du) Dutch

(Eng) English
(Est) Estonian
(Fin) Finnish
(Fr) French
(Ger) German
(Heb) Hebrew
(Hin) Hindi
(Hun) Hungarian
(Ir) Irish
(It) Italian
(Jap) Japanese
(Kor) Korean
(Mx) Manx
(Nor) Norwegian
(Pol) Polish
(Port) Portuguese
(Rus) Russian
(Scot) Scottish
(Sl) Slovakian
(Sp) Spanish
(Swe) Swedish

(Swi) Swiss
(Ukr) Ukrainian
(Wel) Welsh

Ackroyd *(Eng)* Dweller at the oak clearing
Adler *(Ger)* Dweller at the sign of the eagle
Altman *(Ger)* Old man
Armstrong *(Eng)* One who was noted for his strength
Arzt *(Ger)* Doctor
Bader *(Ger)* Barber
Ballard *(Eng)* The bald one
Barkan *(Heb)* Son of a Cohen (priest)
Bauer *(Ger)* Farmer (also Bauman, Baumann)
Baxter *(Eng)* Baker (female)
Becker *(Ger)* Baker
Beebe *(Eng)* Dweller on a bee farm

Belcher *(Fr)* Beautiful, beloved

Bell *(Eng)* Dweller at the sign of the bell

Berra *(It)* Dweller in a hut

Bevilaqua *(It)* Teetotaler, one who drinks only water

Bialik *(Sl)* The white-haired one

Black *(Eng)* The dark-haired one

Bleecker *(Du)* One who bleaches clothing

Bogart *(Du)* Worker in an orchard

Boggs *(Eng)* Dweller in a marsh

Borg *(Ger, Swe, Nor)* Dweller in or near a fortified castle

Bouvier *(Fr)* One who took care of cattle

Bradley *(Eng)* Inhabitant of a broad pastureland (brad means broad, and lee means pastureland)

Brenner *(Ger)* Distiller

Breuer *(Ger)* Brewer (also Brewer, Brewster, Brower)

Brody *(Ger)* A place name

Buick *(Du)* One who had a large stomach or paunch

Bullwinkel *(Ger)* Dweller at the corner where bulls were kept

Bumstead *(Eng)* Dweller from Bumpstead (a reedy place) in Essex

Buren *(Du)* Dweller in the neighborhood

Cabot *(Fr)* One with a small head

Caputo *(It)* One with a large or unusual head; stubborn or dull-witted

Carpenter, Charpentier *(Eng, Fr)* One who worked with wood

Carson *(Scot, Eng, Mx)* Dweller at or near a marsh; also garçon or servant; or son of Car, short for Carmichael

Chevrolet *(Fr)* Dweller at the sign of the little goat

Cleaver *(Eng)* Dweller near a cliff

Cloud *(Scot)* Dweller near the rock or mass of stone; son of Leod

Cooper *(Eng)* Barrel maker

Copple *(Eng)* One who came from Copple (peaked hill) in Lancashire; or from Cople (Cocca's pool) in Bedfordshire

Corona *(It)* One who played the king's part in pageants and festivals; dweller at the sign of the crown

Crawford *(Eng)* One who came from Crawford (crow's pass) in Lanarkshire; dweller near a river crossing where crows are

Crocker *(Eng)* Someone who makes pots (crockery)

Crockett *(Eng)* Little, crooked, or deformed person

Cronkite *(Ger, Du)* One who was ill, an invalid; American corruption of Krankheit

Cullen *(Ger)* From Koln, Cologne

Currier *(Eng)* One who dressed, or prepared, leather

Czyz *(Pol)* Dweller at the sign of the yellow or green finch; finchlike

Dannenberg *(Ger)* One who came from the town of Dannenberg (which means pine-tree-covered mountain), the name of three places in Germany

Desai *(Hin)* District officer, descendant of Desai, Hindi title with no English equivalent

Dick *(Ger, Eng)* Large, fat man; descendant of Dick, pet form of Richard

Diener *(Ger)* Server

Disney *(Eng)* One who comes from Isigny (Isina's estate) in Calvados

Dombrowski *(Pol)* Dweller in or near the oak grove

Doolittle *(Fr, Eng)* One who lived *de l'hôtel*, in the mansion; an idler

Douglas *(Eng)* Dweller at the black water or stream; one who came from Douglas in Lancashire

Dresner *(Ger)* From Dresden

Dreyfuss *(Fr)* One who came from Treves

Duchin *(Heb)* One who gave the priestly blessing

Farber *(Ger)* Painter

Fisch *(Ger)* Fisherman, one who dwelt at the sign of the fish

Fleischer *(Ger)* Butcher

Ford, Forde, Forder *(Eng)* Dweller or worker at a stream crossing

Fowler *(Eng)* Bird catcher or gamekeeper

Frank *(Ger)* One who came from Franconia

Fu *(Chi)* Teacher

Gabler *(Eng)* Tax collector

Gebauer *(Ger)* Peasant or tiller of the fields

Gerber *(Ger)* Tanner

Gillick *(Ir)* The son of Ulick, a pet form of William (resolution, helmet)

Grant *(Eng, Fr, Scot)* Large or fat man

Griffin *(Eng)* Dweller at the sign of the half-lion half-eagle; also one with a ruddy complexion

Hallas *(Pol)* Noisy, bustling man

Hallmark *(Eng)* Nickname, half-a-mark, that is, one-third of a pound, possibly for one who paid a coin of that denomination annually as rent for his land; dweller on or near the hill field

Halpern, Halperin *(Heb, Ger)* Money changer; one who came from Heilbronn (holy well) in Wurtemberg

Hooper, Hoopes *(Eng)* One who made hoops, a cooper; one who lives on the hop, a piece of enclosed land in a marsh

Horowitz *(Cz-Sl, Rus)* One who came from Horice or Horitz (mountainous place) in Bohemia; son of the mountaineer

Horvath, Horvat *(Hun)* One who came from Croatia

Jaffee *(Heb)* Pretty

Kaczmarek, Kaczmarski *(Pol)* Descendant of the bartender

Keller *(Fr, Eng, Ger)* One employed in a storeroom, particularly a food storage place; one who made or sold culs or kells, a cap or hairnet for women; one who came from Keller (wine cellar), several places in Germany

Kellerman *(Ger)* Worker or dweller in a wine cellar or tavern

Kessler *(Ger)* Coppersmith, one who sold or made kettles. Jewish Kesslers get their name not from a profession but from the Hebrew name of an ancestor called "Yekutiel," whose nickname was Kessel; Kessler means "one descended from Kessel"

Kim *(Kor)* Gold

Kite *(Eng)* Dweller at the sign of the kite or hawk

Klein *(Ger)* The short man

Klutz *(Ger)* One who came from Klutz (hot, bubbling spring) in Germany

Kosek *(Pol)* Dweller at the sign of the little blackbird

Koski, Koskinen *(Fin)* Dweller at the rapids or near a waterfall

Kramer *(Ger)* Merchant

Kravitz, Kravetz, Kravets, Kravits *(Cz-Sl, Pol, Ukr)* One who made outer garments, a tailor

Krieger *(Ger)* Warrior; Yiddish could mean tavern keeper

Kumamoto *(Jap)* Bear plus base

Kunstler *(Ger)* Skilled artisan, learned man

Kusaki *(Jap)* Grass plus tree

Lahti *(Fin)* Dweller near the bay

Langley, Langlois *(Fr)* The Englishman

Lanier *(Fr)* One who worked with wool

Lapidus *(Fr)* One who dealt in precious stones

Lapin *(Fr, Rus)* One who hunted, raised, or sold rabbits; one who had big feet

Le *(Chi)* Pear tree

Lederer *(Eng, Ger)* One who drove a vehicle, a carter

Ledermann *(Ger)* Leather maker, tanner

Lehrer *(Ger)* Teacher

Lejeune *(Fr)* The young man

Lesser *(Ger)* Custodian of a forest, gamekeeper

Levin, Levine *(Fr, Heb)* One who sold wine; dweller at the vine or vineyard; descendant of the little Levi (united)

Li *(Chi, Kor)* Plums; black

Lichterman *(Ger)* One who lit lamps, a lamplighter

Lichtman *(Ger)* The light-complexioned man; one who made candles

Long *(Eng)* The tall one

Loughlin *(Scot)* One from the land of lochs (lakes)

Lowenthal *(Ger)* One who came from Lowenthal (lion valley)

Lumpp, Lump, Lumpe *(Eng)* Dweller at or near a deep pool or wooded valley; descendant of Lump, pet form of Lambert (land, bright)

Lustig *(Ger)* Happy

MacGowan, McGowan *(Scot, Ir)* Son of the smith

Machado *(Sp, Port)* One who made and sold hatchets; one who used hatchets in his work

Macintosh *(Scot, Ir)* The son of the chief or leader

Maldonado *(Sp)* Descendant of Donald (dark or brown-haired stranger)

Marinello *(It)* Dweller at the sign of the ladybug

Masada *(Jap)* Right plus rice field

Medina *(Sp)* Dweller at or near the market; one who had returned from Medina, the holy city of Islam; one who came from Medina, the name of several places in Spain

Meer *(Du, Ger)* One who dwells near a lake or on the seacoast

Mehler, Mehlman, Melman *(Ger)* One who paints, a painter

Meltzer, Melzer *(Ger)* One who brews, a brewer; also one who came from Meltz

Menaker *(Heb)* One who cleans the kosher meat

Menzies *(Scot)* One who came from Meyners, in Normandy

Metzger *(Ger)* Butcher

Miller *(Eng)* One who ground meal, grain, etc.

Mogilefsky *(Rus)* Dweller near a tomb or grave

Moneypenny *(Eng)* One with much money, a wealthy man; or ironically, a nickname for a poor man

Moody *(Eng)* the bold, impetuous, brave man

Mori *(Jap)* Forest

Morita *(Jap)* Forest plus rice field

Moshiah *(Heb)* Sephardic name, originally signified follower of Sabbatai Tzvi

Nachtman *(Ger)* One who worked as a night watchman

Nagano *(Jap)* Long plus field

Nagel *(Ger)* One who made nails

Nagy *(Hun)* The big man

Nakada *(Jap)* Middle plus rice field

Nakagawa *(Jap)* Middle plus river

Nakamura *(Jap)* Middle plus village

Nakashima *(Jap)* Middle plus island

Nakayama *(Jap)* Middle plus mountain

Nalbandian *(Arm)* The son of the man who shod horses

Ng *(Chi)* Crow; one who came from the province of Kiangsu

Nishi *(Jap)* West

Nishimura *(Jap)* West plus village

Novick, Nowicki *(Cz-Sl, Pol)* One who recently arrived in the area, a newcomer

Oh *(Chi)* Recklessly

Ono *(Jap)* Little plus field

Ostrow *(Pol)* Dweller on a small island in a river

Ota *(Jap)* Thick plus rice field

Ozawa *(Jap)* Little plus swamp

Pafko *(Cz-Sl)* Son of Palko, Czech form of Paul (small)

Palmiero, Palmieri *(It)* One who carries the palm in religious processions; one who granted or sold indulgences

Paluch *(Pol)* One with an unusual finger

Pancake *(Eng)* One who made and sold pancakes

Paredes *(Sp)* Dweller near the walls

Peabody *(Eng)* Nickname for a showily dressed individual

Pereira *(Port)* One who came from Pereira (pear tree); dweller near a pear tree

Perlmuter *(Ger)* Dealer in mother of pearl; possibly a name taken by one whose mother was named Perl

Piazza *(It)* Dweller at or near the square

Picasso *(Sp, It)* One who uses a pick or pickax in his work; one with the characteristics of a magpie

Pinsky, Pinski, Pinsker *(Rus, Ukr, Pol)* One who came from Pinsk, in Belarus

Plumer, Plomer *(Eng)* A dealer in plumes or feathers; also a variant of Plummer, one who worked with or dealt in lead

Podgorny *(Pol, Rus)* Dweller at the foot of the mountain

Poe *(Eng)* Dweller at the sign of the peacock; a nickname given to a proud or gaudily dressed man

Poland, Polan, Polland *(Eng)* Dweller at the homestead on which there was a pool, or through which a stream flowed; one who made and sold the long, pointed shoes worn in the 14th century

Pollack *(Ger, Fr)* One who came from Poland

Polsky *(Pol)* One who came from Poland, probably one who acquired the name outside of Poland

Pomerantz, Pomerance, Pomeranz *(Fr)* One who sold oranges

Portnoy *(Rus)* One who made outer garments, a tailor

Postman, Postmann *(Ger)* One who came from Postau

Power, Powers *(Eng, Ir)* The poor man, a pauper; one who had taken a vow of poverty

Profeta *(It)* One who played the part of the Prophet in plays or pageants

Profitt, Proffit *(Eng, Scot, Fr)* One who acted the part of the Prophet in medieval pageants; a rich man

Ptashkin *(Rus)* Dweller at the sign of the small bird; one who trapped and sold small birds

Puttkamer *(Ger)* One who cleaned rooms

Quaglia, Quagliani *(It)* Dweller at the sign of the quail

Quayle *(Mx)* Son of Paul

Rabe *(Ger, Fr)* Descendant of the rabbi or teacher; dweller at the sign of the crow

Rabin *(Fr)*, **Rabinovich, Rabinowitz** *(Rus)* Descendant of the rabbi or teacher

Rader *(Ger)* One who made wheels, a wheelwright; one who occupied the office of alderman; one who came from Raden (moor, reedy place); one who thatched with reed

Raitt, Rait, Raite *(Scot)* One who came from Rait (fort), the name of several places in Scotland

Raja, Rajah *(Hin)* Title of an Indian king, prince, or chief

Ramsay, Ramsey *(Scot, Eng)* One who came from Ramsay (ram's isle) in Scotland; or from Ramsey (wild garlic island), the name of places in Essex and Huntingdonshire in England

Rao *(Hin)* A Hindi title; also Italian name

Raudsepp *(Est)* One who worked in iron, a smith

Rausch *(Ger)* The excitable or hurried man; dweller near rushes

Reiber *(Ger)* One who worked at the baths, giving patrons a rubdown

Reifsneider, Reifsnyder *(Ger)* One who made barrel hoops

Reigle, Reigel *(Ger)* Dweller at the sign of the heron

Reiser *(Ger)* One who left to go to war; one from Reiser

Reiter *(Ger)* One who rode a horse, a cavalryman; one who cleared land for tilling

Resnick *(Pol, Rus, Ukr)* One who sold meat, a butcher; one who slaughtered animals for meat according to Jewish ritual

Richter *(Ger)* One who held the office of judge or magistrate

Riegel *(Ger)* Dweller at the town fence; descendant of Ricoald (rule, power)

Ritchie, Ritchey *(Scot, Eng)* Descendant of little Rich, a pet form of Richard (rule, hard)

Rizzo *(It)* One who had curly or wavy hair

Rockne *(Nor)* An ancient farm name said to be older than written history

Rockower *(Ger)* One who came from Rockow (lowland)

Rogalski *(Pol)* Dweller near the Rogalskie (place visited by horned animals), lake in Poland

Rothbart *(Ger)* Red beard

Rovin, Rovine, Rovins, Rovinsky *(Rus, Pol)* Dweller at a canal or ditch

Rozier *(Fr)* Dweller near a rosebush

Ruder, Ruderman *(Ger)* Nickname for a sailor

Rudnick, Rudnicki, Rudnik *(Pol)* One who worked in a mine; dweller near a mine; one who came from Rudnik (red), the name of many places in Poland and the Ukraine

Rusk *(Swe, Dan)* The valiant, brave, active man

Russell *(Eng)* The little red-haired man

Rychlak *(Pol)* One who was always early or ahead of time

Rys *(Eng)* Dweller near rushes or in the brushwood

Sadowski *(Pol)* Dweller at or near an orchard

Saks *(Heb)* Acronym for *zera kedoshim Spiro*, descendants of the martyrs of Speyer (Spiro), in Germany

Saltz, Saltzman, Saltzmann *(Ger)* One who processed and sold salt

Sammoka *(Heb)* The red-haired one

Sandler *(Ger)* One who carted sand; one who repaired shoes, a cobbler

Sanford *(Eng)* One who came from Sandford (sandy ford), the name of several places in England

Sangster *(Eng)* One who sang in church; a member of the chorus

Sato *(Jap)* Help plus wisteria

Savage *(Eng, Ir)* Wild or fierce man; one who had rough manners

Sayers, Sayre, Sayres, Sayer *(Eng)* One who sold silk or serge; one who assayed or tested metals, or tasted food; descendant of Saer or Sayer

Schatz *(Ger, Heb)* Treasure; acronym for *shaliah tzibur*, leader of prayers in synagogue

Schenker *(Ger)* One who kept a public house, a publican

Scherer *(Ger)* One who shaved another, a barber; one who caught moles

Schlesinger *(Ger)* One who came from Silesia, or one who came from Schleusingen, in Thuringia

Schmucker, Schmuckler, Schmukler *(Ger)* One who decorates, embellishes, or ornaments things

Schneider *(Ger)* Tailor

Schreiber *(Ger)* Secretary or scribe

Schreiner *(Ger)* Cabinetmaker

Schubert *(Ger)* One who made and sold shoes

Schulman *(Ger)* School or synagogue man

Schuster *(Ger)* Shoemaker, cobbler

Schweizer, Schweitzer *(Ger)* One who came from Switzerland

Scott *(Eng)* One who came from Scotland; originally the word also included the Irish, one who came from Ireland

Selznick *(Ukr)* One who was thought to resemble a drake or a dragon

Seto *(Jap)* Rapids plus door

Shain, Shaine, Shaines *(Ger)* Beautiful or handsome person

Shanahan *(Ir)* Grandson of little Seanach (old, wise)

Shane *(Ir)* Descendant of Eion or Seon, Irish forms of John

Shapiro, Shapira, Shapero, Shapera *(Ger)* One from Speyer, in the middle ages spelled Spira, and by Jews spelled Shapira, in Bavaria

Shevchuk, Shevchenko *(Ukr)* The son of the shoemaker

Shimada *(Jap)* Island plus rice field

Shimizu *(Jap)* Pure plus water

Shirley *(Eng)* One who came from Shirley (wood belonging to the shire), the name of several places in England

Shoemaker *(Eng)* One who made and sold shoes and boots

Silberg *(Ger)* One from Silberg, the name of two places in Germany

Simonetti *(It)* Descendant of little Simon

Simson *(Eng)* Descendant of Sim or Simon

Sinclair *(Scot, Eng)* One who came from St. Clair, the name of several places in Normandy; a follower of St. Clare

Skelton *(Eng)* One who came from Skelton (the hill, or bank, manor), the name of parishes in Yorkshire and Cumberland

Skolnik, Skolnick *(Cz-Sl, Ukr)* The student, or one connected in some way with a school; an important functionary of the synagogue in the early Jewish communities

Skowron, Skowronski *(Pol)* Dweller at the sign of the lark; one who trapped larks

Skulsky *(Ukr, Rus)* One with a prominent cheekbone

Sleeper *(Eng)* One who made scabbards for swords; one who polished or sharpened swords

Sloan, Sloane *(Ir)* Grandson of Sluaghan (soldier, warrior)

Slocum *(Eng)* Dweller in a valley of blackthorn and sloe trees

Smethhurst *(Eng)* Dweller at the wood on smooth or level land; variant of Smithhurst

Smith *(Eng)* Worker in metals

Sobel, Soble, Sobol, Sobelman *(Pol, Rus)* Dweller at the sign of the sable; one who trapped and sold sables

Song *(Chi)* To dwell (a dynasty name)

Spector, Specter, Spekter *(Rus)* A title meaning "inspector," used by Hebrew teachers in old Russia, which, when registered with the police, enabled them to live in areas forbidden to Jews

Speier *(Eng)* One who acted as a spy or watchman

Spitalny *(Pol)* One who worked in or dwelled near a hospital

Spivak *(Pol, Ukr, Cz-Sl)* Cantor, one who sang in church or synagogue, especially a solo singer

Springfield *(Eng)* One who came from Springfield (spring or stream in open country), in Essex

Stamm *(Ger)* Dweller near an unusual tree trunk

Stanley *(Eng)* One who came from Stanley (stony meadow), the name of several places in England; dweller at a rocky meadow

Stastny *(Cz)* The happy, lucky, joyful man

Steadman *(Eng)* Dweller on a farmstead, a farm worker; one responsible for the care of warhorses

Stein *(Ger)* Dweller near a stone or rock, often a boundary mark; one who came from Stein, the name of numerous villages in Germany and Switzerland; descendant of Staino; a dweller in or near a stone castle

Steinhauer *(Ger)* One who cuts and builds with stone

Stengel *(Ger)* Dweller near a small pole or stake

Stern, Sterne *(Eng, Ger)* The severe, austere man; dweller at the sign of the star, alluding to the Star of David

Sternberg *(Ger)* One who came from Sternberg (star mountain), the name of ten places in Germany

Stock *(Eng, Ger)* Dweller near a tree stump; dweller near a foot bridge

Storr *(Eng)* The big man; the strong, powerful man

Stroh *(Ger)* One who sold thatch for roofs

Studebaker *(Ger)* One who prepared or sold pastries

Sullivan *(Ir)* Grandson of Suileabhan (black-eyed)

Sussman, Susman *(Ger)* Sweet man, an affectionate person

Sutherland, Sutherlan, Sutherlin *(Eng)* One who came from the county of Sutherland (southern land) in Scotland

Sutter *(Eng)* One who made shoes, a shoemaker

Suzuki *(Jap)* Bell plus tree

Svoboda *(Cz-Sl, Pol, Ukr)* Liberty or freedom, a name suggesting a freeman, not a serf

Sweeney, Sweeny *(Ir, Eng)* Descendant of Suibhne (little hero); dweller on the island where pigs were kept; descendant of a peaceful or quiet man

Szabo *(Hun)* One who made outer garments, a tailor

Szasz *(Hun)* One who came from Saxony, a Saxon

Tabak, Taback, Tabachnick *(Pol)* One who prepared and sold snuff

Tagliaferro *(It)* One who cut or otherwise worked with iron

Tailleur *(Fr)* One who worked with outer garments, a tailor

Taylor, Tayler, Taylour *(Eng)* One who made outer garments, a tailor

Teitelbaum *(Ger)* The date palm tree, a name selected from Psalms 92:12: "The righteous shall flourish like the palm tree"

Teller *(Eng)* One who made or sold linen cloth

Ten Broeck *(Du)* Dweller at or near the marsh

Ten Eyck *(Du)* One who lived near an oak tree

Teng *(Chi)* Mound

Tenuto, Tenuta *(It)* Beloved, dear person

Tepper *(Eng)* One who furnished articles, especially arrows, with metal tips

Thatcher *(Eng)* One who covered roofs with straw, rushes, or reeds

Thayer *(Eng)* Descendant of Thaider (people, army)

Toomey, Tomey *(Ir)* Grandson of Tuaim (a sound)

Torme, Tormey *(Ir)* Grandson of Tormaigh (increase) or Thormodr

Treadwell *(Eng)* Dweller at a path or road by a stream or spring

Truman *(Eng)* The loyal servant

Tschudi *(Swi)* One who sat in judgment, a judge

Tsuji *(Jap)* Crossroads

Tuchman *(Ger)* One who deals in cloth

Tucker *(Eng)* One who cleaned and thickened cloth

Tung *(Chi)* To correct

Turner *(Eng)* One who fashioned objects on a lathe

Tuttle *(Eng)* Dweller at a toot-hill, (a hill with a good outlook to detect an enemy's approach);

also one who came from Tothill (lookout hill), the name of places in Lincolnshire and Middlesex

Tyler *(Eng)* One who made, sold, or covered buildings with tiles

Unruh *(Ger)* An agitator or troublemaker; one who was careless, restless, or indolent; one who came from Unruh in Germany

Updike, Updyck *(Du)* Dweller on the dike

Uyeda *(Jap)* Plant plus rice field

Uyeno *(Jap)* Upper plus field

Vaccaro, Vaccari, Vaccarello *(It)* One who tended cows

Voorsanger *(Du)* Cantor, singer

Wagner *(Ger)* Wagoner

Weber *(Ger)* Weaver

Wechsler *(Ger)* Money changer

Wright *(Eng)* One who worked in wood or other hard material; a carpenter

Yamashita *(Jap)* Mountain plus below

Youngman *(Eng, Ger)* The young servant

Correspondence Log

Family Name _____

Date	Wrote to	Address	Subject	Reply

Abstract of Citizenship Papers

(Declaration of Intention, Petition)

My Name _____ Today's date _____

Type of document _____ Where I found the document _____

Court where document was filed _____ Volume # _____ Page or petition# _____ Date filed _____

Applicant's name _____ Address _____

Name of ship to America _____

Where it left from _____ When _____ Where it arrived _____ When _____

Marriage information:

Name of spouse _____ Birthdate _____ Birthplace _____

Date of marriage _____ Place _____

Children:

Name _____ Birthdate _____ Birthplace _____

Name _____ Birthdate _____ Birthplace _____

Name _____ Birthdate _____ Birthplace _____

Witnesses listed on document:

Name _____ Address _____

Name _____ Address _____

Physical description of applicant:

Height _____ Weight _____ Race _____ Complexion _____

Eye Color _____ Hair color _____ Occupation _____

Other documents I found _____

_____

Notes _____

G-639 Freedom of Information Act Request Form

If your ancestors became citizens after 1906, use this form to request their naturalization and citizenship papers. You can find the downloadable version of this at *http://www.ins.gov/graphics/ formsfee/forms/g-639.htm.*

U.S. Department of Justice
Immigration and Naturalization Service

OMB NO. 1115-0087

Freedom of Information/Privacy Act Request

The completion of this form is optional.
Any written format for Freedom of Information or Privacy Act requests is acceptable.

START HERE – Please type or print and read instructions on the reverse before completing this form.

1. Type of Request: *(Check appropriate box)*
   - ☐ Freedom of Information Act (FOIA) *(Complete all items except 7)*
   - ☐ Privacy Act (PA) *(Item 7 must be completed in addition to all other applicable items)*
   - ☐ Amendment *(PA only, Item 7 must be completed in addition to all other applicable items)*

2. Requester Information:

Name of Requester:	Daytime Telephone:
Address *(Street Number and Name):*	Apt. No
City:	State:	Zip Code:

By my signature, I consent to the following:
Pay all costs incurred for search, duplication, and review of materials up to $25.00, when applicable. *(See Instructions)*
*Signature of requester:*_____
   - ☐ Deceased Subject - **Proof of death must be attached.** *(Obituary, Death Certificate or other proof of death required)*

3. Consent to Release Information. *(Complete if name is different from Requester)(Item 7 must be completed)*

Print Name of Person Giving Consent:	Signature of Person Giving Consent:

By my signature, I consent to the following: *(check applicable boxes)*
   - ☐ Allow the Requester named in item 2 to see ☐ all of my records or ☐ a portion of my record. If a portion, specify what part *(i.e. copy of application)*

(Consent is required for records for United States Citizens (USC) and Lawful Permanent Residents (LPR)

4. Action Requested *(Check One):*   ☐ Copy   ☐ In-Person Review

5. Information needed to search for records:
Specific information, document(s), or record(s) desired: *(Identify by name, date, subject matter, and location of information)*

Purpose: *(Optional: you are not required to state the purpose for your request; however, doing so may assist the INS in locating the records needed to respond to your request.)*

6. Data NEEDED on SUBJECT of Record: *(If data marked with asterisk (*) is not provided records may not be located)*

* Family Name	Given Name:	Middle Initial:
*Other names used, if any:	* Name at time of entry into the U.S.:	I-94 Admissions #:
* Alien Registration #:	* Petition or Claim Receipt #:	* Country of Birth:	*Date of Birth or Appx. Year
Names of other family members that may appear on requested record(s) *(i.e., Spouse, Daughter, Son):*			
Country of Origin *(Place of Departure):*	Port-of-Entry into the U.S.	Date of Entry:
Manner of Entry: *(Air, Sea, Land)*	Mode of Travel: *(Name of Carrier)*	SSN:
Name of Naturalization Certifications:	Certificate #:	Naturalization Date:
Address at the time of Naturalization:	Court and Location:	

Form G-639 (Rev. 7-25-00)N

7. Verification of Subject's Identity: *(See Instructions for Explanation)(Check One Box)*

☐ In-Person with ID   ☐ Notarized Affidavit of Identity   ☐ Other *(Specify)*_____

Signature of Subject of Record: Date: _____

_____   Telephone No.: (   ) -

NOTARY *(Normally needed from individuals who are the subject of the records sought) (See below)*
or a sworn declaration under penalty of perjury.
Subscribed and sworn to before me this _____ day of _____ in the Year _____

Signature of Notary _____   My Commission Expires _____

OR

If a declaration is provided in lieu of a notarized signature, it must state, at a minimum, the following: (Include Notary Seal or Stamp in this Space)

If executed outside the United States: "I declare (certify, verify, or state) under penalty of perjury under the laws of the United States of America that the foregoing is true and correct.

Signature:_____

If executed within the United States, its territories, possessions, or commonwealths: "I declare (certify, verify, or state) under penalty of perjury that the foregoing is true and correct.

Signature:_____

Further Reading

I read through many sources while researching this book. Most of them would be useful to anyone who wants to do more exploring in the fascinating, never-ending field of genealogy.

Immigration

Allen, Leslie. *Liberty: The Statue and the American Dream.* New York: Statue of Liberty/Ellis Island Foundation with National Geographic Society, 1985.

Antin, Mary. *The Promised Land.* Boston: Houghton Mifflin, 1912.

Archdeacon, Thomas J. *Becoming American: An Ethnic History.* New York: The Free Press, 1983.

Chermayeff, Ivan, Fred Wasserman, and Mary J. Shapiro. *Ellis Island: An Illustrated History of the Immigrant Experience.* New York: Macmillan Publishing Company, 1991.

Foner, Nancy. *From Ellis Island to JFK: New York's Two Great Waves of Immigration.* New Haven: Yale University Press, 2000.

Handlin, Oscar. *The Uprooted.* 2nd edition. Boston: Atlantic Monthly Press, 1973.

Heaps, Willard A. *The Story of Ellis Island.* New York: Seabury Press, 1967.

Kraut, Alan M. *The Huddled Masses: The Immigrant in American Society. 1880–1921.* Arlington Heights, Illinois: Harlan Davidson, Inc., 1982

Morton Allan Directory of European Passenger Steamship Arrivals: For the years 1890 to 1930 at the Port of New York and for the years 1904 to 1926 at the Ports of New York, Philadelphia, Boston, and Baltimore. Baltimore: Genealogical Publishing Co., 1979.

Novotny, Ann. *Strangers at the Door: Ellis Island, Castle Garden, and the Great Migration to America.* Old Greenwich, Connecticut. Chatam Press, 1991.

Shapiro, Mary J. *Gateway to Liberty: The Story of the Statue of Libery and Ellis Island.* New York: Vintage Books, 1986.

Stern, Gail F., editor. *Freedom's Doors: Immigrant Ports of Entry to the Untied States.* Catalog to exhibit published by the Balch Institute, Philadelphia, 1986.

Wheeler, Thomas, editor. *The Immigrant Experience: The Anguish of Becoming American.* New York: Dial Press, 1971.

Yans-McLaughlin, Virginia, and Marjorie Lightman. *Ellis Island and the Peopling of America: The Official Guide.* Written with the Statue of Liberty/Ellis Island Foundation. New York: The New Press, 1997.

Beginning Genealogy

Beller, Susan Provost. *Roots for Kids: A Genealogy Guide for Young People.* White Hall, Virginia: Betterway Publications, 1989.

Boyer, Carl III. *How to Publish and Market Your Family History.* 2nd edition. Newhall, California: Carl Boyer III Publisher, 1982.

Cosgriff, John and Carolyn. *Climb It Right: A High-Tech Genealogy Primer.* 2nd edition revised. Radford, Virginia: Heritage Press, 1986.

Crandall, Ralph. *Shaking Your Family Tree: A Basic Guide to Tracing Your Family's Genealogy,* Dublin, New Hampshire: Yankee Publishing, 1986.

Croom, Emily Anne. *Unpuzzling Your Past: A Basic Guide to Genealogy.* 2nd edition. White Hall, Virginia: Betterway Publications, 1989.

Hilton, Suzanne. *Who Do You Think You Are?: Digging for Your Family Roots.* Philadelphia: Westminister Press, 1976.

Kyvig, David E., and Myron A. Marty, *Nearby History: Exploring the Past Around You.* Nashville, Tennessee: American Association for State and Local History, 1982.

Lichtman, Allan. *Your Family History: How to Use Oral History, Family Archives & Public Documents to Discover Your Heritage.* New York: Vintage Books, 1978.

Pellowski, Anne. *The Family Storytelling Handbook: How to Use Stories, Anecdotes, Rhymes, Handkerchiefs, Paper and Other Objects to Enrich Your Family Traditions,* New York: Macmillan Publishing Co., 1987.

Perl, Lila. *The Great Ancestor Hunt: The Fun of Finding Out Who You Are.* Boston: Houghton Mifflin, 1989.

Shoumatoff, Alex. *The Mountain of Names: A History of the Human Family.* New York: Simon & Schuster, 1985.

Stone, Elizabeth. *Black Sheep and Kissing Cousins: How Our Family Stories Shape Us.* New York: Times Books, 1988.

Weitzman, David. *My Backyard History Book.* Boston: Little, Brown. 1975.

Westin, Jeane Eddy. *Finding Your Roots: How Every American Can Trace His Ancestors—At Home and Abroad.* Los Angeles: J. P. Tarcher, Inc, 1977.

Williams, Ethel W. *Know Your Ancestors: A Guide to Genealogical Research.* Rutland, Vermont: Charles E. Tuttle, Co., 1965.

Zimmerman, William. *How to Tape Instant Oral Histories.* 4th Printing. New York: Guarionex Press, 1988.

General Genealogy

Boy Scouts of America. *Genealogy* (one of the merit badge series). Irving, Texas: Boy Scout Publishing, 2000.

Crichton, Jennifer. *Family Reunion: Everything You Need to Know to Plan Unforgettable Get-togethers.* New York: Workman Publishing, 1998.

Galford, Ellen. *The Genealogy Handbook: The Complete Guide to Tracing Your Family Tree.* Pleasantville, New York: The Readers Digest Association, 2001.

Hartley, William G. *The Everything Family Tree Book: Finding, Charting, and Preserving Your Family History.* Holbrook, Massachusetts: Adams Media Corporation, 1999.

Horowitz, Lois. *Dozens of Cousins: Blue Genes, Horse Thieves, and Other Relative Surprises in Your Family Tree.* Berkeley, California: Ten Speed Press, 1999.

Luebking, Sandra, editor. *The Source: A Guidebook of American Genealogy.* Revised Edition. Salt Lake City, Utah: Ancestry Publishing, 1997.

Advanced Genealogy

Cerny, Johni, and Arlene Eakle. *Ancestry's Guide to Research: Case Studies in American Genealogy.* Salt Lake City, Utah: Ancestry Publishing, 1985.

Eakle, Arlene, and Johni Cerny. *The Source: A Guidebook of American Genealogy.* Salt Lake City, Utah: Ancestry Publishing, 1984.

Everton, George B., Sr., editor. *The Handy Book for Genealogists.* 7th edition. Logan, Utah: Everton Publishers, 1981.

Groene, Bertram H. *Tracing Your Civil War Ancestor.* Winston-Salem, North Carolina: J.F. Blair, 1973.

Guzik, Estelle M., editor. *Genealogical Resources in the New York Metropolitan Area.* New York: Jewish Genealogical Society, 1989.

Neagles, James C. and Lila Lee. *Locating Your Immigrant Ancestor: A Guide to Naturalization Records.* Logan, Utah: Everton Publishers, 1975.

Internet Genealogy

Crowe, Elizabeth Powell. *Genealogy Online.* 5th Edition. New York: Osborne-McGraw Hill, 2001.

Helm, Matthew L., and April Leigh Helm. *Genealogy Online for Dummies.* 3rd edition. Foster City, California: IDG Books Worldwide, 2000.

Howells, Cyndi. *Netting Your Ancestors: Genealogical Research on the Internet.* Baltimore: Genealogical Publishing Co., 1999.

Lamb, Terri Stephens. *e-Genealogy: Finding Your Family Roots Online.* Indianapolis, Indiana: Sams Publishing, 1999.

McClure, Rhonda. *The Complete Idiot's Guide to Online Genealogy.* Indianapolis, Indiana: Alpha Books, 2000.

Richley, Pat. *The Everything Online Genealogy Book.* Holbrook, Massachusetts: Adams Media Company, 2000.

Ethnic Groups

Baxter, Angus. *In Search of Your British and Irish Roots: A Complete Guide to Tracing Your English, Welsh, Scottish and Irish Ancestors.* Baltimore: Genealogical Publishing Co., 1986.

_____. *In Search of Your European Roots: A Complete Guide to Tracing Your Ancestors in Every Country in Europe.* Baltimore: Genealogical Publishing Co., 1985.

_____. *In Search of Your German Roots: A Complete Guide to Tracing Your Ancestors in the Germanic Areas of Europe.* Baltimore: Genealogical Publishing Co., 1987.

Blockson, Charles L., and Ron Fry. *Black Genealogy,* New York: Prentice-Hall, 1977.

Cohen, Chester G. *Shtetl Finder Gazeteer: Jewish Communities in the 19th and Early 20th Centuries in the Pale of Settlement of Russia and Poland, and in Lithuania, Latvia, Galicia, and Bukovina, with Names of Residents.* Bowie, Maryland: Heritage Books, Inc., 1989.

David, Rabbi Jo. *How to Trace Your Jewish Roots: Discovering Your Unique History.* New York: Citadel Press. 2000.

Kurzweil, Arthur. *From Generation to Generation.* New York: Schocken, 1982.

_____. *My Generations: A Course in Jewish Family History.* New York: Behrman House, 1983.

Meltzer, Milton. *World of Our Fathers.* New York: Dell Publishing, 1976.

Mokotoff, Gary, and Warren Blatt. *Getting Started in Jewish Genealogy.* Bergenfield, New Jersey: Avotaynu, Inc., 1999.

Redford, Dorothy Spruill, with D'Orso, Michael, *Somerset Homecoming.* New York: Doubleday, 1988.

Rose, James, and Alice Eichholz, editors. *Black Genesis: An Annotated Bibliography for Black Genealogical Research.* Detroit: Gale Books, 1977.

Smith, Jessie Carney. *Ethnic Genealogy: A Research Guide.* Westport, Connecticut: Greenwood Press, 1983.

Streets, David H. *Slave Genealogy: A Research Guide with Case Studies.* Bowie, Maryland: Heritage Books, 1986.

Names

Hook, J.N. *The Book of Names: A Celebration of Mainly American Names, People, Places, and Things.* New York: Franklin Watts, 1983.

_____. *Family Names: The Origins, Meanings, Mutations, and History of More than 2,800 American Names.* New York: Macmillan Publishing Co., 1982.

Kaganoff, Benzion. *A Dictionary of Jewish Names and Their History.* New York: Schocken Books, 1977.

Lambert, Eloise, and Mario Pei. *Our Names. Where They Came From and What They Mean.* New York. Lothrop, Lee and Shepard Co., 1960.

Meltzer, Milton. *A Book About Names.* New York: Thomas Y. Crowell, 1984.

Pine. L.G. *The Story of Surnames.* Rutland, Vermont: Charles E. Tuttle Co., 1966.

Smith, Elsdon C. *American Surnames.* New York: Chilton Publishing, 1969.

_____. *The Book of Smith.* New York: Nellen Publishing, 1974.

_____. *New Dictionary of American Family Names.* New York: Harper and Row, 1973. Gramercy Publishing reprint, 1988.

Index

A

B

Photo Credits

Frontispiece: Brown Brothers

Foreword

p. ix: Ron Frishman Photography

Introduction to the First Edition

p. ix: Michael Mauney/timepix

Chapter One: Ancestor Detectors at Work

p. 2: *(left)* National Archives; *(right)* Ira Wolfman. **p. 4:** Ira Wolfman. **p. 6:** Victoria & Albert Museum. **p. 7:** Courtesy of Alex Haley. **p. 8:** *(left)* Photofest; *(center and bottom right)* Courtesy of Alex Haley. **p. 9:** Courtesy of Doubleday. **p. 10:** *(right)* Courtesy of Beth Yarnelle Edwards; *(center and bottom)* Courtesy of Jessica Pearlman. **p. 11:** Courtesy of Carl Glassman. **p.12:** Courtesy of Magda Bogin. **p. 13:** Courtesy of Natasha Bogin. **p. 14:** *(both)* Courtesy of the Taylor Family. **p. 15:** Courtesy of Boy Scouts of America. **p. 18:** *(both)* Courtesy of Anny and Lily Holgate.

Chapter Two: Getting Started

p. 23: Family Record for Andrew Bickford and Olive Clark, Joshua Pool (1787–?). Gloucester, Essex County, Massachusetts: c. 1820. Watercolor, pencil, and ink on paper, 15″×12″. Collection of the American Folk Art Museum, New York. Gift of Ralph Esmerian. 1998.17.6 Photo by John Parnell, New York. **p. 25:** Picture Collection, New York Public Library. **p. 32:** Ira Wolfman. **p. 34:** Picture Collection, New York Public Library. **p. 35:** *(top)* Courtesy Jessica Pearlman; *(bottom)* Minnesota Historical Society. **p. 36:** *(both)* Ira Wolfman. **p. 37:** *(left)* Picture Collection, New York Public Library; *(center and right)* Courtesy of Manuscript Collection, NY Genealogical & Biographical Society.

Chapter Three: Let's Talk About . . . Us!

p. 45: Ira Wolfman. **p. 46:** Comstock. **p. 49:** *(left)* Yivo Institute for Jewish Research; *(right)* Ira Wolfman. **p. 50/51:** Ira Wolfman. **p. 52:** Postcard Collection of Miriam Weiner. **p. 53:** Ira Wolfman. **p. 54:** Florida State Archives. **p. 55:** Courtesy the Kahn family. **p. 56:** Lawrence Migdale/Pix. **p. 57:** Picture Collection, The New York Public Library.

Chapter Four: What's Your Name?

p. 61: Corbis-Bettmann. **p. 63:** Corbis-Bettmann. **p. 69:** Corbis-Bettmann. **p. 70:** Lawrence Migdale/Stock Boston. **p. 72:** Bob Daemmrich/The ImageWorks.

Chapter Five: How We Got Here

p. 74: Corbis-UPI. **p. 76:** The New York Historical Society. **p. 77:** Picture Collection, The New York Public Library. **p. 79:** Association of American Railroads, Washington, D.C. **p. 80:** Culver Pictures. **p. 82:** Chicago & North Western Railway. **p. 83:** Corbis-UPI. **p. 84:** Historical Association of Southern Florida. **p. 85:** Louise Gubb/The ImageWorks. **p. 87:** Florida State Archives. **p. 89:** Ellis Island Immigration Museum. **p. 90:** Library of Congress. **p. 91:** Ellis Island Immigration Museum. **p. 94:** The Mariner's Museum, Newport News, Virginia. **p. 95:** *(top right)* William Williams Collection, U.S. History, Local History, and Genealogy Division, The New York Public Library; *(bottom left)* Corbis-Bettmann; *(bottom right)* Augustus F. Sherman Collection, Ellis Island Immigration Museum. **p. 98:** Corbis-Bettmann. **p. 99:** AP/WideWorld. **p. 100:** Library of Congress. **p. 101:** Brown Brothers. **p. 102:** *(both)* Ellis Island Immigration Museum. **p. 103:** Ellis Island Immigration Museum. **p. 104:** William Williams Collection, U. S. History, Local History, and Genealogy Division, The New York Public Library. **p. 108:** Jay Brady, 1993.

Chapter Six: Becoming an American

p. 111: Library of Congress. **p. 112:** Picture Collection, New York Public Library. **p. 113:** Nancy Richmond/The Image Works. **p. 114:** Jacob A. Riis Collection, Museum of the City of New York. **p. 115:** *(both)* Lewis W. Hine Collection, U.S. History, Local History, and Genealogy Division, The New York Public Library. **p. 117:** Kit Barry. Brattleboro, Vermont. **p. 119:** Corbis-Bettmann. **p. 121:** Dennis Brack/Black Star. **p.122:** Courtesy of Paul Gamarello.

Chapter Seven: The Great Record Hunt

p. 124: Ira Wolfman. **p. 125:** Collection of Miriam Weiner. **p. 126:** Postcard Collection of Miriam Weiner. **p. 128:** Metaform, Ellis Island Immigration Museum. **p. 129:** Collection of Miriam Weiner. **p. 133:** Corbis-Bettmann. **p. 136:** Picture Collection, The New York Public Library. **p. 139:** Collection of Miriam Weiner. **p. 141:** Collection of Miriam Weiner. **p. 142:** Courtesy of Boy Scouts of America. **p. 147:** Ellis Island Immigration Museum. **p. 148:** State Archives of Michigan. **p. 149:** Collection of Miriam Weiner. **p. 150:** Augustus F. Sherman Collection, Ellis Island Immigration Museum. **p. 151:** *(top)* Ellis Island Immigration Museum; *(center right)* Lewis W. Hine Collection, U. S. History, Local History, and Genealogy Division, The New York Public Library. **p. 152:** Images from the Past, Bennington, Vermont.

Chapter Eight: Catching Your Ancestors with a Net

p. 157: Tony Freeman/PhotEdit. **p. 161:** *(both)* Courtesy of the Church of Jesus Christ of Latter-day Saints. **p. 164:** Image State. **p. 165:** Rich Frishman Photography.

Chapter Nine: Where the Records Are

p. 170: *(both)* Images from the Past, Bennington, Vermont. **p. 171:** Library of Congress. **p. 172:** Jo Nordhausen © 1985 American Library Association. **p. 173:** National Archives. **p. 175:** The Church of Jesus Christ of Latter-day Saints. **p. 177:** Dennis Brack/Black Star. **p. 178:** Gail Mooney/Corbis.

Chapter Ten: "My Story's a Little Different"

p. 180: Ken Shung. **p. 181:** Adapted from *Real Parents, Real Children: Parenting the Adopted Child* by Holly van Gulden and Lisa Bartels-Rabb. **p. 182:** Florida State Archives. **p. 183:** Montana Historical Society. **p. 185:** Ira Wolfman. **p. 187:** Ken Shung.

Chapter Eleven: Getting Connected

p. 190: Ellen Fisher Turk. **p. 191:** Minnesota Historical Society. **p. 192:** Workman Archives. **p. 194:** AFP/Corbis. **p. 195:** Bob Daemmrich Photography. **p. 196:** Ted Spiegel/Corbis. **p. 197:** *(both)* Courtesy the Chin family.